ELECTION INTERFERENCE

Russian interference in the 2016 US presidential election produced the biggest political scandal in a generation, marking the beginning of an ongoing attack on democracy. In the run-up to the 2020 election, Russia was found to have engaged in more "information operations," a practice that has been increasingly adopted by other countries. In *Election Interference*, Jens David Ohlin makes the case that these operations violate international law, not as a cyberwar or a violation of sovereignty, but as a profound assault on democratic values protected by the international legal order under the rubric of self-determination. He argues that, in order to confront this new threat to democracy, countries must prohibit outsiders from participating in elections, enhance transparency on social media platforms, and punish domestic actors who solicit foreign interference. This important book should be read by anyone interested in protecting election integrity in our age of social media disinformation.

Jens David Ohlin is Vice Dean and Professor of Law, Cornell Law School. His work stands at the intersection of three related fields: criminal law and procedure, international law, and the laws of war. Trained as both a lawyer and a philosopher, Professor Ohlin has tackled diverse research questions that include the philosophical foundations of international law, collective criminal action, and the role of new technologies in war. He is the author of leading textbooks in international law and criminal law.

Election Interference

INTERNATIONAL LAW AND THE FUTURE
OF DEMOCRACY

JENS DAVID OHLIN

Vice Dean and Professor of Law
Cornell Law School

CAMBRIDGE
UNIVERSITY PRESS

CAMBRIDGE
UNIVERSITY PRESS

University Printing House, Cambridge CB2 8BS, United Kingdom

One Liberty Plaza, 20th Floor, New York, NY 10006, USA

477 Williamstown Road, Port Melbourne, VIC 3207, Australia

314–321, 3rd Floor, Plot 3, Splendor Forum, Jasola District Centre,
New Delhi – 110025, India

79 Anson Road, #06–04/06, Singapore 079906

Cambridge University Press is part of the University of Cambridge.

It furthers the University's mission by disseminating knowledge in the pursuit of
education, learning, and research at the highest international levels of excellence.

www.cambridge.org
Information on this title: www.cambridge.org/9781108494656
DOI: 10.1017/9781108859561

First published 2020

Printed in the United Kingdom by TJ International Ltd. Padstow Cornwall

A catalogue record for this publication is available from the British Library.

Library of Congress Cataloging-in-Publication Data
NAMES: Ohlin, Jens David, author.
TITLE: Election interference : international law and the future of democracy / Jens David
Ohlin, Cornell University, New York, School of Law,
DESCRIPTION: Cambridge, United Kingdom ; New York, NY : Cambridge University Press,
2020. | Includes bibliographical references and index.
IDENTIFIERS: LCCN 2020002617 (print) | LCCN 2020002618 (ebook) | ISBN 9781108494656
(hardback) | ISBN 9781108859561 (ebook)
SUBJECTS: LCSH: Election law. | Self-determination, National. | Sovereignty. | Presidents –
United States – Elections – 2016.
CLASSIFICATION: LCC K3304 .O35 2020 (print) | LCC K3304 (ebook) | DDC 342/.07–dc23
LC record available at https://lccn.loc.gov/2020002617
LC ebook record available at https://lccn.loc.gov/2020002618

ISBN 978-1-108-49465-6 Hardback
ISBN 978-1-108-79682-8 Paperback

For my children
Clara & Chris

Contents

Acknowledgements

In writing this book, I benefited from correspondence and discussions, both online and in person, with a wide variety of legal scholars on multiple continents. They are too numerous to mention, but I am in their debt. I am privileged to call myself a member of the venerable "invisible college" of international lawyers.

I have also benefited from feedback, advice, and support from my colleagues, friends, and students at Cornell Law School. I also gratefully acknowledge that my research is supported by Cornell.

I would also like to thank my editor, Matt Gallaway, and the rest of the team at Cambridge University Press, for working so diligently on the book's acquisition, production, and marketing.

Lastly, I acknowledge the unfailing support of my wife, Nancy, who encouraged me to write this book and had constant faith in the project's validity and necessity.

Introduction

1. WHAT HAPPENED

On February 19, 2016, Twitter user @evagreen69 logged onto her twitter account and typed out the following tweet: "Texas Democrats Indicted for Buying Votes With Cocaine ... #tcot #PJNET #ccot #WakeUpAmerica #RedNationRising." The tweet's central allegation was shocking – and ultimately a conspiracy theory. In fact, Texas Democrats were never indicted for buying votes with cocaine. The story was entirely fictional, though the tweet reported the event as factual news. In order to increase the visibility of the tweet, @evafreen69 used two well-known conservative hashtags, #WakeUpAmerica and #RedNationRising. And this was not the first time that @evagreen69 had tweeted. For example, one prior tweet from 2015 was a retweet of the following statement from another account, @Xamerican: "Michelle Obama Tells San Bernardino Victims' Families That She Will Rap For Them."

Based on these and other tweets, Twitter users could be forgiven for assuming that @evagreen69 was an American voter. But she was not. According to Twitter, these tweets were just among the millions of tweets that were composed or retweeted from accounts controlled by individuals at the Internet Research Agency (IRA) troll farm in St. Petersburg Florida.[1] The massive number of tweets composed by individuals (or automated bots) associated with the IRA troll farm reveals something telling about modern election interference. To have an impact, it was not necessary for the IRA to compose tweets that received a huge amount of engagement – retweets or likes numbering in the 100,000s. Rather, the IRA developed the opposite strategy: swarm social media platforms with a large number of tweets, each of which could have a small amount of engagement but collectively could amplify particular themes, hashtags, and memes. Some of the tweets were vicious and scandalous, others silly or comical. Some of the tweets disparaged Clinton or praised Trump,

---

[1] These tweets were included in the massive database of tweets released by Twitter after the 2016 election and identified as coming from IRA-controlled accounts.

while other tweets amplified leftist talking points – raising questions about the goal of the IRA and the overall strategy it was using to achieve it.

During the early morning hours after election day, as news media organizations officially "called" the election for Donald Trump in the middle of the night, a nation woke up to learn that Trump was the next President of the United States. For those who voted for him, Trump's election was the fulfillment of a promise to fundamentally recalibrate the political spectrum. For those who voted against him, the result was traumatic. Later, the Office of the Director of National Intelligence released a report explicitly concluding that Russia interfered in the election and detailing those efforts. For months following the election, Clinton voters wondered aloud whether the results of the election could be overturned on account of Russia's interference (it could not). Trump responded defensively and boastfully to suggestions that his election was illegitimate.

Trump also offered conflicting statements about whether Putin intervened in the election. During various public appearances he denied that there was any interference, then later conceded that his own intelligence agencies had concluded that there was interference. During a press conference following an official visit with Putin, Trump noted that Putin had denied intervening in U.S. politics and Trump said he had no reason to doubt Putin.[2] After an uproar, Trump claimed that he had misspoken (by adding an errant negative) and had meant to say that there *were* reasons to doubt Putin.[3]

Although election interference is not new, Russia's social media strategy for election interference, writ large, represented a new form of interference in the political affairs of the United States. The advent of social media electioneering raised a number of important political questions. Would Trump have been elected in the absence of Russian interference? Why did the Russians intervene? Why was Trump acting so obsequiously towards Putin? Did the Russians have some form of leverage or *kompromat* over Trump? Was Trump an unwitting Russian asset? If Trump realigned American foreign policy toward Russia and away from traditional allies, was this realignment part of his presidential prerogative based on his constitutional authority over foreign policy?

While political commentators were debating these questions, international lawyers were engaged in a parallel conversation, one that was more technical but just as consequential. International lawyers were asking whether Russia's interference violated international law. Did Russia do something wrong by operating a troll farm to promote divisive rhetoric in the American political landscape? Did the use of cyber technologies turn the Russian interference into an illegal cyber-attack that triggered a right of response, a form of cyber self-defense? International lawyers

---

[2]   Trump's exact words during the press conference were: "[he] just said it's not Russia. I will say this: I don't see any reason why it would be."

[3]   See Dartunorro Clark, *24 hours later, Trump claims he misspoke in Helsinki, meant to say Russia did have reason to meddle in election*, NBC NEWS (July 17, 2018).

generally fell into two camps, with one camp viewing the interference as illegal and another camp viewing it as regrettable but probably lawful under existing legal frameworks. But everyone agreed that Russia's aggressive use of social media technology was a game-changer.

My own intuition was that the "illegal" camp had it right – Russia did violate international law – but that the "illegal camp" had the wrong reasons for reaching this conclusion. The "illegal camp" argument was that Russia had violated American sovereignty during the run up to the 2016 election, but this argument did not sit well with me. I had the different idea that Russia had violated the American people's right of self-determination. I found that not only was I disagreeing with the considered views of many important international lawyers, but that by invoking self-determination I was almost talking a different language – despite the fact that self-determination is widely assumed to be a collective right protected by international law and codified in many human rights treaties. I wrote this book to articulate my view and defend my argument.[4]

2. METHODOLOGY

The analytical framework for this study is international law. One question that arises is why international law is the appropriate lens through which to understand election interference. It certainly is not the only framework that might be used. In recent years, though, public discourse has become increasingly legalized. In prior generations, the public might have debated whether a particular foreign policy arrangement was moral or "just," but today, the public also asks whether a particular course of action is lawful under international law. Many readers want to know whether international law prohibits election interference and this book is designed to answer that question. The legal question does not supplant the moral question, but simply adds to it.

It is crucial to articulate what this book is not. It is not a work of political science. Political scientists seek to explain a particular phenomenon – why it occurs – and to trace causal pathways. This is a worthwhile endeavor, but it is far different from the task of this book. This book focuses on whether election interference is illegal or not. On this question, international law scholars are split. Some have argued that it violates a core prohibition of nonintervention against the political affairs of another state, while others disagree and note that political intervention is only prohibited in very limited circumstances. Despite the disagreement, these camps share a common assumption: that election interference should be analyzed under the rubric of nonintervention and sovereignty. As will be explained below, I side with the camp

---

4   The argument was first explored, in embryonic form, in Jens David Ohlin, *Did Russian Cyber Interference in the 2016 Election Violate International Law?*, 95 Tex. L. Rev. 1579 (2017).

that says election interference is illegal under international law, but I do so for a completely different reason.

If you do not care about international law – or do not think that it makes a difference to the world – then this is not the book for you. This book starts from the assumption that international law matters, that is, that we should care about what it says. If you think that international law has nothing to contribute to the conduct of foreign affairs – that it does not and should not matter whether something is illegal or not – then you should probably stop reading this book right now.[5] Continuing to read this book will only bring you frustration and annoyance.

There are plenty of people in the world who do not care about international law and find it useless or irrelevant. My book is not designed to convince them otherwise. Skeptics or "realists" about international law often consider it epiphenomenal or not likely to change the behavior of other nation-states. Realists about international law might assume that Russia, China, or Iran are not going to forego election interference simply because it is illegal under international law; under this view, international law has little to contribute to the practical conversation about how to combat election interference. Realists would rather look for hard-nosed coercive mechanisms to solve the problem or might resign themselves to living in a world with election interference. Or realists might look to technical solutions to election interference that could be implemented by social media platforms or tech firms. But the question of legality might be secondary (or worse, distracting) to them.

I find this way of looking at the world fundamentally misguided, but this book is not designed to show why international law is relevant. It simply assumes the relevance of international law. Most readers care about international law and what it has to say about election interference, simply because most readers want their state to comply with international law. They might also believe – correctly, as it turns out – that international legal mechanisms could be useful as a way to push back against election interference. Even before we consider legal mechanisms such as countermeasures that are designed to induce compliance among law-breaking states, we should recognize that international law has enormous rhetorical power to structure international relations. Before the question of enforcement arises, labeling some behavior as compliant with international law – and other behavior as violating it – can have powerful consequences for the way states relate to each other on the world stage.

---

[5] For a discussion of this issue, see Francis A. Boyle, *The Irrelevance of International Law: The Schism between International Law and International Politics*, 10 CAL. W. INT'L L.J. 193, 198 (1980) (explaining that "when international political scientists assert the irrelevance of international law, they are not concerned with the vast multitude of relatively inconsequential international relations it governs. Instead they refer to that portion of international relations which, they claim, escapes the effective control of international law and international organizations altogether – conflict over matters of 'vital national interest'"). Some political scientists might argue that election interference is precisely the type of behavior that is destined to "escape" the effective control of international law.

For those looking for a full defense of international law, and its relevance, you should read my prior book, *The Assault on International Law*, which explains why international law matters.[6] In that book, I take up the realist challenge and argue why states should comply with international law, even in the absence of any world government that has the coercive power to enforce it. I argue that states are rationally justified in complying with international law because it is part of an overall strategy of "constrained maximization," a term that I borrow from the philosophical literature on rational choice theory.[7] States do better when they participate in the international legal order than when they ignore it and get branded as a rogue nation. Furthermore, states should follow through on their legal commitments because doing so is rationally justified as part of an overall strategy of constrained maximization. Although it might be tempting to make international legal commitments and then shirk those commitments when they become inconvenient, this is extremely myopic. States are rationally justified in following through on their commitments because doing so is part of an overall plan that will make the state better off in the long run.

For the same reasons, I think that states should comply with the prohibition on election interference. Of course, not every state agrees and some states – including Russia – ignore international expectations about the sanctity of the democratic process. For these and other reasons, this book also addresses what responses international law might offer to confront the problem of election interference, and what measures each state might take, consistent with international law, to protect the integrity of their elections. This includes regulations to prohibit outsiders – foreigners – from participating in elections.

Also, this book is not a work of history. One might wonder if election interference is a new phenomenon or simply the latest chapter of an old story. Certainly, states have interfered in the internal politics of foreign states and for reasons of strategic self-interest have used covert operatives to support political movements or remove governments.[8] The advent of new technology – including social media troll farms and the use of cyber-intrusion methods to hack confidential information – may have radically transformed that older process of intervention, which previously took place using conventional, nondigital methods. A work of history would tell the story of these ancient and recent interventions, with the hope of gaining insight into whether the new interventions are different in kind or only different in degree from what has come before. But as noted above, this book is not a work of history and we should leave to historians this difficult task. The one area where the history of intervention is briefly considered is in the context of customary international law. Customary

---

[6] See JENS DAVID OHLIN, THE ASSAULT ON INTERNATIONAL LAW (Oxford University Press, 2015).

[7] The phrase comes from the philosopher David Gauthier. See DAVID GAUTHIER, MORALS BY AGREEMENT 15 (Oxford University Press, 1986) (discussing constrained maximizers).

[8] For a discussion, see generally STEPHEN KINZER, OVERTHROW: AMERICA'S CENTURY OF REGIME CHANGE FROM HAWAII TO IRAQ (Times Books, 2006).

international law is built from the raw materials of state practice and *opinio juris* (acting from a sense of legal obligation). The history of election interference is marginally relevant for deciding whether states have tacitly acknowledged that election interference is ongoing and whether they consider it a violation of international law. On the other hand, the history is not dispositive, because even if states have engaged in election interference from time immemorial, it still might be illegal. (Many behaviors are illegal even though they are widespread.)

There is a strong temptation to instrumentalize international law – to think of it as a tool to solve international problems.[9] That impulse shows up equally in the case of election interference, tempting us to ask how the norms, processes, and mechanisms of international law could be used to solve the "problem" of election interference. To a certain extent, this impulse is natural, expected, and justified, but in another respect, law has its autonomy and there is value in determining the content of international law before asking what it can do for us. Consequently, the aim of this project is to determine the scope and content of the international legal rules pertaining to election interference. It is perfectly respectable to ask that question without needing to provide an answer as to how international law can improve the situation.

3. SUMMARY OF THE ARGUMENT

The argument in this book unfolds over eight chapters. Chapter 1 asks: What is election interference? To answer that question, I look mostly at the Russian intervention during the 2016 election – with full knowledge that this case study might leave out other forms of election interference. Nonetheless, the inspiration behind the study is to understand whether, and why, Russia's interference in the 2016 election violated international law, and whether similar efforts by other nations would be illegal. Although Russian interference included multiple facets, Chapter 1 focuses on two of the most prominent: the theft and release of private information (such as emails stolen through hacking), and the use of social media troll farms to spread disinformation and amplify division in the electorate. The Russians also attempted to infiltrate advocacy organizations. Chapter 1 argues that the use of social media platforms for political discussions – a technology that was unavailable just decades ago – creates the psychological conditions that allow information operations to be as successful as they are. Specifically, social media platforms allow users to build networks of like-minded friends and curate a feed of news items that either promotes an echo chamber or at the very least heightens partisan intensity. Modern election interference through social media activity can harness this dynamic in order to subtly alter the political discourse of the electorate.

---

[9] *See generally* M. Patrick Cottrell and David M. Trubek, *Law as Problem Solving: Standards, Networks, Experimentation, and Deliberation in Global Space*, 21 TRANSNAT'L L. & CONTEMP. PROBS. 359 (2012–2013).

Although it is unlikely that social media interference can inject new beliefs or opinions into the political discourse, there is ample empirical evidence that it can amplify some opinions and heighten the intensity of political beliefs.

The book then considers a variety of plausible legal frameworks for understanding election interference. Chapter 2 is meant to debunk a promising line of inquiry: that Russian election interference was illegal because it constituted an act of "war" against the United States. In some situations, a cyber-attack can constitute an illegal act of war, thus suggesting that the cyber-war rubric is a helpful one for understanding modern election interference, especially interference that is accomplished through cyber methods. The basic intuition here is that cyber-attacks sometimes qualify as "armed attacks" under international law, thus making the election interference an opening salvo in an armed conflict. On deeper analysis, however, Chapter 2 reveals that the cyber-war analogy is inapt. A discussion of the legal rules regarding cyber-attacks reveals that there are specific doctrinal requirements that must be met before a cyber-attack can be regulated by the international legal rules governing armed conflict. Most importantly, a cyber-attack must accomplish a particular type and amount of physical damage – such as destroying tangible objects, killing people, or under some contested accounts disabling a computer system – in order to constitute an "attack" in the legal sense of that term. These technical requirements fit uncomfortably with the paradigm of election interference which often does not involve this type of destruction or disabling of a target. This observation is not meant to minimize the unique and devastating harm of election interference, but rather is designed to humbly note that we need to continue the intellectual inquiry in order to find the distinctive harm of election interference. Cyber-war turns out to be a metaphor with limited utility for understanding election interference.

Chapter 3 turns the page and considers a different lens for evaluating election interference: the international prohibition on "interventions" against the sovereignty of another state. This rule of nonintervention is a pillar of the international legal system and is arguably implicit in the very notion of a Westphalian legal order (an international community of sovereign states, each one pledging not to interfere in the affairs of the others). As Chapter 3 reveals, most scholars view the nonintervention rule as related to the concept of sovereignty: an intervention against another state is prohibited when it violates the sovereignty of that state. Just as in Chapter 2 and the discussion of cyber-war, the international legal rules regarding nonintervention impose specific doctrinal requirements, most of which do not line up with the case of election interference. Sovereignty is usually violated under international law when the intervening state engages in some coercive act, but it is hard to identify an element of coercion in modern cases of election interference. To be sure, election interference is problematic and damaging, but its wrongfulness does not flow from any coercive quality. Similarly, an intervention might be illegal if it "usurps" a government function, but this too fails to adequately describe cases of election interference – at least if the election interference takes place during the deliberative process. (A case of a foreign state tampering with vote counting might be different.) We will need to search for a better rubric for understanding the wrongfulness of election interference.

Chapter 4 proposes a new framework for understanding election interference, one that has been systematically ignored by international lawyers – practitioners and scholars alike. International law recognizes that every people enjoys the collective right of self-determination. This chapter argues that the right of self-determination, properly understood, provides a powerful concept for explaining the distinctive harm of election interference. When the Russians intervened in the 2016 election, they denied the right of the American people to decide their own destiny through the democratic process. Why have international lawyers steadfastly ignored the explanatory power of self-determination? Simply put, international lawyers have assumed that self-determination only applies to stateless peoples, but that once a people receives a state, the concept of self-determination fades away to be replaced by the protection of sovereignty as a governing framework. This chapter is devoted to the proposition that this basic assumption about self-determination is wrong.

Chapter 5 tries to develop the concept of self-determination by looking at the ways that democratic societies, especially the United States, protect their electoral process by enacting what I call "boundary regulations" that set criteria for membership in the political community. These rules include the prohibition on foreign voting, the prohibition on foreign contributions and spending, and a registration requirement for foreign agents. Each of these regulations, in their own way, helps ensure that the political process is dominated by insiders rather than outsiders. The key move of the chapter is to unite this entire conceptual apparatus together as individual pieces of a larger whole: the fulfillment of a people's right to self-determination through democratic institutions. However, democratic institutions require protection and each of the boundary regulations is an example of that protection. The goal of many of these boundary regulations is *transparency* – in other words, to ensure that the public is aware of when foreign powers are attempting to influence our democratic process. This is precisely the danger of modern election interference, which acts covertly so that the foreign power's participation in the democratic process remains hidden from the rest of the electorate. Chapter 5 ends with a policy suggestion to improve transparency on the Internet: get social media platforms to label posts that have a foreign origin (either voluntarily or through a legal mandate).

Chapter 6 responds to an oft-heard objection to boundary regulations, such as campaign finance regulations, that target foreign speakers. The objection is that restrictions on campaign contributions and spending violate the First Amendment. Also, the transparency rules suggested in the prior chapter might compromise the possibility for purely anonymous political speech, which might raise concerns among First Amendment absolutists. Chapter 6 meets this challenge by arguing that foreigners located outside the territory of the United States have no constitutional right to participate in American elections, nor do they have a right to engage in extraterritorial political speech. Modest transparency regimes, such as labeling foreign political speech as foreign, would be consistent with both the First Amendment and international human rights protections on freedom of speech. Indeed, since free speech absolutism is a distinctively American constitutional phenomenon, international law imposes fewer constraints in this area than U.S. constitutional law.

Chapter 7 considers other responses to election interference, especially the role that criminal prosecutions can play in broadcasting information to the public about the nature of foreign interventions in the democratic process. While we are usually inclined to think of criminal prosecutions as oriented around punishment of the guilty, the criminal process has an important role to play in getting information into the hands of the public. This information-sharing element of the criminal process can be useful for combating election interference. By initiating criminal investigations and prosecutions, state authorities can inform the public of details of foreign election interference in a way that may deprive that interference of its effectiveness, since most interference on social media platforms requires deception in order to work properly. (Although there are other ways that the government can disclose information to the public, the government often fails to do so, and the criminal process forces public disclosure because open access to the courts is a legal requirement.) Unfortunately, the U.S. government response to election interference is controlled by counterintelligence agencies that have limited experience with information disclosure; these agencies are built to keep and protect secrets, not disclose information to the public, and the institutional structures of these agencies are built for the intelligence threats of a prior era. Chapter 7 closes with a wish list for major reforms in the counterintelligence community so that its agencies can be geared toward disclosing information to the public about foreign information operations.

Chapter 8 pivots towards individual conduct and addresses the particular harm posed by individuals who solicit interference from a foreign state during a federal election. Two examples of solicitation come immediately to mind. The first is Trump's request during the 2016 campaign that Russia engage in email hacking, and the second is Trump's solicitation of interference from Ukraine during a phone call with its president in the fall of 2019. A variety of federal and state statutes might apply to these cases of solicitation, although this book will argue that Congress should respond by enacting a new federal statute explicitly criminalizing the solicitation of foreign involvement in federal elections. The chapter closes by responding to the objection that the President's foreign affairs power allows him to decide, without congressional interference, how to conduct foreign policy, up to and including requesting intervention from foreign states in American elections. This view is exposed for precisely what it is – a monarchical view of the presidency that in any event conflicts with Congress' preeminent power to enact the boundary regulations necessary to protect democratic institutions.

1

What Is Election Interference?

INTRODUCTION

The phenomenon of election interference is complicated and multifaceted. Before engaging in a study of election interference's legality under international law, it is imperative that we define the behavior that we are evaluating. What exactly is election interference? What do we mean when we say that one state has interfered with a foreign state's election?

The history of election interference is extensive. The Russian interference in the 2016 election did not emerge from a vacuum; states have, for generations, interfered in the domestic political affairs of their allies and rivals alike, either through propaganda or other information operations.[1] However, the present chapter is not a historical study, but rather is an attempt to articulate the current phenomenon of election interference, which in today's age is pursued with cyber-attacks and social media tools. Although the Russian interference in the 2016 election is not the only example of cyber election interference, it is certainly the most well-known and the best studied, and the one that has inspired people to ask the very question that this monograph seeks to answer: Does election interference violate international law? So, before answering that question, it makes sense to describe the Russian interference, its exact contours, its consequences, and its purposes.

The Russian interference in the 2016 election was not an isolated event but was, rather, a cluster of related techniques, each of which will be described in the following sections. There is wide agreement in government and intelligence circles about what happened, though the Trump administration has at times stated contradictory things about whether the interference occurred, or contradictory

---

[1] See Ashley Deeks, Sabrina McCubbin and Cody M. Poplin, *Addressing Russian Influence: What Can We Learn from U.S. Cold War Counter-Propaganda Efforts?*, LAWFARE (Oct. 25, 2017) (describing Russian interference as "the latest iteration of a practice Moscow has used for nearly a century"). During the 1980s, the American government created the "Active Measures Working Group" (AMWG) to counter Russian information operations. *See* Fletcher Schoen and Christopher J. Lamb, *Deception, Disinformation, and Strategic Communications: How One Interagency Group Made a Major Difference*, 11 STRATEGIC PERSPECTIVES 7–8 (2012).

characterizations of the interference.[2] There was: (1) hacking of email accounts and the public release of information stolen from these accounts; (2) social media campaigns, including paid advertisements on Facebook and postings on Twitter engineered by so-called troll farms; and (3) the infiltration of advocacy organizations such as the National Rifle Association, with the goal of influencing the domestic political landscape. These activities raise two important issues, including: (4) are the actors who engage in this interference private actors or state agents, and does it make a difference?; and (5) based on the methods used, what conclusions can be drawn about Russia's strategic objectives in interfering in the 2016 elections? These questions must be answered in order to answer the fundamental question of this volume, that is, whether election interference violates international law, and if yes, in what way. Fundamentally, this volume will draw a portrait of democracy as an internal decision by a polity which becomes at best corrupted, and at worst is rendered meaningless, if outsiders are entitled to participate in that decision. The dilemma will be how to articulate this disruption in a way that is cognizable under current doctrines of public international law.

1. THEFT AND RELEASE OF PRIVATE INFORMATION

Hackers working for units within Russian military intelligence (GRU) conducted repeated attempted or successful hacking of email accounts belonging to the Democratic National Committee (DNC), the Democratic Congressional Campaign Committee (DCCC), Clinton Campaign Chair John Podesta, other staff members, and Hillary Clinton's private email server. In addition to exfiltrating massive amounts of data and subsequently releasing them, the GRU implanted sophisticated malware on these computer systems in order to cull passwords and set up encrypted data transfers from these systems to GRU-controlled computer servers. As the following section demonstrates, this hacking was more than a mere nuisance: it was a systematic effort to obtain massive amounts of private information and release it to the public at moments in time that were most damaging to the Clinton campaign and most helpful to the Trump campaign.[3]

The Russian hacking of democratic emails ramped up in March of 2016. Hackers with the GRU targeted the email accounts of many prominent Democratic organizations and individuals. According to the Mueller Report, the GRU did not limit its hacking attempts to the email accounts of prominent individuals but attempted to hack *hundreds* of email accounts belonging to members of these organizations,

---

[2]   See, e.g., Angie Drobnic Holan, 2017 *Lie of the Year: Russian Election Interference is a "Made-Up Story,"* POLITIFACT (Dec. 12, 2017).

[3]   See Ido Kilovaty, *Doxfare: Politically Motivated Leaks and the Future of the Norm on Non-Intervention in the Era of Weaponized Information,* 9 HARV. NAT'L SEC. J. 146, 149 (2018) (referring to the hacking and release as a form of "organizational doxing"), *citing* Bruce Schneier, *Organizational Doxing,* SCHNEIER ON SEC. (July 10, 2015).

including low-level employees and volunteers.[4] Initially, the GRU hacking efforts involved simple spear-phishing, that is, sending fraudulent emails to users with a request to have them enter login credentials. By fooling authorized users to enter their login credentials in fake websites that look like their real counterparts, the GRU gained access to multiple email accounts. Reportedly, Clinton campaign chair John Podesta fell for this ruse, as did many others within the democratic organizations. Based on these early efforts, the GRU was able to steal "tens of thousands of emails" from Podesta and other democratic operatives.[5]

The GRU also used spear-phishing to gain access to the actual DCCC network, presumably after a network IT administration fell victim to a spear-phishing effort. From there, the GRU was also able to gain access to the DNC network, because the two organizations had installed a virtual private network (VPN) to connect the two computer networks. The GRU used this access to install several types of malware on the two computer networks, including software dubbed "X-Agent" and "X-Tunnel" and "Mimikatz."[6] The malware programs were designed to steal further credentials, take screenshots, and set up a data transfer between the infected servers and GRU-controlled computer servers. The data transfer allowed the GRU to extract huge amounts of data from the infected servers.

The treasure trove of documents stolen from the DNC and DCCC servers allowed the GRU to create a large database of emails and documents that could be searched by keyword, thus allowing them to create custom "tranches" of stolen documents curated according to a particular topic or a particular individual. So, for example, the GRU could create a data-collection of emails related to John Podesta or emails and documents related to opposition research on candidate Trump, or other topics.

The GRU then created a sophisticated pipeline for distributing the stolen emails and documents. The GRU registered the domain name "dcleaks.com" – a domain name that suggested that the hacked emails had been leaked by a DNC insider rather than stolen by an outside hacker, much less a hacker working for a foreign government.[7] The GRU created a DCLeaks website which included links to the stolen documents, again arranged in particular "tranches" to make the documents more readily viewable and to avoid the best documents getting lost amid a massive data-dump.

---

[4] *See* Robert S. Mueller III, Department of Justice Special Counsel, *Report On The Investigation Into Russian Interference In The 2016 Presidential Election* 36–40 (2019) [hereinafter cited as "Special Counsel Report"].

[5] *Id.* at 37.

[6] *Id.* at 38.

[7] *See* Office of the Director of National Intelligence, Intelligence Community Assessment, *Assessing Russian Activities and Intentions in Recent US Elections*, ICA 2017-01D, at ii (Jan. 6, 2017) [hereinafter cited as "Intelligence Community Assessment"] ("We assess with high confidence that Russian military intelligence (General Staff Main Intelligence Directorate or GRU) used the Guccifer 2.0 persona and DCLeaks.com to release US victim data obtained in cyber operations publicly and in exclusives to media outlets and relayed material to WikiLeaks.").

But the GRU was not content to simply render the DNC files public – they also needed to direct people, including journalists, to the dcleaks.com website. For this reason, the GRU began publicizing the DCLeaks website on social media platforms, including Facebook.[8] To do this, the GRU needed to create a Facebook page for a fake organization called DCLeaks, where it could publicize the supposed "leak" and also correspond with journalists to encourage them to download the stolen files.[9] The GRU also created a Twitter presence for DCLeaks, again allowing them to publicize the stolen information and to correspond with journalists about the archives.[10] The GRU hackers did not reveal their true identities to the journalists, all the while holding themselves out as members of a hacker collective called DCLeaks.

The GRU campaign worked effectively. A number of journalists downloaded the documents and published stories about them. The documents included information about donors to the democratic party and to the Clinton campaign, private correspondence about the Bernie Sanders campaign, internal strategy documents, and emails suggesting that the Clinton campaign had received an advanced look at audience questions to be posed to Clinton during a CNN Town Hall event. The latter revelation proved particularly damaging to both Clinton and to the DNC. The emails suggested that Donna Brazile, a former interim chair of the DNC, and then CNN commentator, had provided the content of questions to Clinton. Brazile was subsequently fired from CNN. More importantly, though, the revelation deepened a suspicion that current and former members of the DNC were working directly with the Clinton campaign to get her elected.[11]

The revelation of this DNC–Clinton alleged collusion, which was further supported by other emails on other topics, had a significant impact on the news cycle. During the primary season, Clinton was locked in a highly competitive, and bitter, primary challenge against Sen. Bernie Sanders. Supporters of Sanders complained that the DNC was favoring Clinton during the primaries, and that the debate procedures and the primary and caucus rules were being written and administered in a way favorable to Clinton. The knowledge that a CNN employee with close ties to the DNC may have helped Clinton during a supposedly neutral event only fostered the feeling among Sanders supporters that the primary process was "rigged" in Clinton's favor. This suggests a strategic plan behind the Russian effort. The internal schism in the democratic party would hurt Clinton's chances of getting elected because some Sanders supporters might refuse to vote for Clinton during the general election by either voting for a third-party candidate, staying home and not participating in the general election, or switching their vote to Trump.[12] Or, even if

---

[8] Special Counsel Report, *supra* note 4, at 42–4.
[9] *Id.* at 42.
[10] *Id.*
[11] *See* Michael Shear and Matthew Rosenberg, *Released Emails Suggest the D.N.C. Derided the Sanders Campaign*, N.Y. TIMES (July 22, 2016).
[12] *See* Jason Le Miere, *Bernie Sanders Voters Helped Trump Win and Here's the Proof*, NEWSWEEK (August 23, 2017) (citing data analysis from *Political Wire*).

Clinton did win the general election, the split in the democratic party would weaken Clinton's standing and increase the chaos surrounding her, making her a weaker president. Furthermore, many of the emails were released to the public at around the same time that Trump's campaign was dogged by the revelation of his "Access Hollywood" tape, which included a taped conversation of Trump making lewd comments about sexual harassment and assault. The release of the Clinton emails helped to change the news cycle at a time when some political observers questioned whether Trump's campaign could recover from the near-fatal blow of the Access Hollywood tape.

The support of third-party candidates is an easy way for a foreign state to wreak havoc in the political process and there are reports that the Russians used that strategy again in the 2020 election cycle. In October 2019, Hillary Clinton suggested that Russian operatives were drumming up support for Rep. Tulsi Gabbard on social media platforms in the hopes that she would mount an independent run for the White House.[13] The existence of a third-party candidate could split the anti-Trump vote between Gabbard and the Democratic nominee, thus increasing the likelihood that Trump would get elected – the outcome desired by the Russian government. Also, Gabbard supported a U.S. withdrawal from Syria, a policy outcome that aligned with Russian strategic interests, since Russia was allied with Syrian President Bashar Al-Assad.[14] This episode demonstrates the perceived strategy of supporting third-party candidates as a form of election interference (though at this time it is unclear if Gabbard's online support was augmented by Russian troll farms, as Clinton asserted). If real, such troll farm support for a third-party candidate can not only tip the balance toward a favored candidate during the general election, but it also has the secondary effect of sowing division and discord within one of the major parties.

The Office of Special Counsel report on Russian interference does not discuss whether the GRU hacking had a measurable impact on the outcome of the 2016 general election. This is an empirical question that would require a statistical analysis. Certainly, some of the hacked emails helped foster a public perception

---

[13]   Clinton stated on a podcast that "I'm not making any predictions, but I think they've got their eye on somebody who is currently in the Democratic primary and are grooming her to be the third-party candidate. She's the favorite of the Russians. They have a bunch of sites and bots and other ways of supporting her so far." To be clear, Clinton was not alleging that Gabbard was working with the Russians, but rather that the Russians might be acting independently to covertly support Gabbard's candidacy.

[14]   Gabbard responded to Clinton's accusation: "Great! Thank you @HillaryClinton. You, the queen of warmongers, embodiment of corruption, and personification of the rot that has sickened the Democratic Party for so long, have finally come out from behind the curtain. From the day I announced my candidacy, there has been a concerted campaign to destroy my reputation. We wondered who was behind it and why. Now we know – it was always you, through your proxies and powerful allies in the corporate media and war machine, afraid of the threat I pose. It's now clear that this primary is between you and me. Don't cowardly hide behind your proxies. Join the race directly." (https://twitter.com/TulsiGabbard/status/1185289626409406464)

that Clinton was hostile to religion – a view that helped Trump consolidate support among traditional social conservatives and motivated his supporters to vote for him on election day.[15] But the deeper point is that the (potential or real) harm to Clinton explains the GRU motivation for its hacking efforts and also explains why Donald J. Trump Jr. coordinated with Wikileaks regarding the release of the hacked emails and about the dissemination of other negative stories about Clinton, including the false allegation that Clinton had ordered a drone to target Assange.[16]

Ultimately, the GRU decided to extend their publicity efforts beyond the DCLeaks project. The GRU created an online persona called "Guccifer 2.0" to correspond with Wikileaks over Twitter and other social media platforms to coordinate their efforts to release hacked emails and documents.[17] The outreach was successful and Wikileaks also released the DCLeaks material. Given Wikileaks' established pedigree, the appearance of the material on the Wikileaks website encouraged journalists to pay even more attention to the material, resulting in more news articles.[18] Unlike DCLeaks, which was an unknown entity, Wikileaks was an established organization with a well-known, albeit controversial, founder, Julian Assange. According to published reports, Trump confidante Roger Stone corresponded with Guccifer 2.0 about the plan to release the hacked documents. The Russian government had a preexisting relationship with Wikileaks and had collaborated with Assange on other projects.[19]

Whether wittingly or unwittingly, Wikileaks continued the charade that the leaked documents were released by an insider rather than by foreign hackers interfering in the election. At the time, conservative media had begun reporting the falsehood that the murder of DNC staffer Seth Rich was somehow connected to the release of the hacked documents. This rumor was particularly damaging to the Clinton campaign. First, it suggested that an insider unhappy with the campaign,

---

[15] See Christina Lam, A *Slap on the Wrist: Combatting Russia's Cyber Attack on the 2016 U.S. Presidential Election*, 59 B.C. L. Rev. 2167, 2201 (2018) (noting that former New Hampshire Governor John H. Sununu said that some of the hacked e-mails "revealed an underlying sense of religious bigotry" on the Clinton campaign).

[16] Special Counsel Report, *supra* note 4, at 60 ("On October 12, 2016, WikiLeaks wrote again that it was 'great to see you and your dad talking about our publications. Strongly suggest your dad tweets this link if he mentions us wlsearch.tk.' WikiLeaks wrote that the link would help Trump in 'digging through' leaked emails and stated, 'we just released Podesta emails Part 4.' Two days later, Trump Jr. publicly tweeted the wlsearch.tk link.").

[17] Special Counsel Report, *supra* note 4, at 42.

[18] See Intelligence Community Assessment, *supra* note 7, at 3 ("Moscow most likely chose WikiLeaks because of its self-proclaimed reputation for authenticity.").

[19] *Id.* at 3 ("The Kremlin's principal international propaganda outlet RT (formerly Russia Today) has actively collaborated with WikiLeaks. RT's editor-in-chief visited WikiLeaks founder Julian Assange at the Ecuadorian Embassy in London in August 2013, where they discussed renewing his broadcast contract with RT, according to Russian and Western media. Russian media subsequently announced that RT had become 'the only Russian media company' to partner with WikiLeaks and had received access to 'new leaks of secret information.' RT routinely gives Assange sympathetic coverage and provides him a platform to denounce the United States.").

rather than outside forces, had released the hacked emails. Second, it suggested that someone within the DNC or the larger Clinton orbit had murdered Seth Rich in retaliation for his leaking of the documents. In reality, none of this was true. Rich was tragically victimized by street violence and the hacking was conducted by the GRU – not by insiders. However, Wikileaks helped to foster the "insider leak" idea. The Mueller Report notes that Assange was asked during media interviews about Wikileaks' interest in the Seth Rich murder, and Assange noted that they were concerned about "anything that might be a threat of Wikileaks sources" – a comment that implied without directly stating that Rich was a Wikileaks source.[20] Assange stated that he was not asserting that Rich's murder was directly connected to Wikileaks while simultaneously describing Rich as "potentially connected to our publication" – a statement that was either false or obfuscating.[21]

The GRU also launched cyber-attacks against Hillary Clinton's personal email account. The Special Counsel Report asserts that the GRU had not even attempted to hack this domain name until Trump made his July 27, 2016 speech in Florida in which he stated: "Russia, if you're listening, I hope you're able to find the 30,000 emails that are missing. I think you will probably be rewarded mightily by our press."[22] Although it is unclear whether the two events are directly connected, the timing is striking. For the first time, the GRU attempted to infiltrate Clinton's personal network later that day on July 27, 2016.[23] Once again, the GRU used a simple spear-phishing technique in an attempt to gain login credentials from users on the Clinton network. According to the Mueller Report, the email addresses that the GRU targeted were not publicly known, so it is unclear how the GRU was able to identify these email addresses for targeting. Around this time, the GRU also targeted cloud-based services used by the DNC, successfully gaining access to large amounts of data.

Most of the GRU efforts were focused on stealing information related to the Clinton campaign and sowing discord by releasing that information to the public. While the information was a mixture of true information (the emails) and extravagant falsehoods that were then generated from these attacks (the Seth Rich story, the Pizza-gate conspiracy theory), the release of the information served the GRU goals of interfering in the election by controlling the news-cycle, damaging Clinton's legitimacy, and buttressing Trump's chance of getting elected. It should be noted that the GRU did not hack email accounts belonging to Trump and his close associates; or, if they did, they certainly never released that information to the public. This was a one-sided social media campaign to steal and release information that might be damaging to the Clinton campaign.

[20]   Special Counsel Report, *supra* note 4, at 48.
[21]   *Id.* at 48.
[22]   *Id.* at 49.
[23]   *Id.*

The GRU also infiltrated and hacked into computer accounts maintained by state and local board of elections and other election infrastructure. It is unclear what the GRU's goal was in these attacks. They might have been preparing to launch an election-day cyber-attack against election infrastructure to disrupt the process of casting ballots, if that became necessary. Or the goal might have been to gain information in order to launch a future attack that could change election results – again if that became a strategic objective in the future. Or the GRU might have tried these objectives in the 2016 election and failed. Either way, what is significant is that the GRU efforts to target election infrastructure were the least significant of its hacking efforts. The GRU did not focus its efforts on the *direct* manipulation of election results but rather on the *indirect* manipulation of the electioneering process. In other words, the Russian interference focused less on the electoral process of casting ballots and counting votes, and more on the electoral process of deliberation. In a sense, both are important elements of democracy, though the former is the most bureaucratic aspect of the democratic process. The latter is the heart and soul of democracy – the contest of ideas, the laying out of competing visions for the future of our country, and the debate and deliberation that this occasions. The Russians interfered in that fundamental process, which in a sense is less technologically difficult than changing vote tallies but in a conceptual sense is far more ambitious because it requires social and psychological engineering. It involves nothing less than corrupting an entire political debate by introducing new information in strategic ways. The hacking of the DNC, DCCC, and Clinton campaign emails, and their coordinated release through DCLeaks and Wikileaks, was designed to alter the course of those political deliberations in ways that served the strategic goals of the GRU and the Russian government. These information operations represented a perversion of the American political discourse, in part because the true source of the disclosures was not fully transparent.

In this sense, it is important to distinguish between hacking and release of information that might have been conducted by American citizens and hacking that was conducted by foreign agents. Any hacking conducted by Americans would have been illegal, and possibly criminal under federal law, but would not have corrupted the political process in the same way. The foreign nature of the 2016 hacking altered the political discourse because the public was not aware of why the emails were stolen or why they were disseminated – at least not at the time when they were released (the GRU's involvement was revealed later by the U.S. government). It is for this reason that it was so important for the GRU to present themselves, through DCLeaks and Wikileaks, not as foreign actors but as insiders to the American political process, harnessing First Amendment values to steal and release insider information. Had the public known that the Russians were involved, the hacked emails would have been viewed more suspiciously. But as an allegedly internal squabble, the interference was more successful. Part of the strategic efficacy of the Russian interference was its lack of transparency, that is, its masquerading as

American political activity when it was not. The hacking of the DNC and Clinton emails followed this paradigm exactly.[24]

2. SOCIAL MEDIA CAMPAIGNS

The GRU used Facebook and Twitter for more than just directing the public to the DCLeaks operation. Additionally, Russian operatives conducted an extensive media campaign using Facebook and Twitter to engage in foreign electioneering.

According to the Mueller Report, firms connected to the Russian government purchased advertisements on Facebook that were overtly political in nature. Represented in terms of total dollar amounts, the Facebook advertisements were not significant. The Internet Research Agency (IRA) spent about $100,000 on more than 3,500 advertisements. However, the content of these advertisements was tightly targeted to generate negative sentiment against Hillary Clinton. According to the Report, one IRA-purchased advertisement displayed a picture of Clinton with the following words: "If one day God lets this liar enter the White House as a president – that day would be a real national tragedy."[25] The advertisement played on themes already in circulation: that Hillary Clinton, like her husband, former President Bill Clinton, was not a trustworthy individual. Other advertisements purchased by the IRA included the provocative hashtag "#HillaryClintonForPrison2016," a hashtag that echoed one of Trump's favorite campaign rally chants: "Lock Her Up!" The IRA also purchased advertisements on Instagram to encourage young Trump supporters to post photos with the hashtag "#Kids4Trump."[26]

Facebook either failed to recognize that these advertisements were purchased by foreign actors, in violation of federal election law, or did not care to check.[27] Either way, the advertisements echoed divisive, grassroots political issues that would harm Clinton's campaign and potentially buttress the Trump campaign. As will be discussed in subsequent chapters, foreign election spending is illegal in the United States because of a concerted political decision to limit electioneering to members of the American polity who are participating in the election. (For similar reasons, noncitizens are not permitted to vote in elections.) In order to avoid the

---

[24] See Kilovaty, *supra* note 3, at 151 ("Massive volumes of damaging, sensitive, or classified information can be exfiltrated and released almost instantaneously, a development that challenges notions of sovereignty, non-intervention, and friendly relations. The damage that can be inflicted by leaking sensitive information can be enormous – political processes can be disrupted; fundamental human rights, like privacy and self-determination, can be violated; and the opinions of citizens can be manipulated by the release of materials that a foreign government selects.").

[25] Special Counsel Report, *supra* note 4, at 25.

[26] *Id.*

[27] See generally Brian Beyersdorf, *Regulating the "Most Accessible Marketplace of Ideas in History": Disclosure Requirements in Online Political Advertisements After the 2016 Election*, 107 CAL. L. REV. 1061, 1063 (2019) ("Nearly a year after the 2016 presidential election, Facebook, Twitter, and Google executives acknowledged to Congress that Russia's disinformation campaign exploited their online platforms to influence the election.").

legal prohibition on foreign spending on elections, it was important for the Russian organizations and individuals who purchased the social media advertisements to maintain the fiction that the advertisements originated with an American source. Consequently, the advertisements presented themselves as inside communications despite their outside origins.

But the paid advertisements on Facebook represented only a small fraction of the Russian social media campaign. The larger initiative, and by far the more expensive, was the creation of a Russian social media "troll farm" – a group of computer specialists who created thousands of fake online social media accounts on Facebook and Twitter. These accounts posted original content written by computer specialists, but the accounts also retweeted articles and posts that the troll farm found online. In addition to the accounts that were personally managed by members of the troll farm, the organization also created thousands of so-called "bot accounts" that were programmed to automatically retweet posts and articles from other accounts. One consequence of this strategy was to create an echo chamber. By retweeting and reposting and giving greater prominence to some online activities, the troll farm was able to alter the political discourse by encouraging and amplifying divisive political rhetoric.

The specialists worked for the Internet Research Agency (IRA), which was owned by a Russian oligarch with close ties to Putin and the Kremlin. IRA employees could be described as hackers, though this is a slightly misleading description. Although they were involved in the creation of fictitious accounts and the use of automation tools to amplify the messages that they circulated on social media, their primary responsibility was content creation and content dissemination. Consequently, it might be more appropriate to refer to them as "active-measures" agents or information operatives.

According to the Office of the Special Counsel, whose prosecutors filed an indictment against the IRA and some of its employees, the social media campaign began well before the 2016 presidential election. In 2014, the IRA started the process of creating fake social media platforms. According to the Special Counsel, the first wave of social media accounts were not fake individual users, but fake organization accounts that mimicked real U.S. Organizations, such as the Tennessee Republican Party.[28] Other accounts simply pretended to represent grassroots organizations that did not exist but that were associated with well-known causes, such as the Tea Party or the Black Lives Matter movement. By creating fake accounts for both conservative and liberal movements, the troll farm was able to ensure that its divisive messages and inflammatory rhetoric were not simply ignored. So, for example, a fake account pretending to be connected to the Black Lives Matter movement would post something strident at which point a fake Tea Party account could repost and comment

---

[28] USA v. Internet Research Agency LLC et al., Indictment, at para. 36 (Feb. 16, 2018) [hereinafter cited as "IRA Indictment"].

derisively on the original post. The consequence of this strategy was that real social media users sympathetic to a Tea Party message would have their feelings intensified by reading the exchanges.

Some of the social media campaigns had a more direct strategy in mind – voter suppression. For example, fake Facebook and Twitter accounts attempted to popularize a "voter boycott" of the general election as a protest against some right-wing behavior. Although it is unclear whether this particular IRA effort affected voter turnout, it is not coincidental that the vast majority of these voter boycott efforts were directed at left-leaning voters who were encouraged to stay home to protest systems of discrimination in society.[29] If this effort had a tangible effect, it would depress voter turnout among Democrats while leaving voter turnout for likely Republican voters unchanged.

The scope of the social media campaign was unprecedented. In 2018, Twitter released a dataset of more than 10 million tweets from troll farms and related accounts. Although the dataset included propaganda tweets from sources other than Russia (primarily Iran), a large percentage of the tweets were the work of Russian troll farms. Indeed, Twitter announced that 3,841 accounts were associated with the IRA and 770 accounts had links to Iran. The dataset revealed the important role played by bot accounts that automatically retweeted the work of accounts personally managed by IRA employees. In essence, the bot accounts functioned as "force multipliers" that magnified the effect, and the investment, of the IRA efforts.

The IRA troll farm focused on particular issues over which they could have an impact by intensifying the political discourse. For example, according to the Mueller Report, the IRA created Facebook groups called "Secured Borders," "Stop All Immigrants," and "Stop All Invaders."[30] Focusing on illegal immigration, the need for border security, and Trump's plan to build a border "wall," helped intensify anti-immigrant sentiment among potential Trump voters.

According to the Special Counsel, IRA employees even "acknowledged that their work focused on influencing the U.S. presidential election."[31] The goal of the IRA troll farm's work is therefore beyond reasonable doubt and its impact was wide-ranging. Social media posts and tweets generated by IRA-associated accounts were viewed by tens of millions of Americans, according to the Special Counsel.[32] For example, the report quotes Facebook as concluding that IRA Facebook accounts reached between 29 million and 126 million Americans.

---

[29] See Jon Swaine, *Russian propagandists targeted African Americans to influence 2016 US election*, THE GUARDIAN (Dec. 17, 2018) (noting that one "popular bogus Facebook account created by the Russians, Blacktivist, attracted 4.6 million 'likes'" and that the page said that "black people should vote for the Green party candidate, Jill Stein, and that 'not voting is a way to exercise our rights'"). The turnout among African-American voters declined in the 2016 election when compared with the 2012 election.

[30] Special Counsel Report, *supra* note 4, at 25.

[31] *Id.* at 24.

[32] *Id.* at 26.

The IRA troll farm made a special effort to ensure that its Twitter postings originated from accounts that appeared to be associated with American residents, while in reality they were being composed by IRA employees in Russia.[33] This strategy was important because its messages would have been largely ignored if they originated from overtly Russian accounts. Few American social media users would care what a Russian resident thought about illegal immigration, but social media posts from Americans on this topic have greater currency. For this reason, IRA social media accounts were carefully curated to appear American, with American handle names and biographies that suggested an American connection. For example, Twitter accounts included names such as @TEN_GOP or @Pamela_Moore13.[34] The latter purported to be an individual from Texas. Many of the biographies for these accounts announced that the account holders were either supporters of President Trump or held views that were central to Trump's campaign messaging, such as anti-immigrant sentiments. When creating fake accounts targeting the American political landscape, IRA employees eschewed Russian-sounding names, biographical details that were foreign, or Russian political interests.[35]

It is hard to gauge how many of these accounts were successful in duping Americans into believing that the tweets were home-grown American views rather than stimulated by a foreign campaign of disinformation. However, there was little in these accounts to make users suspicious and at the time there was limited news publicity regarding Russian troll farm accounts on Twitter and Facebook. Furthermore, mainstream journalists were certainly duped by at least some of the posts because they authored newspaper and website articles that quoted postings on social media accounts and presented them as being American in origin when in fact they were later discovered to have originated from the IRA troll farm.[36] The Special Counsel also noted that prominent American citizens such as cable TV host Sean Hannity, Trump confidante Roger Stone, and former Pentagon official Michael Flynn all engaged with or retweeted IRA-generated posts, suggesting that IRA material not only successfully masqueraded as American content but also gained significant traction in our online political discourse.[37] To take just one notable example, Donald Trump Jr. retweeted a post from an IRA account on November 7, 2016.[38] The IRA tweets were not simply authored, published, and ignored, but rather helped to spark and intensify political discussions during the 2016 election cycle.

---

[33] *Id.*

[34] *Id.* at 27.

[35] *Id.* at 22–8. The Russian government also engineered social media campaigns, in the Russian language, that were focused on Russian domestic political issues and which targeted a domestic Russian audience.

[36] Special Counsel Report, *supra* note 4, at 27.

[37] *Id.* at 28.

[38] *See id.* at 34 (referring to Trump Jr.'s retweeting of a November 7, 2016 post on Twitter from the account of @Pamela_Moore13, which was identified as an IRA-linked account).

One of the boldest IRA operations involved the creation of Facebook and Twitter accounts associated with fake grassroots organizations. These are sometimes referred to as "AstroTurf" campaigns, although the phrase AstroTurf may not be entirely accurate in this context. Usually, an AstroTurf organization is created, funded, or organized by a corporate entity or its allies while using a name or other branding to falsely suggest that the organization was spontaneously organized by a group of like-minded citizens concerned about a particular topic. In short, an AstroTurf organization is a corporate lobbying organization that brands itself as a grassroots concern. The IRA organizations, however, did not even exist – at least not beyond their social media presence. The IRA would create fake accounts on Facebook and Twitter and then later announce the scheduling of a protest, political rally, or meeting, and encourage followers of the social media account to attend the event.[39] This strategy was somewhat less effective than the general IRA project of sowing political division on Facebook or Twitter, but they did manage to stage several events. The Special Counsel's Report was able to identify "dozens" of events organized by the IRA in the United States – some of which were sparsely attended but a few events managed to attract "hundreds" of attendees. The IRA also used its social media accounts to increase participation at events that they did not directly organize. They also tried to network these events with Trump campaign officials.[40]

In order to maximize the impact of the events, the IRA would sometimes organize counterprotests or countermeetings. To make this happen, the IRA needed to create left-leaning grassroots organizations or to generate anger about the protests among existing left-leaning organizations. In one sense this strategy sounds counterintuitive, because it required initiating or amplifying anti-Trump messages – a strategy which was seemingly at odds with the rest of the IRA messaging on social media. But on deeper reflection the overall strategy was both logical and inevitable. The grassroots events would be ineffectual if they were poorly attended or if they were ignored. The whole point of a public event is for it to generate public reaction, which is not likely to happen if the event is ignored. The best way to get an event noticed, and even to generate attendance at an event, is to get both sides of the issue angry about it.

---

[39] For example, in one Facebook message, an IRA employee wrote: "Hi there! I'm a member of Being Patriotic online community. Listen, we've got an idea. Florida is still a purple state and we need to paint it red. If we lose Florida, we lose America. We can't let it happen, right? What about organizing a YUGE pro-Trump flash mob in every Florida town? We are currently reaching out to local activists and we've got the folks who are okay to be in charge of organizing their events almost everywhere in FL. However, we still need your support. What do you think about that? Are you in?" *See* IRA indictment, *supra* note 28, at para. 69.

[40] For example, IRA employees wrote: "Hello [Campaign Official 1], [w]e are organizing a state-wide event in Florida on August, 20 to support Mr. Trump. Let us introduce ourselves first. "Being Patriotic" is a grassroots conservative online movement trying to unite people offline. . . . [W]e gained a huge lot of followers and decided to somehow help Mr. Trump get elected. You know, simple yelling on the Internet is not enough. There should be real action. We organized rallies in New York before. Now we're focusing on purple states such as Florida." *See* IRA Indictment, *supra* note 28, at para. 76.

Since IRA employees worked in Russia and were not able to attend the IRA-inspired events, the IRA would recruit American citizens to serve as surrogate organizers. While the IRA employee might continue to be involved in the online promotion of the event, a real American would be recruited to be designated as a "leader" or other organizer of the event. The Special Counsel report concludes that the IRA "recruited U.S. persons from across the political spectrum," meaning both Trump supporters and Democratic-leaning social justice activists.[41] It appears that none of these individuals were aware that they had corresponded with Russian agents.[42] Had they known that they were corresponding with Russian operatives, it is doubtful that the recruited individuals would have agreed to act as surrogate organizers for the events. As in other IRA endeavors, lack of transparency was a necessary precondition for success.

It should be noted that these activities were undertaken by the IRA, not by the Trump Campaign. However, it would be a mistake to conclude that there were *no* contacts at all between the Trump Campaign and the IRA. Rather, the Special Counsel's investigation revealed that the IRA specifically targeted its social media efforts at prominent individuals associated either formally or informally with the Trump Campaign, such as the previously mentioned Roger Stone and Michael Flynn. Specifically, the report notes that "in a few instances, IRA employees represented themselves as U.S. persons to communicate with members of the Trump Campaign in an effort to seek assistance and coordination on IRA-organized political rallies inside the United States."[43] So, while there was coordination between Russian agents and surrogates of the Trump Campaign, those contacts were presumably made in ignorance of the Russian origins of these communications.[44]

3. INFILTRATION OF ADVOCACY ORGANIZATIONS

The Russian government also intervened in U.S. politics by arranging for a Russian asset to infiltrate the National Rifle Association (NRA). Although this was apparently an isolated endeavor that was not repeated with other political organizations, the operation constitutes a template by which future interference operations might be conducted.

---

[41]   *See* Special Counsel Report, *supra* note 4, at 31.

[42]   According to the Justice Department indictment, the IRA "staged political rallies inside the United States, and while posing as U.S. grassroots entities and U.S. persons, and without revealing their Russian identities and organization affiliation, solicited and compensated real U.S. persons to promote or disparage candidates. Some Defendants, posing as U.S. persons and without revealing their Russian association, communicated with unwitting individuals associated with the Trump Campaign and with other political activists to seek to coordinate political activities."

[43]   Special Counsel Report, *supra* note 4, at 33.

[44]   Also, there were direct contacts with members of the Trump family and Wikileaks regarding the dissemination of hacked documents.

In 2016 and 2017, Russia citizen Maria Butina made contact with American officials, posing as a Russian gun-rights activist interested in working with the NRA and other Second Amendment enthusiasts in the United States. At the time, Butina's activities in the United States were being directed by Aleksandr Torshin, a former politician in Russia who had also worked for the Russian Central Bank. Her work was also funded by a wealthy Russian named Konstantin Nikolaev. Justice Department prosecutors alleged that Torshin was connected to Russian intelligence services and was handling Butina as an asset of the Russian government. Butina was arrested and charged in 2018 with being an unregistered asset of the Russian government. The Foreign Agent Registration Act requires foreign agents, including lawyers and lobbyists, to register with the U.S. government if they are working on behalf of a foreign government within the United States.[45] In the past, the statute has been inconsistently enforced. It is sometimes used as a law enforcement tool against intelligence assets who work for foreign governments but fail to fulfill their reporting obligations because they wish to continue their work clandestinely or covertly.

According to the Justice Department, the goal of Butina's work in the United States was to establish "'back channel lines of communication" with U.S. officials and "penetrate the U.S. national decision-making apparatus to advance the agenda of the Russian Federation."[46] The NRA was presumably selected because of its proximity to power in right-leaning political circles.[47] Butina would attend special events that were frequented by U.S. officials while she posed as a Russian gun-rights activist seeking to develop links between her organization and the NRA, which she asserted shared a common agenda.

However, Butina's interest was not limited to the Second Amendment. Rather, her interest in the Second Amendment is best viewed as the instrument by which she engaged in her information operation, rather than its goal. According to the Justice Department, one of Butina's alleged co-conspirators wrote: "Unrelated to specific presidential campaigns, I've been involved in securing a VERY private line of

---

[45]   22 U.S.C. § 612 ("No person shall act as an agent of a foreign principal unless he has filed with the Attorney General a true and complete registration statement and supplements thereto as required by subsections (a) and (b) of this section or unless he is exempt from registration under the provisions of this subchapter. Except as hereinafter provided, every person who becomes an agent of a foreign principal shall, within ten days thereafter, file with the Attorney General, in duplicate, a registration statement, under oath on a form prescribed by the Attorney General.").

[46]   *See* Affidavit in Support of An Application For A Criminal Complaint, at para. 14.

[47]   For a discussion, see Norman I. Silber, *Foreign Corruption of the Political Process Through Social Welfare Organizations*, 114 Nw. U. L. Rev. 104, 109 (2019) ("According to a Statement of Offense by the United States Attorney for the District of Columbia, senior staff and board members of a 'gun rights organization' communicated with Russians in the United States, and also visited Russia. These allegations have led to speculation that foreign contributions might have been made from Russia or another country, using the NRA, an affiliate, or some 501(c)(4) organization as a conduit, during the period of the 2016 election campaign. The NRA has denied using foreign funds for political activities, but reports indicate that federal authorities have investigated whether the NRA used foreign donations to support political campaigns. To date, all investigations have resulted in no charges or official accusations that the NRA used foreign funds to support domestic political campaigns.").

communication between the Kremlin and key [Republic] leaders through, of all conduits, the [NRA]."[48] This email demonstrates that the infiltration of the NRA was the means rather than the ends of the Butina influencing operation, because the NRA is a key locus of important individuals in the right-wing and conservative ecosystem. It is the ideal environment to meet and interface with key Republican politicians, policy experts, and thought leaders.

Furthermore, Butina attended the Nevada Freedom Festival in 2015 and asked Trump, then a candidate for the GOP nomination for president, whether he would continue the administration's policy of leveling "damaging" sanctions against Russia.[49] Trump responded by suggesting that he would be in favor of changing America's strategy of pushing back against Russia: "Obama gets along with nobody. The whole world hates us ... And yet they make money with us ... With me we're going to make money on them, and they're going to like us ... I believe I would get along very nicely with Putin. I don't think you would need the sanctions ... I think we would get along really well. I really believe that."[50]

Although Butina did not work directly on the sanctions issue, her colloquy with Trump suggested a possible motivation for Russia and its agents to insinuate themselves with U.S. officials. If Butina and others could convince American officials – either Trump or anyone else in a position of policy influence – that America should drop its sanctions and develop a less antagonistic stance towards Russia, this would promote Putin's and Russia's economic and strategic interests. Nor would this result need to be achieved directly through some quid pro quo. It would be enough to open up a policy debate about American approaches to Russia that might lead to a change in sanctions policy.

Butina did more than simply attend a few NRA or gun rights conferences. Butina also organized "friendship and dialogue" dinners, according to the Justice Department, which were designed to bring together Russians and Americans to discuss topics of mutual interest.[51] She also attended the politically important National Prayer Breakfast – twice – in order to develop contacts with prominent American politicians and policy makers.[52] Butina even discussed with "associates" of the organizer of the 2017 National Prayer Breakfast the possibility that President Putin might attend a future national prayer breakfast, along with other heads of state.[53] Although this suggestion did not bear fruit, Butina wrote in subsequent emails that the goal of having a "handpicked" delegation of Russians at the 2017 breakfast was designed to "establish a back channel of communication ... "[54] Butina

---

[48] See Affidavit, *supra* note 46, at para. 31.
[49] See Sara Dorn, *Alleged spy once asked Trump about Russia, was a regular at GOP events*, N.Y. Post (July 19, 2018).
[50] *Id.*
[51] See Affidavit, *supra* note 46, at para. 8.
[52] *Id.* at para. 24.
[53] *Id.* at para. 29.
[54] *Id.* at para. 40.

wrote after the breakfast the following email to one of the organizers of the event: "the gift of you [sic] precious time during the National Prayer Breakfast week – and for the very private meeting that followed. A new relationship between two countries always begins better when it begins in faith. Once you have a chance to rest after last week's events, I have important information for you to further this new relationship. I would appreciate one brief additional meeting with you to explain these new developments. I remain in Washington, D.C. pursuing my Master's Degree at American University. My schedule is your schedule!"[55] Like the infiltration of the NRA, the infiltration of the national prayer breakfast was selected because of its proximity to cultural and political power, especially in Republican circles.

The affidavit supporting the Justice Department's prosecution of Butina noted that "Russian influence operations are a threat to U.S. interests as they are low-cost, relatively low-risk, and deniable ways to shape foreign perceptions and to influence populations. Moscow seeks to create wedges that reduce trust and confidence in democratic processes, degrade democratization efforts, weaken U.S partnerships with European allies, undermine Western sanctions, encourage anti-U.S. political views, and counter efforts to bring Ukraine and other former Soviet states into European institutions."[56]

It is tempting to view Butina as an off-books diplomat who simply sought back-channel communications with American officials, while failing to register as a foreign agent with the Justice Department, as the Foreign Agent Registration Act (FARA) requires. But it is important to view Butina's actions in context. Although Butina was not directly involved in corrupting the electoral process, as the IRA was, she sought to insinuate herself into the political process at the behest of the Kremlin. She was not practicing diplomacy, either officially or unofficially, in any of its traditional manifestations. She was working behind the scenes to influence U.S. political discourse in such a way that it would alter its current policy and adopt a new policy of appeasement towards Russia. Moreover, it is important to see Butina's efforts within the context of the rest of Russia's information operations: the hacking of democratic emails and their dissemination through DCLeaks and Wikileaks, social media campaigns on Facebook and Twitter, and the creation of fake grassroots organizations to intensify divisive political rhetoric. Taken together, they represent a coordinated campaign of election interference.

4. PSYCHOLOGICAL CONDITIONS FOR INFORMATION OPERATIONS

The information operations conducted by the Russian government, especially the troll farm activity conducted by the IRA, did not occur in a vacuum. Users of social media are in some ways susceptible to these information operations, based on the

[55]   *Id.* at para. 46.
[56]   *Id.* at para. 11.

nature of online activity and the psychological profile of its users. First, users of Facebook and Twitter often surround themselves, online, with like-minded individuals, making them particularly susceptible to troll farm activity. Second, social media posts that elicit anger may produce heightened partisan loyalty. (In theory, this increase in intensity might increase voter turnout.) Troll farm activity harnesses both of these factors in order to influence the electorate. These two factors will now be described in greater detail.

Facebook and Twitter are based on the idea that their users "curate" their own online experience by building networks of associates. On Facebook, users create a network of "friends" whose social media posts the user will then see, including any news items that the friend reposts or decides to share over Facebook. Similarly, Twitter users select which accounts to "follow," thus creating a feed of posts that the user can scroll through. The key point is that the decision of who to follow or friend is not a random one. On Facebook, users will "friend" people for a particular reason, either because they already know the person, because they are a friend of a friend, or because the user wishes to subscribe to the individual's social media updates. On Twitter, users will follow another account because the user has some reason to think that they will want to read the posts from that account. These are not random decisions. Just as someone selects a TV channel because they expect to enjoy its programming or subscribes to a newspaper because they expect to like its articles, social media users curate their online experience with specific goals in mind.

Common sense suggests that this process of curating a social media feed makes it more likely that users will surround themselves with like-minded individuals, rather than those they disagree with.[57] One reason for this outcome might be cognitive dissonance, the uncomfortable feeling of having conflicting thoughts or beliefs. A form of cognitive dissonance might appear in relationships when a group of friends have inconsistent beliefs.[58] Specifically, imagine a person *a* who has an enjoyable relationship with a friend, *b*. However, *b* has another friend, who we will call *c*, that *a* does not like, perhaps because of some disagreement on a particular topic. In this case, cognitive dissonance results, which is uncomfortable for *a*. In the end, *a* may try to convince *b* that they are wrong about *c* in order to get *b* to drop *c* as a friend. Or, if *b* refuses, *a* might distance themselves from *b*. Although not everyone has the same level of intolerance for cognitive dissonance, and some people are fine with having disagreements among their networks of associates, the tendency to avoid

[57] *See* S. Iyengar and K. S. Hahn, *Red Media, Blue Media: Evidence of Ideological Selectivity in Media Use*, 59 J. COMMUNICATION 19–39 (2009); E. Lawrence, J. Sides, and H. Farrell, *Self-segregation or Deliberation? Blog Readership, Participation, and Polarization in American Politics*, 8 PERSPECTIVES ON POLITICS 141, 152 (2010) (concluding that "[b]oth sides of the ideological spectrum inhabit largely cloistered cocoons of cognitive consonance, thereby creating little opportunity for a substantive exchange across partisan or ideological lines").

[58] *See* FRITZ HEIDER, THE PSYCHOLOGY OF INTERPERSONAL RELATIONS (Lawrence Erlbaum Associates, 1958) (harmonious situations preferred to unbalanced or negative relations).

cognitive dissonance may explain why people tend to associate themselves with like-minded individuals.

On the Internet, this phenomenon can quickly produce what information scientists refer to as an echo chamber.[59] An echo chamber results when a social media user is surrounded by like-minded individuals.[60] Instead of resulting in sophisticated deliberation over contested ideas or values, the chamber amplifies existing core beliefs or values, though details might be debated.[61] The echo chamber effect makes social media users particularly susceptible to troll farm activity. It may be difficult for troll farms to implant a core value in the mind of a social media user who sees the fraudulent social media posting. However, what the troll farm activity *can* accomplish is to amplify the echo chamber effect, that is, to increase the decibel level of the echo.[62] During the 2016 election, the IRA created thousands of posts to amplify particularly divisive rhetoric or to increase the level of anger among social media users who viewed the fraudulent posts.

Some scholars have speculated that the echo chamber effect on the Internet may lead to increased group polarization.[63] Group polarization occurs when a group displays more extreme beliefs than what its members would be inclined to believe if they had not joined the group. In other words, the existence of the group intensifies the beliefs of the members of the group. In political situations, this makes liberals more liberal and conservatives more conservative, just by spending time (either online or in person) with their like-minded peers. Troll farms harness this psychological phenomenon to increase the level of group polarization. In the absence of the phenomenon of group polarization, it would be hard for troll farms to have an effect on the online discourse.[64]

---

[59] *See* J. CAPPELLA AND K. JAMIESON, ECHO CHAMBER: RUSH LIMBAUGH AND THE CONSERVATIVE MEDIA (Oxford University Press, 2008).

[60] *See, e.g.,* CASS SUNSTEIN, REPUBLIC.COM 2.0 60 (2009) (stating that "group polarization ... raises serious questions about any system in which individuals and groups make diverse choices, and many people end up in echo chambers of their own design" and coining the term "cyberpolarization").

[61] An echo chamber might also be enhanced by the existence of confirmation bias. Confirmation bias exists when an individual gathers, remembers, or analyzes evidence differently depending on whether the evidence confirms or discounts the individual's preexisting hypothesis. Conflicting information is not sought out, or, if the individual is confronted with that conflicting evidence, the individual may discount its significance. The result is that, for individuals exhibiting this cognitive error, a hypothesis is more likely to be repeatedly confirmed rather than disproven. On social media, users curate their own experience by selecting which accounts to follow and then may discount opinions that they disagree with.

[62] CASS SUNSTEIN, REPUBLIC.COM 2.0 at 60–1 (noting that "groups of like-minded people, engaged in discussion with one another, will end up thinking the same thing that they thought before – but in more extreme form").

[63] *See, e.g.,* Michael A. Beam, Myiah J. Hutchens and Jay D. Hmielowski, *Facebook News and (De) polarization: Reinforcing Spirals in the 2016 US Election,* 21 INFORMATION, COMMUNICATION & SOCIETY 940 (2018).

[64] However, the empirical evidence is mixed, with some scholars concluding that echo chamber effects might be overstated. *See, e.g.,* Elizabeth Dubois and Grant Blank, *The Echo Chamber is Overstated: The Moderating Effect of Political Interest and Diverse Media,* 21 INFORMATION, COMMUNICATION &

Why would it serve troll farms to heighten divisions on social media? There is some empirical evidence that increased anger results in increased distrust in government.[65] If the result of our hyper-polarized political environment is that Americans are more distrustful of their government and its institutions, the electorate will spend more time fighting with itself rather than joining together to fight a common adversary such as a foreign power. Also, distrust will decrease the amount of political capital that the government enjoys, possibly inducing governmental paralysis. At the same time, anger increases *partisan* loyalty, with the result that voters show increased affinity to their political in-group.[66]

If political deliberations on social media platforms were ideal examples of political participation, troll farm activity would be harmless. But group polarization, echo chambers, and anger are very real phenomena on the Internet. By exploiting these psychological features, troll farm social media posts increase anger, reduce confidence in government institutions, and increase partisan intensity. The result that this has on the outcome of an election will depend on the dynamics in each election. Increased voter turnout will benefit some candidates over others.[67] Whether it is empirically valid or not, the IRA may have believed that posting incendiary information would promote hatred of Clinton, trigger anger toward liberal causes, and increase the intensity of support for Donald Trump among some social media users.

5. PRIVATE ACTORS OR STATE AGENTS

The electoral interference described above would not be so worrisome for international lawyers if it were conducted by private actors. If the social media campaigns were conducted by private individuals and organizations with no connection to

SOCIETY 729, 725 (2018) (suggesting that "[p]eople who are politically interested often want to understand political situations in detail and understand alternative perspectives" and for these people "there is value and relevance in avoiding echo chamber"). *Compare with* Lawrence et al., *supra* note 57, at 152 ("Discourse in the political blogosphere is more compatible with accounts that emphasize the importance of clashes of interest, sharp disagreement, and conflict in deliberation, and suggest that some of the claims of more optimistic scholars of deliberation are utopian.").

[65] *See* Steven W. Webster, *Anger and Declining Trust in Government in the American Electorate*, 4 POLITICAL BEHAVIOR 933, 934 (2018) (noting that "while the anger that is so prevalent within contemporary American politics may bring positive benefits (e.g. increased participation and clarified choices at the ballot box), it is likely that this anger-fueled partisan antipathy has the negative consequence of diminishing individuals' evaluations of American government").

[66] *See* STEVEN W. WEBSTER, AMERICAN RAGE: HOW ANGER LOWERS POLITICAL TRUST, WEAKENS DEMOCRATIC VALUES, AND FORGES PARTISAN LOYALTY (Cambridge University Press, forthcoming).

[67] See Susan Jacobson, Eunyoung Myung and Steven L. Johnson, *Open Media or Echo Chamber: The Use of Links in Audience Discussions on the Facebook Pages of Partisan News Organizations*, 19 INFORMATION, COMMUNICATION & SOCIETY 875 (2016) (noting "increased political engagement as a potential benefit of the polarization created by selective exposure"); Natalie Jomini Stroud, *Polarization and Partisan Selective Exposure*, 60 J. COMMUNICATION 556, 557 (2010) (noting that "exposure to likeminded interpersonal views is connected to higher levels of political participation").

a foreign government, then it is doubtful that the behavior would be fit for regulation by public international law. But there is little question that the IRA functioned as an arm of the Russian government and that the international legal rules regarding attribution are sufficient to make the Russian government responsible for its actions.

The IRA was funded by Yevgeny Viktorovich Prigozhin, who controlled a group of companies called Concord, including Concord Catering. The Mueller report refers to "reports that other Russian entities engaged in similar active measures operations targeting the United States" and that "[s]ome evidence collected by the Office corroborates those reports ... "[68] The IRA had an office building in St. Petersburg, Russia, where its employees created the fake social media accounts described above. However, their mere existence is insufficient to generate state responsibility for Russia; Russia is only responsible if there is the requisite connection between the government and the IRA sufficient to meet the applicable legal standard.

Although Prigozhin's connections to Putin are a matter of public record, the Special Counsel Report redacted most of the material related to their relationship, in part because releasing the information would run the risk of harm to an "ongoing matter," presumably the indictment of the IRA filed by the Justice Department.[69] The indictment named as defendants not just the IRA, Concord Management and Consulting, and Concord Catering, but also Prigozhin personally and several other IRA employees whose identities could be confirmed by the Justice Department. Although the individual named defendants did not appear in person at an initial hearing, because they were located in Russia, lawyers for the corporate defendants appeared in court to represent the corporations. This proved to be a brilliant legal tactic. Unlike the individual employees who risked arrest and confinement if they appeared in the United States, the corporate defendants could send attorneys to make an appearance on their behalf without running the risk that the corporations would be subject to any meaningful punishment – because the corporate defendants appear to have no assets located in the United States, effectively making them judgment proof. Consequently, even if the corporate defendants were convicted at trial, any punishment leveled against them by a federal district court will be mostly ineffectual. Furthermore, by officially appearing for the criminal proceedings, the corporate defendants were able to assert discovery rights, that is, asking for documents from the Justice Department that it collected in the course of its investigation of the IRA and the Concord entities.[70] Lawyers for the Justice Department worried that production of the documents to the corporate defendants would run the risk that

---

[68] *See* Special Counsel Report, *supra* note 4, at 14.

[69] The Office of the Director of National Intelligence referred to him as a "close Putin ally." *See* Intelligence Community Assessment, *supra* note 7, at 4.

[70] *See, e.g.*, United States v. Concord Mgmt. & Consulting LLC, No. 18-CR-32-2 (DLF), 2019 WL 2247792, at *2 (D.D.C. May 24, 2019) ("Concord seeks a list of all unindicted co-conspirators known to the government.").

the documents or their content could be transmitted in some form to the Russian government, or individuals closely connected to it.[71]

According to the IRA Indictment, individuals associated with the IRA traveled to the United States "for the purpose of collecting intelligence to inform Defendants' operations."[72] At least part of the purpose of the trip was to secure the services of computer servers and networks housed in the United States that would conceal the foreign nature of the materials created and posted by the Russian employees of the IRA. The IRA included separate departments for graphical services, data analysis, search-engine optimization, information-technology support, and financial affairs.[73] The IRA also included a "translator project" department which created the content for the social media posts that targeted the American public.[74]

Funding for the IRA activities came from Concord accounts and reportedly its budget was more than 1,250,000 USD per month. This money provided the funding not only for the IRA's interference in the 2016 election but also information operations targeting Russian "domestic audiences."[75]

In one particularly brazen episode, IRA employees organized a public birthday message to Prigozhin – in the United States. IRA employees, through fake social media accounts, arranged for a political rally to be held outside the White House. Participants at the rally were duped into holding a sign that said "Happy 55th Birthday Dear Boss" – a reference to Prigozhin because the event occurred on June 1, his birthday.[76] (The individuals holding the signs apparently believed that the signs referred to a fictitious American who had founded the political group, not a Russian.)

Under international law, the conduct of an organization or group of individuals can be attributed to a state for the purposes of establishing state responsibility. The key criterion is the concept of control. In this case, if the Russian government controlled the actions of the IRA, then the conduct of the IRA is attributable to the Russian government for purposes of determining whether Russia violated international law by virtue of the IRA's election interference. In the context of a military organization, the International Court of Justice (ICJ) has stated that a state bears responsibility for the action of the military organization, in particular violations of International Humanitarian Law (IHL) or Human Rights Law, if the state had "effective control" over the organization's conduct.[77] The UN International

---

[71] *Id.* at *3 ("at the government's request, the Court has restricted access to the vast majority of those documents to protect national security concerns, pending investigations, and personally identifiable information").

[72] *See* IRA Indictment, *supra* note 28, at para. 5.

[73] *Id.*

[74] *Id.* at para. 10.

[75] *Id.* at para. 11.

[76] *Id.* at para. 12.

[77] *See* Military and Paramilitary Activities in and against Nicaragua (Nicar. v. U.S.), Judgment, 1986 I.C. J. Rep. 14 (June 27).

Criminal Tribunal for the former Yugoslavia (ICTY) has disagreed with this for-mulation of the control requirement, preferring instead to support an "overall control" test that would only require a looser form of control over the organization that commits the wrongdoing.[78] Subsequent to those ICTY opinions, the ICJ has reiterated its support for the effective control requirement, and reaffirmed its rejec-tion of the overall control test, noting that it must "be shown that this 'effective control' was exercised, or that the State's instructions were given, in respect of each operation in which the alleged violations occurred, not generally in respect of the overall actions taken by the persons or groups of persons having committed the violations."[79] The difference between the two approaches involves the level of granularity when analyzing state control. The overall control test simply requires control over strategic goals and procurement of resources, whereas the effective control test requires more specific control over individual operations.

However, these dueling precedents have occurred in the context of cases invol-ving attribution of military activities. Setting aside the debate between effective and overall control, it is unclear whether the control requirement would work the same way for nonmilitary operations. For example, article 8 of the ILC Draft Articles on State Responsibility simply states that "the conduct of a person or group of persons shall be considered an act of a State under international law if the person or group of persons is in fact acting on the instructions of, or under the direction or control of, that State in carrying out the conduct."[80] Indeed, Brownlie writes in his treatise that "the same principles apply to this category of officials [armed forces], but it is probably the case that a higher standard of prudence in their discipline and control is required, for reasons which are sufficiently obvious."[81] All of this makes abun-dantly clear that state responsibility is predicated on governmental control, although the exact contours of the control requirement are either ill-defined or are the subject of contestation.[82]

The factual conditions that establish the Russian government's alleged control over the IRA have been redacted from public documents released by the U.S. government, so this evidence cannot be scrutinized here. However, the Office of the Director of National Intelligence concluded that the influence cam-paign was ordered by Putin, though much of the evidence for that conclusion has

---

[78]   *See* Prosecutor v. Tadić, ICTY Appeals Chamber Judgment, Case No. IT-94-1-A (July 15, 1999).

[79]   *See, e.g.,* Application of the Convention on the Prevention and Punishment of the Crime of Genocide (Bosnia and Herzegovina v. Yugoslavia), 2007 I.C.J. 2 (Feb. 26), para. 400.

[80]   *See* International Law Commission, Report on the Work of Its Fifty-second Session, UN GAOR, 55th Sess., Supp. No. 10, at 124, UN Doc. A/55/10 (2000) (also known as the "ILC Draft Articles on State Responsibility").

[81]   IAN BROWNLIE, PRINCIPLES OF PUBLIC INTERNATIONAL LAW 449–50 (7th edn., Oxford University Press, 2008).

[82]   For a discussion, see Natalia Perova, *Disentangling "Effective Control" Test for the Purpose of Attribution of the Conduct of UN Peacekeepers to the States and the United Nations,* 86 NORDIC JOURNAL OF INTERNATIONAL LAW (2017) (arguing that the "interpretation of 'effective control' as an 'ability to prevent' is the correct one").

not been declassified.[83] At some later point in time, if that evidence is publicly released, we can evaluate its significance. In the meantime, this issue must be bracketed, though it is perhaps enough to note that the U.S. government has publicly stated that the Russian government directed or controlled the election interference engaged by the IRA and that its actions are properly attributable to the Russian government and to Putin specifically. None of the U.S. intelligence agencies has ever publicly referred to the IRA as a purely private enterprise or as a rogue element of Russian society that operates outside the will of the Russian government. Moreover, the U.S. intelligence community concluded that the Russian government approved particular influence campaigns rather than simply providing resources for a general effort.[84] This view, if correct, would support a finding of state responsibility even under the strictest possible standard, that of effective control.

6. STRATEGIC GOALS: DISRUPTING DEMOCRACY, INFLUENCING OUTCOMES

What motivated the Russians to interfere in the 2016 election and what did they hope to accomplish? The answer to the former question requires consideration of why a potential Hillary Clinton presidency was considered so problematic from the perspective of President Putin.

The answer lies in Clinton's past work as Secretary of State. While she served in the State Department, Clinton took an aggressive stance against the Putin regime. Many of Clinton's comments were inspired by Russian intervention in Eastern Ukraine, Crimea, and other regions. But Clinton was also concerned about democracy deficits within Russia and made comments that described Putin in tyrannical terms. For example, in an event in California in 2014, Clinton stated, referring to Putin, that "Now if this sounds familiar, it's what Hitler did back in the '30s. All the Germans that were ... the ethnic Germans, the Germans by ancestry who were in places like Czechoslovakia and Romania and other places, Hitler kept saying they're not being treated right. I must go and protect my people, and that's what's gotten everybody so nervous."[85]

Putin may have grown concerned that a Clinton administration would pursue regime change in Russia as an official policy of a Hillary Clinton administration.

---

[83] *See* Intelligence Community Assessment, *supra* note 7, at 1 ("We assess with high confidence that Russian President Vladimir Putin ordered an influence campaign in 2016 aimed at the US presidential election, the consistent goals of which were to undermine public faith in the US democratic process, denigrate Secretary Clinton, and harm her electability and potential presidency.").

[84] *Id.* at 2 ("We assess that influence campaigns are approved at the highest levels of the Russian Government – particularly those that would be politically sensitive.").

[85] *See* Philip Rucker, *Hillary Clinton says Putin's actions are like "what Hitler did back in the '30s,"* WASH. POST (March 5, 2014). Clinton also apparently described Putin's mission as "restor[ing] Russian greatness." *Id.*

The United States has occasionally sought to spark democracy in foreign countries. In the context of Russia, a Clinton preference for democratic reform in Russia and the Clinton preference for a less aggressive Russia might be viewed by Putin as related concepts. In other words, Putin might have attributed to Clinton an assumption that a democratic Russian government would be more sympathetic to American interests and less aggressive on the global stage.[86] All of this adds up to two possibilities. First, that Putin viewed Clinton as an existential threat to his leadership of Russia. And second, that Putin considered it possible that a future Clinton presidency would interfere in the domestic politics of Russia and therefore decided to preemptively interfere in American domestic politics to ensure that Clinton's policies could never be enacted.[87]

The Justice Department concluded that the IRA's activities were clearly designed to support Trump and "disparag[e]" Clinton.[88] The Director of National Intelligence (DNI) flatly stated that "Putin and the Russian Government developed a clear preference for President-elect Trump."[89] The Russian government had taken notice of candidate Trump's statements in favor of pursuing a pro-Russian policy, which would have helped Russia in conflict zones such as Syria and the Ukraine.[90] In contrast, Clinton was likely to continue economic sanctions designed to punish Russia for the annexation of Crimea and its intervention in Eastern Ukraine.[91] Some have even suggested that Putin was "humiliated" by the U.S. decision to invade Iraq in 2003 over Russia's objections – an event that evidenced our "post-Soviet world order, where one superpower reigned."[92]

Even if the IRA had not succeeded in getting Trump elected, the goal of "disparaging" Clinton had an independent rationale. Doing so would weaken Clinton's political power, in the event of her electoral victory, by reducing her

---

[86] See Allison Denton, *Fake News: The Legality of the Russian 2016 Facebook Influence Campaign*, 37 B.U. INT'L L.J. 183, 186 (2019) (concluding that "Russia's preference for Trump over Clinton is unsurprising").

[87] I am not suggesting here that Clinton would have interfered in Russian domestic affairs, nor that any such interference would necessarily have violated international law. Rather, I am simply asserting that if Putin believed that Clinton might interfere in Russian politics by, for example, supporting the work of opposition leaders or pro-democracy activists in Russia, then this would have motivated Putin's desire to prevent Clinton from being elected in the 2016 election.

[88] See IRA Indictment, *supra* note 28, at para. 6.

[89] See Intelligence Community Assessment, *supra* note 7, at ii.

[90] See *id.* at 1. The DNI also noted that "Moscow also saw the election of President-elect Trump as a way to achieve an international counterterrorism coalition against the Islamic State in Iraq and the Levant (ISIL)." *Id.*

[91] See Allison Denton, *Fake News: The Legality of the Russian 2016 Facebook Influence Campaign*, 37 B.U. INT'L L.J. 183, 186 (2019) ("election of Clinton would have presented obstacles to ending sanctions").

[92] Michael R. Sinclair, *The Rising Dragon and the Dying Bear: Reflections on the Absence of A Unified America from the World Stage and the Resurgence of State-Based Threats to U.S. National Security*, 46 SYRACUSE J. INT'L L. & COM. 115, 148 (2018), *citing* Julia Ioffe, *What Putin Really Wants*, THE ATLANTIC (Jan/Feb 2018).

credibility and legitimacy.[93] The Director of National Intelligence concluded that the goal of Russia's information operation was to "denigrate Secretary Clinton, and harm her electability and potential presidency."[94] At the point in time when the Russians believed that Clinton's election was inevitable, the goal of the operation was to weaken and delegitimize her presidency, but when the Russians believed that Trump's election was possible, the goal of the operations subtly changed to also help Trump get elected, if possible.[95] This transition may have happened mid-way through the general election, when Trump began to consolidate power over the Republican party and also experienced a rise in polls in key battleground states.

To understand this strategic goal, it is important to understand that presidents, like all political leaders, have various degrees of power that are not reducible to their official constitutional authorities. Rather, political leaders have political and cultural capital that waxes and wanes depending on the particular moment. A political leader with maximum political capital has more options at his or her disposal to act on their desired agenda. In contrast, a political leader with low political capital will be constrained and will have fewer options at their disposal. For example, some political leaders are so hampered by scandal, or so dogged by political rivals, that they have few options for governing. Consequently, a stronger president in the White House has more options for governing. A weak president has fewer options.

The same would hold true for a potential Clinton presidency. With the assumption that Clinton was going to be hostile to Russia, the Russians would rather have a weak Clinton in office than a strong one, because a strong and emboldened Clinton would have significant political capital to spend – political capital that could be spent on countering Russian interests (and perceived Russian expansionism) across the world. At its most extreme, an emboldened Clinton might seek to promote pro-democracy elements in Russia in order to weaken Putin's grip on power. However, even in the absence of this developed antipathy, Putin may simply have concluded that the growing international democratic order, and its preference for democratic regimes, is a threat to Putin's legitimacy and power.[96]

None of this is meant to suggest that Putin's interference in the 2016 election was *justified* on account of political self-defense. Rather, it simply suggests that the Russians were strongly motivated to interfere in the 2016 election and that doing

---

[93] *See* Michael R. Sinclair, *The Rising Dragon and the Dying Bear: Reflections on the Absence of A Unified America from the World Stage and the Resurgence of State-Based Threats to U.S. National Security*, 46 SYRACUSE J. INT'L L. & COM. 115, 153–4 (2018) (concluding that "[b]y all measures, the Russian use of cyber tools to exert influence over the 2016 Presidential election was a cohesive integrated campaign in furtherance of the Russian political objective of both denying the presidency to Secretary Clinton and sowing dissent and confusion amongst the American electorate").

[94] *See* Intelligence Community Assessment, *supra* note 7, at ii.

[95] *Id.* ("When it appeared to Moscow that Secretary Clinton was likely to win the election, the Russian influence campaign began to focus more on undermining her future presidency.").

[96] *Id.* at 1 (concluding that "[i]n trying to influence the US election, we assess the Kremlin sought to advance its longstanding desire to undermine the US-led liberal democratic order, the promotion of which Putin and other senior Russian leaders view as a threat to Russia and Putin's regime.").

so was meant to maximize the strategic interests of the Russian Federation. Putin hoped to gain a specific advantage by interfering in the 2016 election, and the interference represented a rational calculation that by spending a small amount on information operations, he could weaken an inevitable Clinton presidency or in the alternative embolden a friendlier Trump administration. When viewed through this lens, the election interference represented a powerful form of *Kriegsraison* – not in a literal sense of a rationale for armed conflict but in a metaphorical sense: the Clausewitzian state interest of the Russian government that guided its efforts. Just as Clausewitz viewed the state's deployment of military force as inevitably tied to, and possibly justified by (according to some interpretations), a particular state interest that would be vindicated by the use of military force, operations that fall below the threshold of the use of force can be viewed in the same light. The Russians had a particular objective in mind and rationally constructed an information operation to advance their strategic interests.

CONCLUSION

Since the interference in the 2016 election was designed to advance Russia's strategic interests, one might be tempted to consider it as a legitimate diplomatic activity, as a form of pernicious but ultimately permissible form of propaganda.[97] A full assessment of the legality of this interference will unfold over the course of this monograph, but even before laying out the details of this legal analysis in future chapters, there are already reasons why we should reject the label of this operation as merely a legitimate form of traditional diplomatic activity dressed up in modern cyber clothing.

First, the conduct was mostly clandestine and unacknowledged.[98] During Putin's well-publicized meeting with Trump, Trump reported back to the media that Putin had specifically denied interfering in U.S. elections.[99] The unacknowledged nature of the activity, while not necessarily dispositive on the question of legality, does

---

[97] Several scholars have noted that the deployment of propaganda is not, per se, illegal under international law. *See* Michael N. Schmitt, *"Virtual" Disenfranchisement: Cyber Election Meddling in the Grey Zones of International Law*, 19 CHICAGO J. INT'L L. 30, 50 (2018); Allison Denton, *Fake News*, at 202; Ashley C. Nicolas, *Taming the Trolls: The Need for an International Legal Framework to Regulate State Use of Disinformation on Social Media*, 107 GEO. L.J. ONLINE 36, 38 (2018) (noting that "[t] hroughout history, psychological operations have been inherently limited in scope and considered legal insofar as they did not constitute perfidy or violate the prohibition of intervention" and concluding that "[n]ot all interference equates to intervention"). *See generally* Kilovaty, *supra* note 3, at 161 (surveying the views of other scholars and noting that the "traditional understanding of intervention does not conform easily to the emerging role that states are playing in cyberspace").

[98] *See* Kilovaty, *supra* note 3, at 153 (noting that "doxfare" is "comprised of covert and overt elements").

[99] *See* Julie Hirschfeld Davis, *Trump, at Putin's Side, Questions U.S. Intelligence on 2016 Election*, N.Y. TIMES (July 16, 2018) (quoting Trump as saying, referring to his own intelligence agencies: "They said they think it's Russia . . . . I have President Putin; he just said it's not Russia").

nonetheless cast the activity in a particular light. It is a form of statecraft that attempts to remain shielded from international scrutiny.

Second, the interfering conduct lacked transparency.[100] The Russian agents working through the IRA masqueraded as Americans while posting on social media platforms. The corrosive nature of their conduct flowed not from the content of their messages but rather the content of the message *combined* with their duplicity over their national identity. To see why this is the case, consider the nature of democracy and the special role that elections play in democratic societies. Elections allow a political group to make a decision about how they should be governed; indeed, this is the very definition of *politics*, a word derived from the Greek word for the city-state (*Polis* and *Politika*). By definition, elections are for insiders, otherwise the election becomes the expression of the will, not of the city-state, but of the world community, thus eviscerating the distinction between the polity and its outer boundaries. As long as the world is composed of peoples who find their ultimate expression in states, the democratic notion of an election will require drawing (and zealously guarding) boundaries between insiders and outsiders.

The Russian information operation interfered with this process, which already marks it as distinct from other forms of statecraft.[101] We leave aside for the moment whether the interference violated international law or not. Whether the democratic process is protected, by international law, against this interference, will require further examination in the coming chapters. Chapter 2 will focus on whether interference is illegal as a form of cyber warfare, while Chapter 3 will focus on whether election interference is illegal under international law as a violation of sovereignty. For the moment, it is enough to note that election interference is a form of interference whose principal target is neither the security of the foreign state (as traditionally construed) nor its territorial sovereignty, but rather its political independence. This distinguishes

---

[100] At least under one definition, traditional "psychological operations" involve the conveyance of truthful information. *See* Nicolas, *supra* note 97, at 39, *citing* ROBERT J. KODOSKY, PSYCHOLOGICAL OPERATIONS AMERICAN STYLE: THE JOINT UNITED STATES PUBLIC AFFAIRS OFFICE, VIETNAM AND BEYOND xiv (2007). However, it should also be noted that the 2010 Department of Defense definition of PSYOPS does not include an explicit reference to truthfulness: "Planned operations to convey selected information and indicators to foreign audiences to influence their emotions, motives, objective reasoning, and ultimately the behavior of foreign governments, organizations, groups, and individuals. The purpose of psychological operations is to induce or reinforce foreign attitudes and behavior favorable to the originator's objectives. Also called PSYOP." *See* Department of Defense, Joint Publication 3-13.2, *Psychological Operations* GL-8 (Jan. 7, 2010). This is contrasted with "propaganda," which the Department of Defense defines explicitly as a form of "adversary communication, especially of a biased or misleading nature." *See id.* at GL-7.

[101] Indeed, the DNI assessment noted that "Russian efforts to influence the 2016 US presidential election represent the most recent expression of Moscow's longstanding desire to undermine the US-led liberal *democratic order*, but these activities demonstrated a significant escalation in directness, level of activity, and scope of effort compared to previous operations." *See* Intelligence Community Assessment, *supra* note 7, at ii (emphasis added).

it from other forms of statecraft that harm a state, its nationals, or its leaders. For example, a foreign state might impose economic sanctions which interfere with another state's ability to conduct business. Or a foreign state might close its borders to nationals from a third state, which interferes with their free movement. These other forms of statecraft might be classified as interference, but they have neither the same consequences nor the same modalities as election interference.

At its simplest, election interference is a distinct form of interference, unlike any other. It strikes at the core institution of democracy – the election – whereby the polity deliberates and then decides its destiny.[102] Even where the interference fails to alter the vote tally or tamper with election machines, election interference might still compromise the nature of democratic deliberations.[103] In this regard, the corrosive nature of the social media information operation is the most significant. If the social media posts were written by Russian individuals who transparently identified themselves as Russian, then the social media operations would not have had the same corrosive effect. But by creating specific accounts that appeared to be American, and by engaging in online correspondence pretending to be Americans, the Russian government entered the political arena in a manner designed not only to redirect the political deliberations in ways that maximized Russian interests but also to perfidiously implant political sentiments into the body politic. Consequently, the political deliberations in the 2016 election reflected not just the political sentiments of the American electorate but also the political sentiments of outsiders as well.[104]

Finally, given the success of the Russian election interference, it is clear that future interference is likely. The interference was inexpensive, helped to advance Russian strategic interests, and had few negative consequences for the Kremlin or Putin personally.[105] Economic sanctions leveled against oligarchs associated with

---

[102] *See* Boyd Garriott, *A Constitutional Outlier: Legitimacy As A State Interest and Its Implications in Election Law*, 41 HARV. J.L. & PUB. POL'Y 973 (2018) (stating that a "common theme throughout election law jurisprudence is the idea of *legitimacy*").

[103] *See* Intelligence Community Assessment, *supra* note 7, at iii ("Russian intelligence obtained and maintained access to elements of multiple US state or local electoral boards. DHS assesses that the types of systems Russian actors targeted or compromised were not involved in vote tallying.").

[104] *See* Zephyr Teachout, *Extraterritorial Electioneering and the Globalization of American Elections*, 27 BERKELEY J. INT'L L. 162, 183 (2009) ("The center of the democratic promise is the idea that people control the rules of their own community and collectively direct their laws. They make decisions about the way they want their community to look and then attempt to implement those decisions through a set of rules, punishments, and actions.").

[105] *See* Intelligence Community Assessment, *supra* note 7, at 4 ("Putin's public views of the disclosures suggest the Kremlin and the intelligence services will continue to consider using cyber-enabled disclosure operations because of their belief that these can accomplish Russian goals relatively easily without significant damage to Russian interests.").

Putin have had limited effect and have failed to alter Putin's basic calculation. The age of election interference is upon us.[106]

[106] The DNI refers to Russia's election interference as a "new normal." *See* Intelligence Community Assessment, *supra* note 7, at 5. Specifically, the DNI noted that: "Immediately after Election Day, we assess Russian intelligence began a spearphishing campaign targeting US Government employees and individuals associated with US think tanks and NGOs in national security, defense, and foreign policy fields. This campaign could provide material for future influence efforts as well as foreign intelligence collection on the incoming administration's goals and plans." *Id.*

Election Interference Is Not Cyber-War

INTRODUCTION

Historically, foreign election interference was accomplished through nondigital means. So, for example, a state might drop leaflets on a city urging the residents to take a particular action. Or, the state might broadcast messages over radio or other media. Or, the interfering state might make corrupt deals with local politicians or officials in ways that might constitute meddling. In today's world, however, these prosaic forms of interference have been replaced with their digital counterparts: the use of email hacking and fraudulent social media presence to influence the public and consequently interfere with an election. Because the method of election interference has shifted to the digital domain, there is a strong temptation to view the legality of election interference through the international legal rules governing cyber-attacks. In other words, one common assumption made by commentators is that election interference should be understood as a subcategory or particular instantiation of cyber-attacks. Although the international law governing cyber-activity is still emerging, the greatest clarity in that area stems from the international law regarding cyber-war. The majority view among international lawyers is that the regular rules governing kinetic warfare – that is, physical military movements – also apply to cyber-warfare.[1] So, for example, an attack that would violate the law of war if conducted by planes and tanks would also violate the law of war if the same effects are produced by a cyber-attack launched by a team of hackers acting as state-cyber-combatants.

We will discuss this particular argument in greater detail below, but for the moment the key point is that there is a strong temptation to understand election

[1] For an expression of this point of view, see Jody M. Prescott, *Building the Ethical Cyber Commander and the Law of Armed Conflict*, 40 RUTGERS COMPUTER & TECH. L.J. 42, 47 (2014) ("As nations move toward securing the means to conduct cyber conflict that begins to approach our common understandings of war, a consensus appears to be emerging among international organizations concerned with the implementation of LOAC, and in academia, that LOAC at least applies to those actions in cyberspace that either result in, or are intended to result in, injury to humans and damage to geophysical things.").

interference through the lens of cyber-war. In other words, some would condemn election interference as illegal under international law because it represents a form of cyber-warfare. Other lawyers and politicians will argue the opposite: that election interference does not violate international law because it does not rise to the level of a cyber-war, as if this is the end of the matter in terms of the legal analysis. What unites these two competing conclusions is the assumption that cyber-warfare is the correct framework for judging the legality of election interference. That assumption is profoundly mistaken.

This chapter will explain why the assumption is mistaken and why the cyber-war framework is unhelpful. Although international law is a broad and sweeping body of law, the legal regulation of warfare is one of the most prominent and successful subdisciplines of international law. So, perhaps it is not surprising that lawyers should jump to cyber-war as an attractive framing device. But the framing device is poor and sucks up oxygen from other more compelling frameworks that international law has to offer.

In order to explain why cyber-war is a poor fit for understanding election interference, this chapter will first explain the basic principles behind the legal regulation of warfare. Then, in Section 2, this chapter will explain how these principles apply in the context of cyber-attacks. Finally, Section 3 will consider the specific case of election interference to show why it does not constitute an illegal cyber-attack in violation of the law of war. But just because it does not violate the rules regarding cyber-war does not mean that it might not violate some other area of international law. The field of international law is at once broader and deeper than the legal regulation of armed conflict. But only by first pushing aside the most obvious framing device can we move toward more compelling and innovative frameworks for understanding the particular harm posed by foreign election interference. This argument will unfold over the course of the subsequent chapters.

1. INTERNATIONAL REGULATION OF WARFARE

A. *The Distinction Between* Jus ad Bellum *and* Jus in Bello

The international legal regulation of warfare is based on the foundational distinction between *jus ad bellum* and *jus in bello* – terms that originate with the Just War philosophical tradition. *Jus ad bellum* regulates the recourse to force, that is, the decision to go to war in the first place. With very few exceptions, states are mostly prohibited from using military force to settle international disputes, but in some situations, the recourse to military force might be justified. In contrast, *jus in bello* regulates the conduct of hostilities during an armed conflict. So, for example, *jus in bello* passes judgment on the tactics used during an armed conflict, such as who can be targeted, in what circumstances, and with what weapons.[2] For example, one of the cardinal rules of *jus in bello* is the rule prohibiting collateral damage that is excessive or disproportionate to the value of the military target.[3] One way of explaining the distinction between *jus ad bellum* and *jus in bello* is that the former covers macro-questions regarding the legality of the overall war, while the latter covers micro-questions regarding the conduct of individual military operations within that war.

The legal domains of *jus ad bellum* and *jus in bello* are legally and conceptually independent, in the sense that a *jus in bello* analysis does not depend on the outcome of the *jus ad bellum* analysis.[4] In other words, both the aggressor state and the victim state are required to follow the same rules regarding the conduct of warfare. The victim state is not entitled to more liberal rules for the conduct of warfare, just because the victim state is on the receiving end of a *jus ad bellum* violation. Conversely, the aggressor state is not subject to more restrictive conduct rules just because the aggressor state has violated *jus ad bellum* principles. In the conduct of cyber-war, this means that whether a state has violated *jus ad bellum* or not is irrelevant to the question of how the rules of *jus in bello* are applied in the context of cyber-attacks. It is important to keep the macro-level and micro-level questions separate.

There has been a recent trend in the philosophical literature to question the canonical separation between *jus ad bellum* and *jus in bello* principles. These "revisionist just war" arguments have pushed back against the classical Just War Tradition, which always assumed that the *jus ad bellum* and *jus in bello* domains were conceptually distinct.[5] Under the revisionist line of thinking, philosophers have suggested that, for example, noncombatants on the victim side should be entitled to fight back against an unjust aggression, whereas under the traditional view, noncombatants are prohibited from participating in hostilities and are there-fore not entitled to the combatant's privilege.[6] Part of the inspiration for the revisionist trend is that the ethical rules regarding killing should be the same for individuals as they are for groups.[7] In other words, the revisionist camp aims to

---

[2]   See GARY SOLIS, THE LAW OF ARMED CONFLICT 7–8 (2nd edn., Cambridge University Press, 2016) (noting that: "All's fair in love and war? Hardly! Any divorce lawyer will attest that 'all' is decidedly not fair in love. Just as surely, all is not fair in war.").

[3]   *Id.* at 292–300.

[4]   See MICHAEL WALZER, JUST AND UNJUST WARS: A MORAL ARGUMENT WITH HISTORICAL ILLUSTRATIONS 21 (3rd edn., Basic Books, 2000) (suggesting that the "two sorts of judgment are logically independent"). *See also* Nathaniel Berman, *Privileging Combat? Contemporary Conflict and the Legal Construction of War*, 43 COLUM. J. TRANSNAT'L L. 1, 27 (2004) (discussing the "indifference of jus in bello to the relative jus ad bellum merits of the parties").

[5]   See Jeff McMahan, *War as Self-Defense*, 18 ETH. & INT'L AFF. 75 (2004).

[6]   See Jeff McMahan, *Innocence, Self-Defense and Killing in War*, 2 J. POL. PHIL. 193–221 (1994).

[7]   McMahan, *supra* note 6, at 198 ("According to virtually all accounts of the right of individual self-defense, the Culpable Attacker is not morally permitted to use lethal violence even to defend himself against his initial victim's self-defensive response.").

harmonize rules of individual morality with rules for group morality, rather than seeing them as separate modes of ethical conduct. Under principles governing personal self-defense, for example, the victim of an unjust attack is entitled to fight back whereas the aggressor is not entitled to use physical force. Revisionists ask why the same should not be true also in the context of warfare.

Whatever one thinks about the philosophical legitimacy of these revisionist arguments, even the philosophers do not contend that their arguments are currently represented in international legal doctrine.[8] The revisionist just war philosophers are making arguments about the deep morality of warfare and even some of them concede that there might be legitimate institutional or pragmatic reasons why international law separates *jus ad bellum* and *jus in bello* into conceptually distinct normative regimes. For example, it might be unworkable to assign to each soldier and to each civilian the task of determining whether a military invasion is justified under *jus ad bellum* before they decide how they should behave.[9] So, the virtue of the current legal regime is that soldiers and civilians alike can fight (or not fight) in a war without having to adjudicate the contentious *jus ad bellum* questions. Whether this separation is consistent with the "deep morality" of warfare or not, it certainly makes life for the professional solider (on both sides) more workable and represents the current state of the legal regulation of warfare. It may even be morally justified as an instrumental matter, because separating the two domains might service the legitimate goal of designing real-world institutions that ensure compliance with rules that are a second-best alternative to the deep morality of war.[10]

B. *The Basic Rules Regarding* Jus ad Bellum

The rules regarding *jus ad bellum* are relatively straightforward to articulate, although they are contentious when it comes to their *application*. The use of military force by one state against another state is only justified if taken in self-defense or in accordance with a Security Council authorization. Article 2(4) of the UN Charter prohibits the use of military force for the resolution of international disputes, but article 51 of the UN Charter carves out cases of self-defense from the basic article 2(4) prohibition.[11] Article 51 imposes various requirements for the exercise of self-defense, including the existence of an armed attack against the victim

---

[8]   *Id.* at 208 ("There are compelling reasons why the laws of war cannot treat the use of violence by Unjust Combatants as criminal.").

[9]   *Id.* at 208.

[10]   *See* Janina Dill, *Should International Law Ensure the Moral Acceptability of War?*, 26 Leiden J. Int'l L. 253–70 (2013).

[11]   Article 2(4) of the UN Charter states: "All Members shall refrain in their international relations from the threat or use of force against the territorial integrity or political independence of any state, or in any other manner inconsistent with the Purposes of the United Nations." Article 51 states that "Nothing in the present Charter shall impair the inherent right of individual or collective self-defence if an armed attack occurs against a Member of the United Nations, until the Security Council has taken measures necessary to maintain international peace and security. Measures taken by Members in the exercise of

state, and a requirement that the Security Council be informed if a state is exercising its legal right of self-defense. Although not explicitly articulated in the text of article 51, international law also imposes additional constraints, including requirements of imminence, necessity, and proportionality.[12] The former requires that the armed attack against the victim state be imminent at the point in time when the victim state uses military force to repel the threat. The latter requirement requires that the defensive force be necessary to stop the threat; if nonmilitary measures are available to resolve the threat, the resort to defensive force is illegitimate (because it is unnecessary at the point in time when it is exercised). Any military response to an attack, undertaken in self-defense pursuant to article 51, would be constrained by the principle of proportionality, meaning that the defensive force must not be disproportionate to the legitimate interest being vindicated by the defensive force.[13]

The Security Council is entitled under Chapter VII of the UN Charter to issue a binding resolution calling on member states to use military force to resolve a threat of or breach of international peace and security.[14] Member states are not *required* to use military force in that situation, but they are *permitted* to do so; the Security Council resolution transforms what would otherwise potentially be a violation of article 2(4) into a lawful police action to enforce international law. The Security Council is therefore a clearinghouse for decisions regarding the lawfulness of military force, although individual states retain the "inherent" right to exercise defensive force even in situations where the Security Council fails to act to authorize military force.[15] The Security Council may also authorize nonmilitary measures under article 41 of the UN Charter.[16] The right to unilateral defense force is particularly important since the Security Council includes five permanent members (China, France, Russia, United States, United Kingdom), each of whom enjoys a veto, that is, the right to veto any resolution coming out of the Security Council.

this right of self-defence shall be immediately reported to the Security Council and shall not in any way affect the authority and responsibility of the Security Council under the present Charter to take at any time such action as it deems necessary in order to maintain or restore international peace and security."

[12] For a discussion of these requirements, see generally YORAM DINSTEIN, WAR, AGGRESSION, AND SELF-DEFENSE (Cambridge University Press, 2012).

[13] For a discussion of the proportionality requirement, see generally MICHAEL A. NEWTON AND LARRY MAY, PROPORTIONALITY IN INTERNATIONAL LAW (Oxford University Press, 2014).

[14] *See* art. 42 ("Should the Security Council consider that measures provided for in Article 41 would be inadequate or have proved to be inadequate, it may take such action by air, sea, or land forces as may be necessary to maintain or restore international peace and security. Such action may include demonstrations, blockade, and other operations by air, sea, or land forces of Members of the United Nations.").

[15] *See* art. 51.

[16] *See* art. 41 ("The Security Council may decide what measures not involving the use of armed force are to be employed to give effect to its decisions, and it may call upon the Members of the United Nations to apply such measures. These may include complete or partial interruption of economic relations and of rail, sea, air, postal, telegraphic, radio, and other means of communication, and the severance of diplomatic relations.").

Consequently, a resolution authorizing the use of force is exceedingly rare and requires universal approval from the world's major powers. Given the possibility for gridlock on the Council, most cases of military force are justified, if at all, under article 51 self-defense.

C. The Basic Rules Regarding Jus in Bello

The rules regarding the conduct of warfare are expressed in major treaty conventions such as the four post-World War II Geneva Conventions, two additional protocols to the Geneva Conventions from 1977, and the Hague Conventions of 1899 and 1907. These treaty sources can be combined with rules of customary international law that equally regulate the conduct of hostilities. The rules regarding the conduct of warfare can be broadly fit into the following categories: targeting, participation in hostilities, tactics in warfare, and weaponry.

For example, the bedrock principle of *jus in bello* is that attacking forces should limit their attacks to enemy combatants, that is, members of enemy military forces or other militia units that meet the requirements of combatancy. Attacking forces are also entitled to attack civilians for such time as those civilians are directly participating in hostilities.[17] It would be incongruous if a state could avoid its nationals being targeted simply by refusing to organize itself into formal military units, hence the exceptional rule that allows targeting of civilians who directly participate in hostilities. Despite this cardinal rule of distinction, civilians may be killed but only as collateral damage.[18] By the phrase "collateral damage," the law means that the civilians were not the object of the attack but were killed as a side effect of an attack on a lawful military objective such as a military asset or military personnel.[19] So the difference between a violation of the principle of distinction and a case of permissible collateral damage is the attitude of the attacker. If the attacker is aiming at the civilian, the attacker has violated the principle of distinction. On the other hand, if the attacker is aiming at a lawful military objective, but still kills a civilian or a group of civilians, the civilians are considered collateral damage. The attacking force may even envision the civilian deaths, and they should still be counted as collateral damage.[20] However, the *jus in bello* imposes a major constraint on the existence of collateral damage by prohibiting collateral

---

[17] This rule is codified in article 51(3) of Additional Protocol I (API) to the General Conventions: "Civilians shall enjoy the protection afforded by this Section, unless and for such time as they take a direct part in hostilities."

[18] The principle of distinction is also sometimes referred to as the principle of discrimination. The two are roughly synonymous, though the word "distinction" is more often used by lawyers and "discrimination" is more common among philosophers of war.

[19] Solis dates the term "collateral damage" to the 1991 Gulf War. *See* SOLIS, *supra* note 2, at 295; SAHR CONWAY-LANZ, COLLATERAL DAMAGE 221 (Routledge, 2006).

[20] The question of mental intent in the context of collateral damage is somewhat complicated and has produced a series of unfortunate statements from international courts. For a discussion of this issue, see Jens David Ohlin, *Targeting and the Concept of Intent*, 35 MICH. J. INT'L L. 79 (2013).

damage that is disproportionate or "excessive" to the anticipated value of the military advantage that will be gained from destroying the military target.[21]

The *jus in bello* also outlaws particular tactics. Killing by perfidy is outlawed, such as pretending to be a civilian to draw out the enemy or waiving a white flag and pretending to surrender, only to kill the enemy during an ambush.[22] These are "dishonest stratagems" as Kant called them, and impermissible as far back as the Lieber Code.[23] Similarly, the *jus in bello* prohibits tactics that increase the suffering of the enemy (*maux superflus*) but do not produce any additional military benefit.[24] So, in other words, it would be illegal to use a weapon that does not increase lethality but only increases the pain that the enemy will suffer before dying. Similarly, particular weapons may be outlawed by particular treaties or conventions, such as nuclear weapons (for some states that have signed nonproliferation accords), chemical weapons, cluster munitions, and landmines, though in each of these cases (other than chemical weapons) several states have refused to sign on to the conventions because they consider the weapon system in question to be necessary for strategic interests. Finally, attacking forces are not permitted to attack soldiers who are *hors de combat* because they are sick or because they have effectively communicated their surrender. Consequently, summarily executing a group of POWs (without legal process or criminal culpability) would constitute a war crime.

The basic structure behind the *jus in bello* is to create a special "war convention," as Michael Walzer once described it. It creates, in other words, a special framework for the conduct of hostilities. Lawful combatants are granted the combatant's privilege: in exchange for opening themselves up to the reciprocal risk of killing, combatants may not be prosecuted by the enemy for lawful acts of belligerency. In exchange, combatants are required to limit their attacks to military objects, thus sparing civilians from the burdens of war, as much as possible as would be consistent with the need to pursue the war effort (banning collateral damage entirely would effectively hamper warfare entirely). The requirement to carry arms openly and to avoid perfidious killing – among other prohibitions – install a basic notion of transparency in the law of war. Combatants do not simply fight for themselves as if they were fighting in a duel. Rather, combatants are representatives of the state, killing on the state's behalf, and therefore combatants and the state "advance and retrograde" together on the field of battle, in Lieber's

---

[21]   See API, art. 51(5) ("Among others, the following types of attacks are to be considered as indiscriminate ... (b) an attack which may be expected to cause incidental loss of civilian life, injury to civilians, damage to civilian objects, or a combination thereof, which would be excessive in relation to the concrete and direct military advantage anticipated.").

[22]   See API, art. 37(1) ("It is prohibited to kill, injure or capture an adversary by resort to perfidy. Acts inviting the confidence of an adversary to lead him to believe that he is entitled to, or is obliged to accord, protection under the rules of international law applicable in armed conflict, with intent to betray that confidence, shall constitute perfidy ....").

[23]   However, it should be noted that "ruses of war are not prohibited." See API, art. 37(2).

[24]   API, art. 35(2) ("2. It is prohibited to employ weapons, projectiles and material and methods of warfare of a nature to cause superfluous injury or unnecessary suffering.").

famous phrase.[25] None of that would be possible without a basic principle of transparency in the application of *jus in bello*, which requires for its operation a tangible and public connection between individual combatants and the state on whose behalf they fight.

2. THE EMERGING CONSENSUS ON CYBER-WAR

The last few years have witnessed a tremendous acceleration of work applying the law of war to the context of cyber-attacks. That being said, there is some uncertainty over the application of core law of war principles to cyber-space. There are several reasons for the uncertainty. The first is that there has been little diplomatic effort to codify specific international rules for cyber-attacks. One reason for the reluctance is that many lawyers believe that existing rules of IHL are adequate to the task of regulating state behavior in cyber-space. Second, some states want to preserve flexibility for their operations conducted in the cyber-realm. Third, the secretive nature of cyber-activities hampers the formation of customary rules. Customary international law develops out of state practice (action) and *opinio juris* (performing the legal action from a sense of legal obligation). But many cyber-attacks are conducted in secret, either covertly or clandestinely, and states often refuse to acknowledge their involvement in cyber-attacks. Other states will sometimes criticize those attacks, but in other situations the difficulty with "attribution" will hamper those public criticisms, thus leading to more private criticism through diplomatic channels.[26] This dynamic scuttles or limits the formation of customary norms. However, despite these limitations, international lawyers have worked hard to explain, through soft-law mechanisms, how the law of war applies in cyber-space. One result of this effort, the Tallinn Manual, brought together experts on cyber-law and sought feedback from state governments.

This section outlines the state of international law regarding cyber-war: subsection A focuses on the role of the Tallinn Manual in constructing these norms; subsection B on whether cyber-wars are armed conflicts under international law; subsection C on the armed attack requirement for self-defense; and subsection D on the application of *jus in bello* principles to cyber-attacks.

---

[25]   Lieber Code, art. 20 ("Public war is a state of armed hostility between sovereign nations or governments. It is a law and requisite of civilized existence that men live in political, continuous societies, forming organized units, called states or nations, whose constituents bear, enjoy, suffer, advance and retrograde together, in peace and in war.").

[26]   *See* Delbert Tran, *The Law of Attribution: Rules for Attributing the Source of A Cyber-Attack*, 20 YALE J. L. & TECH. 376, 386 (2018) (noting that the "difficulty in tracing the source of a cyber-attack has long plagued discussions of cybersecurity, and much of current scholarship has accepted the traditional wisdom that the technological architecture of the internet makes attribution an exceedingly difficult problem"); Collin S. Allan, *Attribution Issues in Cyberspace*, 13 CHI.-KENT J. INT'L & COMP. L. 55 (2013).

A. The Role of the Tallinn Manual

The Tallinn Manual was initiated by the NATO Cooperative Cyber Defence Centre of Excellence, which is located in Tallinn, Estonia.[27] The initiative involved a collaboration of international law and military law experts from across the world, followed by consultation and feedback from governments and their legal advisors. Although the Tallinn Manual is not a source of international law per se, it is relevant to the state of international law for two reasons. First, it may help in the formation of customary international law, as states gravitate towards particular statements of customary rules and norms, providing expression of legal rules for states to either accept or reject through the process of *opinio juris*. Second, the Tallinn Manual is a semi-authoritative statement of how experts believe that the existing law can and should be *applied* in cyber-space. If there is no need to amend or create new law, but simply a need to apply existing law to activities in cyber-space, then there is no requirement that the application be guided by the stringent rules for the *creation* of international law.[28]

The Tallinn Manual focused on a variety of legal questions, including the applicability of *jus ad bellum* and *jus in bello* principles to cyber-attacks, and the use of countermeasures to thwart cyber-attacks. Also, the Tallinn Manual discusses violations of sovereignty that fall below the "armed attack" threshold – violations that will be the focus of the next chapter of this book.[29]

B. Are Cyber-Wars Real Wars As a Matter of International Law?

The first threshold question is whether a cyber-war is a real "war" in the legal sense of that term as used by international lawyers. The answer to that question is yes, depending on the type of damage produced by the conflict, though this answer is a bit controversial.[30] Some legal scholars argue that defining cyber-wars as real "armed conflicts" only functions to give state militaries control over cyber-infrastructure and cyber-governance – questions that necessarily impact civilian life and which ought not to be exclusively managed by state militaries.[31] There is

---

[27] *See* Tallinn Manual on the International Law Applicable to Cyber Warfare (Michael N. Schmitt et al. (eds.), 2013) [hereinafter cited as "Tallinn Manual"].

[28] The strictly defined sources of international law are generally outlined in article 38 of the ICJ Statute.

[29] For our purposes, the Tallinn Manual sections on cyber-war are the most relevant to our analysis.

[30] For example, the philosopher Larry May has argued that cyber-wars should not be understood as real "armed conflicts" in the way that international lawyers use that term. *See* Larry May, The Nature of War and the Idea of "Cyberwar," in Ohlin et al. (eds.), Cyber War: Law and Ethics for Virtual Conflicts 3 (Oxford University Press, 2015) (suggesting that one could look at cyber-attacks as more like embargoes than as armed conflicts).

[31] *See* Mary Ellen O'Connell, *Cyber Security without Cyber War*, 17 J. Conflict & Sec. L. 187, 209 (2012) ("To date, the problem of Internet security has been the domain of international law scholars with expertise in use of force questions. They have sent the message that the Internet may be protected through military force or the threat of military force, analogizing to Cold War deterrence strategy.

wisdom in this criticism, though it is also the case that some cyber-wars should be considered significant enough to qualify as an armed conflict if they result in physical damage.

In terms of the application of international law, there is a widely shared definition for what counts as an armed conflict. International lawyers generally distinguish between international armed conflicts (IACs) between states, and noninternational armed conflicts (NIACs) between a state and a nonstate actor or between two nonstate actors. An IAC is triggered when there is a resort to "armed force" by one state against another state.[32] The standard view, though it is not codified in any treaty, is that there is no intensity threshold for this determination. In other words, an IAC exists between two states when one state uses military force against the other, regardless of how much force is used, or for how long it lasts. An IAC might involve a one-time airstrike by one state's air force, bombing targets in the other state, or the IAC might involve a full-scale land invasion that lasts for months or even years.[33] Either way, military force is traditionally thought of as involving some kinetic activity – the crossing of a border with a military asset, or the use of a confederate to destroy installations or buildings within the target state. It is very hard to think of an international armed conflict being triggered without either a border crossing or some physical destruction of at least some kind.

In contrast, a NIAC requires the existence of violent hostilities between a state and a nonstate actor that reaches a certain level of scope and intensity. So, for example, the state's use of physical force against a nonstate actor, such as a group of rebels, might not constitute an armed conflict if the state simply fires a few shots and arrests the members of the rebel organization. However, if there are sustained hostilities between the state and the nonstate actor that pass a certain threshold, the situation

---

Governments have followed this modelling, pouring resources into the military for keeping the Internet safe and for taking advantage of what it offers to attack opponents. Doing so has required strained analogies of cyber-attacks to conventional kinetic attacks. The Internet is now far less secure than before there was a Cyber Command or a NATO CCDCOE. It is time, therefore, to turn to cyber disarmament and a focus on peaceful protection of the Internet."). *See also* Christopher J. Finlay, *Just War, Cyber War, and the Concept of Violence*, 31 PHILOSOPHY & TECHNOLOGY 357–77 (2018) (preferring to conceptualize cyber-attacks under the broader rubric of "violence" instead of "war"); Ryan Patterson, *Silencing the Call to Arms: A Shift Away from Cyber Attacks As Warfare*, 48 LOY. L. A.L. REV. 969, 975 (2015) (arguing that "alternate legal regimes, including domestic law enforcement and the international principle of non-interference, may prove more effective frameworks to govern malicious cyber activities"). *Compare with* Yoram Dinstein, *Cyber War and International Law: Concluding Remarks at the 2012 Naval War College International Law Conference*, 89 INT'L L. STUD. 276, 283 (2013) ("There is nothing extraordinary in cyber warfare: it is just ordinary warfare with a little bit of extra. Cyber warfare does not merely resemble other forms of warfare: it is warfare. As such, it is directly governed by the jus in bello.").

[32] *See* Prosecutor v. Dusko Tadić, Decision on the Defence Motion for Interlocutory Appeal on Jurisdiction, Case No. IT-94-1-A, October 2, 1995, para. 70 ("an armed conflict exists whenever there is a resort to armed force between States").

[33] *See* International Committee of the Red Cross (ICRC), *How is the Term "Armed Conflict" Defined in International Humanitarian Law?*, Opinion Paper, March 2008, at 2 (citing D. Schindler for the proposition that an international armed conflict exists whenever any arms are used between states).

might graduate from a law enforcement operation to a full-blown NIAC that triggers the application of IHL rules (at least the rules that apply during a NIAC).[34]

Assuming that these articulations are correct statements about the international legal threshold for armed conflict, most cyber-attacks will not rise to the level of an armed conflict. Although the standard for the creation of an armed conflict is more liberal for international conflicts (IACs) than internal ones (NIACs), because the standard allows any use of force, it is unclear whether a cyber-attack would constitute a "use of force" against another state.[35] On this question there is not universal agreement. At first blush, one can distinguish between three examples of cyber-attacks. In the first, one state uses a cyber-attack to cause damage or to destroy a physical building in the target state. For example, the state uses a cyber-attack to cause an electrical power station to overheat, resulting in an explosion and fire that destroys the power station. The second example would be a cyber-attack that is launched against a computer system in the target state, resulting in the physical destruction of the computer system but no other physical destruction. The third example would be a cyber-attack that penetrates a foreign computer system, resulting in the theft or destruction of *information* but no physical damage, not even physical damage to the computer system.

Although experts are divided on some of these questions, there is widespread agreement that the first example would constitute a use of force that would trigger the existence of an armed conflict. In that case, a cyber-war would be a "war" in the sense of an "armed conflict" as international lawyers use the term. As the Tallinn Manual stated in its Rule 11, "A cyber operation constitutes a use force when its scale and effects are comparable to non-cyber operations rising to the level of a use of force."[36] In making this determination, international lawyers sometimes look at the "scale and effects" of the force to determine whether it crosses the relevant threshold.[37] In determining whether a cyber-attack constitutes a use of force, the Tallinn Manual suggests looking at the following criteria: severity, immediacy,

---

[34] Although customary international law arguably imposes the same (or similar) rules of conduct in both types of armed conflict, major treaties regulating *jus in bello* impose different legal regimes in each type of conflict. For example, the full Geneva Conventions apply during IACs, whereas only one article of the Geneva Conventions – Common article 3 – applies during NIACs.

[35] Solis, one of the leading American experts on the law of war, describes the standard in the following terms: "A cyber attack, as opposed to a cyber intrusion, constitutes a 'use of force' if undertaken by a state's armed forces, intelligence services, or a private contractor whose conduct is attributable to the state, and its scale and effects are comparable to non-cyber operations that rise to a level of a use of force." Gary D. Solis, *Cyber Warfare*, 219 MIL. L. REV. 1, 15 (2014).

[36] Tallinn Manual, *supra* note 27, at 45.

[37] *Id.* at 46 (noting that "'scale and effects' is a shorthand term that captures the quantitative and qualitative factors to be analysed in determining whether a cyber operation qualifies as a use of force."). The use of the "scale and effects" language in the Tallinn Manual is a bit unfortunate because it confuses the ICJ standard for armed attack within the context of self-defense for the standard for determining whether something counts as a use of force, despite the fact that the Tallinn Manual concedes that the definitions for a "use of force" and an "armed attack" are designed to "serve different normative purposes." *Id.* at 52. That being said, the confusion is not important,

directness, invasiveness, measurability of effects, military character, state involvement, and presumptive legality.[38] Even a threatened cyber-operation can constitute a use of force under certain circumstances.[39]

The second and third examples are more complicated. Some international lawyers would consider the second example a use of force because it involved the physical destruction of a computer system. The third example is the most difficult, because many lawyers would consider the loss or theft of information to be insufficient to count as a use of force under international law. A small minority of lawyers are more liberal in their interpretation of what counts as a use of force. However, it would seem that the majority has the better of the argument, because it is hard to understand how the mere theft of information could constitute an armed *attack*. Indeed, it seems to be theft or destruction of information, rather than an armed attack. One might argue that the concept of an armed attack should be amended in today's world of cyber-threats, but indeed the whole point of using this legal trigger is to declare the existence of an armed conflict and trigger the application of IHL, and it is unclear how anything would be improved by triggering the application of IHL every time there is a cross-border cyber-attack. Indeed, one should remember that IHL has both a regulating and licensing function, in that it allows privileged (i.e. lawful) combatants to kill each other with personal legal immunity. So, there are some costs to the application of IHL, and placing states in a constant state of armed conflict simply because of a cyber-attack would do little to resolve international disputes peacefully.

In practical terms, what this means for election interference is that most cases of cyber-election interference will not trigger the existence of an armed conflict under international law. If state agents seek to influence an election by surreptitiously posting messages on social media, even if in doing so they pretend to be American citizens, this hardly seems like a "use of force" in the military sense of that term. Even if a state uses a cyber-attack to hack election results and *change* vote tallies, this clearly constitutes a substantial intrusion in the political integrity of another state, though again it is hard to qualify it as a use of force. The changing of the vote tallies would alter – arguably destroy – the legitimacy of the election results, but the problem is that international law views the concept of the use of force through a military lens, while in this case the harm seems decidedly political rather than military.

---

because all parties agree that a cyber operation can, in theory, constitute a use of force under international law.

[38] *Id.* at 48–52 (but noting that the factors are not exhaustive and that "States may look to others, such as the prevailing political environment, whether the cyber operation portends the future use of military force, the identity of the attacker, any record of cyber operations by the attacker, and the nature of the target (such as critical infrastructure)").

[39] *Id.* at 52 (Rule 12: "A cyber operation, or threatened cyber operation, constitutes an unlawful threat of force when the threatened action, if carried out, would be an unlawful use of force.").

In drawing this conclusion, we need to postpone the more general question of whether such interference violates another body of international law and focus for the moment on the narrower question of whether the "war" paradigm is the right way for understanding information operations aimed at undermining the legitimacy of an election. Based on the analysis in this chapter, it is quite clear that the war paradigm is deficient.

The one situation where there might be an argument for classifying election interference as a use of force is if the cyber-attack does more than simply penetrate election infrastructure but actually physically destroys it. So, for example, if a state were to launch a cyber-attack that caused election machines to overheat and become inoperable, there is an argument that such a cyber-attack might constitute a use of force. Or, similarly, if a cyber-attack causes the electrical system at a state board of elections to overheat and cause a fire, this too would create the physical manifestation necessary to constitute a use of force. But if the election interference of 2016 has taught us anything, it is that the most potent forms of interference involve no physical damage at all. The target of this interference is not physical locations or the lives of military or civilian personnel; the target is democratic institutions through the strategic deployment of misinformation. Social media campaigns designed to influence an election are not acts of war, though this conclusion should not blind us to the threat they pose to democratic systems. We will need to leave to the next two chapters whether international law has an alternative paradigm to describe the harm caused by these cyber-attacks.

C. The Armed Attack Requirement for Self-Defense

The prior subsection focused exclusively on the triggering conditions for the existence of an armed conflict (and hence the applicability of IHL). A distinct but related question is what constitutes an "armed attack" under article 51 of the UN Charter. The existence of an armed attack is a condition for the target being permitted to exercise lethal force in response as a defensive measure. It is important to remember that not every violation of international law triggers a right of self-defense in response. Some violations, when they rise to the level of an armed attack, are considered sufficiently serious that the victim state is entitled to unilaterally exercise defensive force even in the absence of Security Council authorization.

The armed attack requirement is not subject to the same intensity requirements as required by the use of force analysis by IHL in the context of a NIAC. However, given the similarities between the two tests, international lawyers have generally assumed that an armed attack for purposes of article 51 requires some physical destruction. In the *Nicaragua* opinion, the ICJ argued that an attack must meet a "scale and effects" criterion in order to qualify as an armed attack – a standard that has had enormous influence in contemporary international legal and diplomatic practice. The Tallinn Manual endorses the "scale and effects" standard in the context of self-defense, though it concedes that even before the complication of cyber-attacks is added to the mix, the standard is somewhat vague and requires contentious application.[40] Governments likely support an "effects" test for evaluating a cyber-attack because it preserves maximum flexibility for using offensive cyber-attacks in many situations that fall below the relevant "effects" threshold.[41]

Consequently, a cyber-attack in some circumstances could qualify as an armed attack that triggers the inherent right to self-defense article in article 51.[42] The destruction must be foreseeable but it need not be immediate.[43] For example, if a cyber-attack produces death or physical destruction, even if that consequence is a "downstream" consequence, it might still qualify as an armed attack, as long as the resulting destruction is a reasonably foreseeable consequence of the cyber-attack.[44] One notable example is a cyber-attack against a water-filtration plant that prevents the target state from maintaining the quality of its water-supply; if civilians ultimately get sick or die, even if that occurs weeks or months after the original cyber-attack, this could qualify as an armed attack for purposes of article 51.[45]

If a military – that is, kinetic – response is going to be authorized by international law, it makes sense to have a demanding trigger. Consequently, the majority of experts who worked on the Tallinn Manual concluded that an armed attack requires an actual or imminent territorial infringement that will cause physical damage to persons or things.[46] The imminence requirement is a preexisting element of the

---

[40] *Id.* at 55 (concluding that "the parameters of the scale and effects criteria remain unsettled beyond the indication that they need to be grave").

[41] *See* Matthew C. Waxman, *Cyber-Attacks and the Use of Force: Back to the Future of Article 2(4)*, 36 YALE J. INT'L L. 421, 434–5 (2011) (concluding that "the U.S. government probably prefers an effects- or consequences-based interpretation of 'force' or 'armed attack' with respect to cyber-attacks not only for what it includes (and therefore what the Charter prohibits and what could trigger self-defense rights), but also for what it excludes. Computer-based espionage, intelligence collection, or even some preemptive cyber-operations or countermeasures designed to disable an adversary's threatening capabilities, for example, would generally not constitute prohibited force because these activities do not produce destructive consequences analogous to a kinetic military attack").

[42] Tallinn Manual, *supra* note 27, at 54 ("The International Group of Experts unanimously concluded that some cyber operations may be sufficiently grave to warrant classifying them as an 'armed attack' within the meaning of the Charter.").

[43] *See* Michael Gervais, *Cyber Attacks and the Laws of War*, 30 BERKELEY J. INT'L L. 525, 538 (2012) (noting that "[c]yber attacks do not always intentionally target the critical infrastructure that they eventually disrupt."). For another defense of the "reasonably foreseeable" standard in this context, see Michael N. Schmitt, *Computer Network Attack and the Use of Force in International Law: Thoughts on a Normative Framework*, 37 COLUM. J. TRANSNAT'L. L. 885, 916 (1999) (arguing that "the nature of the act's reasonably foreseeable consequences would be assessed to determine whether they resemble those of armed coercion").

[44] However, it is certainly true that "it is very difficult from a practical standpoint to predict whether a cyber attack will lead to kinetic harm or not." *See* Stephen Petkis, *Rethinking Proportionality in the Cyber Context*, 47 GEO. J. INT'L L. 1431, 1449 (2016).

[45] This example is explored in the Tallinn Manual, *supra* note 27, at 57.

[46] Tallinn Manual, *supra* note 27, at 54 (Rule 13: "A state that is the target of a cyber operation that rises to the level of an armed attack may exercise its inherent right of self-defense. Whether a cyber operation constitutes an armed attack depends on its scale and effects.").

international legal doctrine on self-defense, though how imminence should be understood for a cyber-attack is more difficult than its kinetic analog. For example, an imminent military attack might be manifested in the form of air, sea, and land forces moving into position to launch a strike or invasion. The public nature of these deployments ensures that the imminent requirement can be transparently evaluated by the court of world opinion. But a cyber-attack that is brewing would not be manifested in the same public manner, because the preparatory works would most likely be private, secret, or unknown.[47]

The physical damage could be caused by a physical attack or by a cyber-attack, but the resulting damage must be physical in nature.[48] The experts concluded that "it is not the nature (injurious or destructive) of the consequences that matters, but rather the extent of the ensuing effects."[49] However, it should be noted that a minority of scholars working on the Tallinn Manual concluded that a cyber-attack that destroys "data," even if it fails to destroy the computer system that houses the data, might in some circumstances constitute an armed attack.[50] A cyber-attack that disrupts the stock exchange and causes financial damage would not produce the requisite physical damage to be considered an armed attack, though there is disagreement on this question, with a minority of scholars suggesting that the negative consequences flowing from such an attack might meet the requirements for an armed attack.[51] Presumably, those scholars who view the "catastrophic effects" of a cyber-attack against a stock market as enough to qualify as an armed attack might also be

---

[47] However, some scholars have disputed that cyber-attacks can never be identified when they are still in the imminence window. *See* Ryan J. Hayward, *Evaluating the "Imminence" of A Cyber Attack for Purposes of Anticipatory Self-Defense*, 117 COLUM. L. REV. 399, 419 (2017) (concluding that "there is ample evidence to believe that investments over the past several years have dramatically improved the United States' monitoring abilities in this arena"). The Tallinn Manual argues that the right to self-defense in response to an offensive cyber armed attack is limited by two temporal limitations. First, the original cyber-attack must have occurred or must be imminent. Second, the defensive response must be immediately necessary to counter the threat. *See* Tallinn Manual, *supra* note 27, at 64–5. This second immediacy requirement is especially important in cases of anticipatory self-defense.

[48] *See* Herbert S. Lin, *Offensive Cyber Operations and the Use of Force*, 4 J. NAT'L SECURITY L. & POL'Y 63, 73 (2010) (suggesting that "effects rather than the modality of an action are the appropriate starting point for understanding how jus ad bellum and the U.N. Charter apply to offensive cyber operations" and concluding that "[e]ffects-based analysis suggests that the ambiguities are fewest when cyber attacks cause physical damage to property and loss of life in ways that are comparable to kinetic attacks and traditional war, because traditional LOAC provides various relevant precedents and analogies").

[49] Tallinn Manual, *supra* note 27, at 56. For example, Lubell argues that it is "at least arguable that computer data is closer to what the drafters wanted to include as objects than to the notion of what they wanted to exclude as aim or purpose." *See* Noam Lubell, *Lawful Targets in Cyber Operations: Does the Principle of Distinction Apply?*, 89 INT'L L. STUD. 252, 268 (2013). Lubell points out that data is, in some circumstances, more precious than physical objects; buildings can be rebuilt, but data that is not backed up (or if the backup tapes are destroyed as well) is gone forever.

[50] *See* Lubell, *supra* note 49, at 267 (concluding that "[t]he problem that arises, which is relatively unique to cyber operations, is whether data can be considered an object. While there is no definitive answer to this question, the currently prevailing view among LOAC experts appears to hold that in most cases data, for the purposes of LOAC targeting, should not be considered an object.").

[51] Tallinn Manual, *supra* note 27, at 56.

willing to view similarly a cyber-attack against election infrastructure or some other form of election cyber-interference.[52] However, this conclusion would appear to stretch the concept of "armed attack" well beyond its original meaning, at least when judged against its functional role in the overall ecosystem of *jus ad bellum*.[53]

So far our discussion has focused on the requirements for triggering a *military* response under article 51 after a state suffers a cyber-attack. However, different rules would apply for a right of *cyber*-defense in response to a first cyber-attack. If both a first cyber-attack and a defensive cyber-response fall below the threshold for armed attacks, then two nations could engage in a tit-for-tat response of increasingly serious cyber-attacks, and none of it will be regulated by either *jus ad bellum* or *jus in bello*.[54] The absence of physical destruction of persons or things will remove the cyber-engagement from the legal regulation of warfare, potentially emboldening states to engage in a wide range of cyber-activities.[55]

The question in today's world is whether states would prefer to continue these cyber-attacks without legal regulation or whether a system of reciprocal constraints on cyber-attacks below the military threshold would be a good idea.[56] Although

---

[52] It should also be noted that the downstream "effects" of a cyber-attack could take weeks or months to be fully manifested – a factor which makes the law of war much more difficult to apply to cyber-attacks, rather than conventional military attacks where the effects are more readily ascertainable in the hours and days after the attack. *See* Stephen Petkis, *Rethinking Proportionality in the Cyber Context*, 47 GEO. J. INT'L L. 1431, 1448 (2016) (concluding that "the principal problem with an 'effects test' in the cyber context is that the nature and gravity of a cyber attack can be incredibly difficult to ascertain at the time the attack occurs. Unlike kinetic action, the true 'effect' of a cyber intrusion may not be known until weeks, months, or years after it is first discovered").

[53] *See, e.g.*, Michael Gervais, *Cyber Attacks and the Laws of War*, 30 BERKELEY J. INT'L L. 525, 536 (2012) (concluding that "in light of the 'object and purpose' of the Charter, 'force' should be read more narrowly. The express aim of the United Nations is to maintain international peace and security, as well as 'to save succeeding generations from the scourge of war'. That suggests the notion of force in 1945 was limited to the military instrument."). Gervais goes on to correctly note that "treating all forms of cyber attack as a use of force would require an implausibly broad reading of Article 2(4) that includes non-physical damage." *Id.* at 537. *But see* Schmitt, *supra* note 43, at 919 (asking whether there should be a presumption that computer attacks fall in the use of force box and suggesting that "the security framework of the Charter would be best effected by application of an inclusivity presumption").

[54] *See* Priyanka R. Dev, *"Use of Force" and "Armed Attack" Thresholds in Cyber Conflict: The Looming Definitional Gaps and the Growing Need for Formal U.N. Response*, 50 TEX. INT'L L.J. 381, 392–93 (2015) (musing that "an alternative solution to better encapsulate non-physical cyber effects, rather than expanding ill-fitted traditional concepts, would be for the international community to create a new threshold for actions that do not meet the traditional use of force threshold but nonetheless constitute a 'breach of the peace' under Article 39 of the U.N. Charter").

[55] *See, e.g.*, Matthew C. Waxman, *Cyber-Attacks and the Use of Force: Back to the Future of Article 2(4)*, 36 YALE J. INT'L L. 421, 434 (2011) (noting that "in addition to the more traditional military defense and deterrence strategies just described, the U.S. government may also be considering legal interpretations flexible enough to permit its own offensive cyber-operations below a certain threshold or against inchoate hostile cyber-activities").

[56] Cyber-attacks that fall below the armed attack threshold would still be subject to international legal regulation, just not under the law of war. *See* Daniel J. Ryan et al., *International Cyberlaw: A Normative Approach*, 42 GEO. J. INT'L L. 1161, 1181 (2011) ("The term 'information operations' may

there have been extensive calls for more regulation, perhaps even a new treaty, to govern cyber-space, the lack of serious development of explicit rules suggests that most states are interested in keeping the law open in order to preserve their flexibility going forward. Indeed, states often refuse to even acknowledge publicly when they have perpetrated or been victimized by a cyber-attack – a reticence that hampers the development of legal norms in this area.

D. *Application of* Jus in Bello *Principles to Cyber-Attacks*

Principles of *jus in bello* apply to cyber-attacks as long as the cyber-attack either triggers an armed conflict or is launched during an armed conflict.[57] Outside the context of an armed conflict, a cyber-attack would be constrained by principles of international human rights law, and general constraints embodied in public international law (including the concept of proportionality), but the more specific rules of *jus in bello* would not apply. But in the context of an armed conflict, there are at least three *jus in bello* rules that are of prime importance to consider: the principle of distinction, the prohibition on excessive collateral damage, and the combatant's privilege.[58] Each will now be considered.

The principle of distinction requires attacking forces to limit their attacks to military objectives. A cyber-attack that takes place during an armed conflict would be subject to the same limitations.[59] So, for example, a state launching a cyber-attack would be prohibited from using a cyber-weapon to disable a purely civilian system, such as a school computer system, an electrical power grid providing electricity to a civilian neighborhood, or a computer system associated with a medical-care facility. This prohibition applies not just to attacks against civilian personnel, but also to attacks against civilian installations and civilian infrastructure. This rule would explicitly permit cyber-attacks against military targets, such as a computer system for any military base, missile system, air-defense system, or even an infrastructure system that provides resources exclusively to a military system. So, for example, it would be consistent with the laws of war to use a cyber-attack to disable an oil refinery that provides oil exclusively to a nation's military, with the goal of denying tanks, Humvees, and other military vehicles the fuel that they need to operate.

---

also include cyber operations that exceed the 'threat or use of force' threshold of Article 2(4) but which do not exceed the threshold of Article 51.95 Disruptive information operations that are narrower in results, less intense, and shorter in duration might fall into this category. Such operations would trigger the Rules of Countermeasures.").

57 *See, e.g.,* Gary D. Solis, *Cyber Warfare*, 219 MIL. L. REV. 1, 2 (2014) (noting that "[w]hether a 500-pound bomb or a computer is used to effect death and destruction, a weapon is a weapon").

58 Strangely, Gary Brown argues that *jus in bello* "has little of interest to say specifically about cyber warfare" and "the places where actual cyber activities and the LOAC intersect are few and, in the scheme of things, not especially relevant." Gary D. Brown, *International Law Applies to Cyber Warfare! Now What?*, 46 Sw. L. REV. 355, 356 (2017).

59 For a discussion of this issue, see Lubell, *supra* note 49, at 252.

Of course, a civilian target may be destroyed as collateral damage, provided that the collateral damage is not excessive or disproportionate to the military advantage gained by destroying the military target. In the context of a cyber-attack, it might be permissible to destroy a civilian computer system if it is a collateral consequence of destroying a military computer system, which might be the case if the two computer systems are linked together. However, if the destruction of the civilian computer system is disproportionate relative to the military advantage conferred by destroying the military computer system, the collateral damage would be disallowed by *jus in bello*.[60] There is some uncertainty about how to apply the concept of collateral *damage* to cyber-attacks. Some scholars have argued that the rule against disproportionate collateral damage should apply even when the damage to the civilian system is limited to loss of *functionality* to a computer system that provides service to the civilian population, even if the computer system is not physically destroyed.[61] The general law-of-war impulse to insulate civilians from the burdens of war applies just as much in cyber-space as it does on the kinetic battlefield.

The much more difficult application of this rule involves dual-infrastructure targets. Many infrastructure targets, such as power plants, oil refineries, water treatment plants and mining facilities, provide general resources for both civilian and military uses.[62] International lawyers have been perplexed by these targets for many years, and the NATO bombing of Serbia in 1999 threw into sharp relief the legal uncertainty over their status. For example, NATO forces attacked bridges that were used by both civilian and military vehicles, and also attacked TV stations that were owned by the government and used to broadcast nationalist propaganda. Although controversial, the prevailing consensus is that dual-use infrastructure targets need to be considered as both civilian and military at the same time and evaluated on that basis. Consequently, while it might be legitimate to destroy the military-side of a dual-use infrastructure target, the destruction of the civilian part (or the civilian percentage) is only justified if it is not excessive or disproportionate to the military advantage gained by destroying the military part. So, for example, the bridge

---

[60] For a discussion of the proportionality analysis related to a cyber-attack, see Jeremy Richmond, *Evolving Battlefields: Does Stuxnet Demonstrate A Need for Modifications to the Law of Armed Conflict?*, 35 FORDHAM INT'L L.J. 842, 891 (2012) (concluding that the Stuxnet cyber-attack against Iran was proportionate because "[g]iven the minimal amount of collateral damage caused by Stuxnet, Stuxnet's commanders were almost certainly reasonable in their calculations").

[61] *See, e.g.*, Eric Talbot Jensen, *Cyber Attacks: Proportionality and Precautions in Attack*, 89 INT'L L. STUD. 198, 206 (2013) (noting that "some have taken the view that damage also encompasses serious interruptions in functionality, such as would require replacing parts or reloading software systems. For example, in the kinetic analogy used above where a cyber attack shut down a communication port but left the rest of the computer unaffected, the computer would still turn on but its actual functionality might be seriously affected. If functionality is considered when determining damage, the kinetic analogy would be of limited value.").

[62] *See* Captain Christopher M. Kovach, *Beyond Skynet: Reconciling Increased Autonomy in Computer-Based Weapons Systems with the Laws of War*, 71 A.F. L. REV. 231, 250 (2014) (noting that "the proliferation of dual-use facilities and systems complicates the ability of cyberweapons to limit their effects solely to lawful targets").

can be destroyed if the civilian harm is not disproportionate to the advantage conferred by denying the *military use* of the bridge. For a cyber-attack, this means that a computer system could be destroyed even if it has some civilian use, but only if that civilian use is not disproportionate to the military advantage. A cyber-attack against a general power grid that supplies power to both the civilian population and the military would be lawful or unlawful depending on the exact proportion of the two uses and the relative harm it would impose on the civilian population weighed against the military value of denying power to the military.[63] The same would hold true for a cyber-attack against an oil refinery.

The combatant's privilege provides immunity to military personnel who fight during an armed conflict: as long as their acts comply with the laws of war, the soldiers cannot be prosecuted by a foreign adversary in a domestic court. The privilege applies to members of armed forces and members of a militia who wear uniforms or a fixed emblem, carry arms openly, have a responsible command structure, and comply with the laws and customs of warfare. In the kinetic context, it is clear what this means. Soldiers should wear uniforms, carry their rifles openly, and comply with the laws of war. Members of the CIA or other civilian agencies who are deployed covertly, without the state acknowledging their link to the forces, are not entitled to the combatant's privilege and could be prosecuted by the enemy upon capture. For a cyber-warrior working for the U.S. government, it is unclear how these requirements should translate.[64] In theory, the cyber-warrior should be wearing a uniform or fixed emblem, although there is little transparency gain from a hacker's wearing a uniform as compared to the transparency gain from an infantry solider wearing a uniform. The problem of remoteness is not unique to cyber-warriors, since missile operators or airmen might never be seen by the enemy either and the general assumption is that these service personnel should wear identifying emblems.

What does it mean for a cyber-warrior to "carry arms openly"? This is genuinely unclear and it is doubtful that there is a nonquestion-begging answer to this question. Military cyber-operations are often unacknowledged in the sense that the U.S. government will not acknowledge its role in an offensive cyber-attack, nor does it release much information about defensive cyber-activities either. To comply with the requirements of carrying arms openly and wearing a fixed emblem, should

---

[63] *See* Duncan B. Hollis, *Why States Need an International Law for Information Operations*, 11 LEWIS & CLARK L. REV. 1023, 1030 (2007) (noting that "[c]omputers and computer networks have become increasingly integral to government, military, and civilian functions. They allow instant communication and provide platforms on which business and government alike can operate. Computers now control both military and civilian infrastructures, including nuclear arsenals, telecommunication networks, electrical power systems, water supplies, oil storage facilities, banking and financial systems, and emergency services").

[64] *See* Logan Liles, *The Civilian Cyber Battlefield: Non-State Cyber Operators' Status Under the Law of Armed Conflict*, 39 N.C. J. Int'l L. & Com. Reg. 1091, 1110 (2014) ("Cyber operations' dual dimensions make applying the LOAC to determine an individual's status more complicated.").

the computer code deployed by the NSA during a cyber-attack contain a line acknowledging that the United States has deployed the malicious computer code, just as American tanks, missiles, and submarines all carry American insignia? Arguably yes, if the analogy to tanks and airplanes is the appropriate analogy.

3. ELECTION INTERFERENCE AND THE LAW OF WAR

Based on the preceding analysis, it is clear that while election interference is certainly destructive, it is not destructive in the way contemplated by the law of war.[65] Consequently, politicians who refer to election interference as an "act of war" almost surely have the legal analysis wrong. Future National Security Advisor John Bolton referred to Russian interference in the 2016 presidential election as an act of war, a "casus belli" that Washington would not and should not accept, and argued that negotiating with Russia was dangerous.[66] Despite their disagreements over how to approach Russia (and their disagreements about Russian election interference), Trump would later appoint Bolton as National Security Advisor. Similarly, Sen. Richard Blumenthal stated: "This was an act of war, in my view." Blumenthal continued: "I've said it in various hearings before this indictment. Interestingly enough the indictment refers to information warfare, that's the term the Russians use."[67] Nikki Haley, at the time US Ambassador to the United Nations, stated that "[w]hen a country can come and interfere in another country's elections, that is warfare," and she also described election interference as Russia's "weapon" of choice in its conflict with the United States.[68] Former Vice President and Secretary of Defense Dick Cheney used similar language.[69] Many pundits and political observers referred to election interference as an act of war:

Call it a different kind of war – asymmetric warfare, or whatever. But it is war. Whatever role Trump played in the attack, whatever he knew or didn't know about

---

[65] As noted above, if a cyber-attack produces physical destruction, it would be regulated by the laws of war. *See* Thomas C. Wingfield, International Law and Information Operations, in Franklin D. Kramer, Stuart H. Starr, and Larry K. Wentz (eds.), CYBERPOWER AND NATIONAL SECURITY (Potomac Books, 2009) 538 (noting that "[i]t should be immaterial whether a refinery was destroyed by a 2,000-pound bomb or by a line of malicious code in its pressure regulation subroutine; what did matter was the size of the hole left in the ground after the attack").

[66] John Bolton, *Vladimir Putin Looked Trump in the Eye and Lied to Him; We Negotiate With Russia at Our Peril*, THE TELEGRAPH (July 10, 2017).

[67] Nicholas Rondinone, *Blumenthal: Russian Interference is "Act of War,"* HARTFORD COURANT (Feb. 24, 2018). Blumenthal also said that: "There was clearly indisputably Russian interference in our last election, an attack on our democracy. Some would regard it, and I believe as well, an act of war." CNN, *Interview with Senator,* 2017 WLNR 26117365.

[68] *See, e.g.,* Associated Press, *Trump UN Envoy: Russia's Election Interference is "Warfare,"* Associated Press (Oct. 19, 2017).

[69] *See* Morgan Chalfant, *Cheney: Russian Election Interference Could be "Act of War,"* THE HILL (Mar. 27, 2017).

it previously, Russia took a hostile strike against this country. And it is, so far, winning.[70]

Or consider the statement from one Democratic lawmaker who said that he had "no doubt" that Russian interference constituted an act of war.[71] Even John McCain referred to it as an act of war.[72] Other politicians referred to the Russian interference as "hybrid warfare" – a category that evokes armed conflict but at least in some usages would be defined as falling below the level of armed conflict. For example, Secretary of Defense Ash Carter said that Russia interfered in "our democratic processes" with hybrid warfare, that is "interference in the internal affairs of nations, short of war."[73]

Most scholars who have considered the issue have correctly analyzed that Russian interference falls outside the scope of armed conflict, though each has struggled to articulate a convincing framing device. For example, Herb Lin has stated that:

> IW/IO is a hostile non-kinetic activity, or at least an activity that is conducted between two parties whose interests are not well-aligned. At the same time, IW/IO is not warfare in the Clausewitzian sense (nor in any sense presently recognized under the laws of war or armed conflict); it is better characterized as hostile or adversarial psychological manipulation. IW/IO has connotations of soft power (more properly, a mix of soft power and sharp power): propaganda, persuasion, culture, social forces, confusion, deception.[74]

Others have similarly concluded that the interference fell below the threshold of armed conflict.[75] Understood in this way, interference is extremely disruptive but not a subject for *jus in bello* regulation.[76]

Outsiders (non-lawyers) often assume that the law of war is designed to regulate every infringement of a state's territorial or political integrity. But that is certainly not the case. The law of war is designed to regulate the use of force and the conduct of

---

[70] Michelangelo Signorile, *Russia Committed An Act Of War And Trump Won't Talk About It*, HUFFINGTON POST (July 16, 2018).

[71] *Dem Calls Russia Meddling "Act of War," Urges Cyber Attack on Moscow Banks*, THE HILL (July 17, 2018) (quoting Rep. Steve Cohen as saying "No question about it" when asked if Russian interference in the election constituted an act of war). Cohen also stated: "It was a foreign interference with our basic Democratic values. The underpinnings of Democratic society is elections, and free elections, and they invaded our country." *Id.*

[72] *See* Jesse Hyde, *The Last Statesman: Inside the Diplomatic World of Jon Huntsman*, DESERET NEWS (Nov. 1, 2018) (noting that Sen. John McCain had referred to it as an act of war).

[73] Robert Burns, *Carter Questions Russia's Desire for Syrian Cease-Fire*, ASSOCIATED PRESS (Sept. 8, 2016).

[74] *See* Herbert Lin, *On the Organization of the U.S. Government for Responding to Adversarial Information Warfare and Influence Operations*, 15 J.L. & POL'Y FOR INFO. SOC'Y 1, 2 (2019).

[75] *See, e.g.*, Ryan Goodman, *International Law and the US Response to Russian Election Interference*, JUST SECURITY (Jan. 5, 2017) (DNC hack not an act of war under international law).

[76] *See* Laura Dickinson, *Not-War Everywhere: A Response to Rosa Brooks's How Everything Became War and the Military Became Everything*, 32 TEMP. INT'L & COMP. L.J. 17, 21–2 (2018) ("Yet perhaps equally important are legal discussions about cyber actions that fall below that threshold. Those actions can be tremendously disruptive, as we have seen in examples as wide-ranging as the Sony hack and the reported interference of Russia in U.S. elections.").

hostilities – concepts which are internal to the concept of warfare. In theory, some types of cyber-attacks might fall under the regulation of the law of war, but most cases of election interference would not. The primary reason for this conclusion is that election interference rarely involves physical damage. In cases where data is destroyed, there is a case to be made that we should label such interference as an act of war. The erasure of the data could be accomplished by physically damaging election computers, or by simply erasing the data without physically destroying the hardware where it resides. In the case of a physical destruction, the election inter-ference might be regulated by the law of war, but in all other cases, not.

The most salient examples of election interference involve either the theft and public release of private information or the posting of political views on social media platforms, often with the goal of disguising the true identity, and national origin, of the account holder. In the case of theft-and-release, a state might steal private information about a candidate – such as emails, text messages, private medical information, or confidential employment records from a human resources depart-ment – and release the damaging information to the public in order to favor a rival candidate.[77] Some of the information might be real and some of the information might be doctored or otherwise misleading. In the case of the second example of election interference, the foreign state might create fake Facebook groups focusing on a particular issue or candidate, in order to drum up excitement for or against a particular candidate, or fake Twitter or Instagram accounts with the same goal in mind. Each of these activities involves foreign interference that arguably interferes with the political process and the political integrity of the target state, but neither involves the kind of physical destruction or territorial infringement that is the *sine qua non* of armed conflict.

There is a strong temptation to reduce all important issues of international law to questions of warfare. Armed conflict is a distinctive moment for international lawyers, full of peril, and the concept of warfare captures the imagination of nonlawyers. Often the critical question (does this conduct violate international law?) gets displaced by the simpler question (is the conduct a war crime?), without first considering whether war is the relevant paradigm or not. But international law is not reducible to the law of war. Public international law is so much richer than just rules regulating the use of force and the conduct of hostilities. We need to resist the temptation to put everything into a war framework. The distinct harm of election interference speaks to broader and more complex questions of political integrity that go well beyond the concept of armed conflict.

---

[77] The Tallinn Manual, *supra* note 27, at 55 concludes that "acts of cyber intelligence gathering and cyber theft, as well as cyber operations that involve brief or periodic interruption of non-essential cyber services, do not qualify as armed attacks." It is unclear whether the experts considered the fact that a mere cyber theft, when used for the purpose of election interference, could have an enormous impact on the target state's political process.

That being said, it is important to recognize the impulse to analyze election interference through the war paradigm. The regulation of warfare is one of the great success stories of international law, because the discourse on warfare, both *jus ad bellum* and *jus in bello*, has been wholeheartedly legalized. International lawyers discuss the rules of warfare with a precision that is almost scientific in nature. For a public grasping for certainty and legality, the law of war is an attractive horizon to steer towards. So, it is no wonder that people gravitate to the war paradigm given how successful international lawyers have been in occupying the field. But the war discussion crowds out alternative legal frameworks for understanding election inter-ference, frameworks that focus on the political significance of elections and the way that foreign interference undermines the political integrity of the state.

The concept of "sovereignty" is one alternative framework.[78] Clearly, a state's violating the sovereignty of another state is illegal under some circumstances. So, it is intuitively plausible to suggest that election interference violates the sovereignty of the target state whose election is disputed, compromised, or influenced by the outside actor. The next chapter will explore "sovereignty" as a more salient legal category than armed conflict and examine both the benefits and the drawbacks of describing election interference in those terms. One noteworthy complication is the fact that the technical and doctrinal requirements for a legal infringement of sovereignty do not line up with common-sense intuitions about what counts as a violation of sovereignty. Consequently, many behaviors that sound as if they should count as sovereignty violations turn out to be perfectly legal – or at the very least contested – according to established doctrines of public international law. It also does not help that the concept of sovereignty is a cluster concept, housing diverse notions such as physical control over territory, control over a population, and expressions of a polity's popular will. This produces a lot of cross-talking since not everyone means the same thing when they utter the word "sovereignty."

One argument for focusing on sovereignty is that international law is much broader than the regulation of war. Just because election interference fails to qualify as an armed attack does not mean that the interference is lawful under international law. Similarly, even though election interference does not trigger a right of self-defense, international law might allow other responses to the interference. Under international law, a state is not required to simply suffer violations falling short of an armed attack. Victim states are entitled to use retorsions and countermeasures in an attempt to get the offending state to back off and cease the illegal behavior.

Countermeasures and retorsions are united by the state's intention behind their use, which is to induce the law-breaking state into compliance in the future. Countermeasures and retorsions differ in the legal status of the action used to induce

---

[78] *See* Michael N. Schmitt and Liis Vihul, *Respect for Sovereignty in Cyberspace*, 95 TEX. L. REV. 1639, 1647 (2017) ("Treating violations of sovereignty as a primary rule of international law, Tallinn Manual 2.0 seeks to add granularity to the circumstances in which a cyber operation might violate a State's territorial sovereignty.").

compliance. In the case of a countermeasure, the state that uses the countermeasure is engaging in conduct that is otherwise illegal; because the illegal conduct is used as a countermeasure to induce compliance, it becomes permissible. In contrast, a retorsion involves action that is already lawful and within the lawful discretion of the state. The classic example of a retorsion is recalling an ambassador, closing an embassy or breaking off diplomatic relations with a state. There is no requirement under international law for a state to have diplomatic relations with another state,[79] and the state may recall an ambassador for any reason or no reason at all. Similarly, imagine that a state *a* plans to sell missiles to state *b*, but becomes angry when state *b* violates international law and refuses to sell the missiles. This would constitute a retorsion because state *a* was under no obligation to sell the missiles in the first place.

Of the two, countermeasures are the more controversial because they involve conduct that would otherwise be illegal. However, it should be noted that countermeasures should not include the use of military force, which are governed by the principles of self-defense. Although the issue is somewhat contested, the majority (and better) view is that the doctrine of countermeasures cannot be used as an exception to the requirements of *jus ad bellum*. If a state wishes to use military force, it needs either Security Council authorization or a defensive claim under article 51 of the UN Charter.

After the Russian interference in the 2016 election, President Obama announced sanctions designed to punish the Russian government for election interference and related behavior, including Russian interference in Ukraine.[80] For example, on April 1, 2015, President Obama issued an executive order declaring that "the increasing prevalence and severity of malicious cyber-enabled activities originating from, or directed by persons located, in whole or in substantial part, outside the United States constitute an unusual and extraordinary threat to the national security, foreign policy, and economy of the United States."[81] On December 28, 2016, Obama amended the earlier executive order and ordered the Treasury Department to freeze the assets of individuals involved in Russian cyber-interference.[82]

---

[79] Of course, international law imposes certain restrictions on how ambassadors should be treated *if* a state is engaging in diplomatic relations with another state, but nothing requires the state to have the diplomatic relations in the first instance.

[80] Christina Lam, *A Slap on the Wrist: Combatting Russia's Cyber Attack on the 2016 U.S. Presidential Election*, 59 B.C. L. Rev. 2167, 2201 (2018).

[81] *See* Exec. Order No. 13694, 80 Fed. Reg. 18,077 (Apr. 1, 2015).

[82] *See* Exec. Order No. 13757 (Dec. 28, 2016). The order was made pursuant to the International Emergency Economic Powers Act, 50 U.S.C. 1701, and the National Emergencies Act, 50 U.S.C. 1601. The executive order covered the following entities: Main Intelligence Directorate (a.k.a. GRU); Federal Security Service (a.k.a. FSB); Special Technology Center (a.k.a. STLC, Ltd. Special Technology Center St. Petersburg); Zorsecurity (a.k.a. Esage Lab); Autonomous Noncommercial Organization "Professional Association of Designers of Data Processing Systems" (a.k.a. ANO PO KSI). The order also included four Russian named individuals.

In December 2016, the Obama administration also expelled thirty-five Russian diplomats who were described as members of Russian intelligence. In a related move, the Obama administration shut down two Russian diplomatic "compounds" that the administration claimed were being used for intelligence collection. Though these compounds were probably connected with domestic intelligence gathering rather than troll farm activity launched from St. Petersburg, the move to shut down the compounds was part of a general package of punitive actions against Moscow. In making this move, Obama stated:

> These actions are not the sum total of our response to Russia's aggressive activities. We will continue to take a variety of actions at a time and place of our choosing, some of which will not be publicized. In addition to holding Russia accountable for what it has done, the United States and friends and allies around the world must work together to oppose Russia's efforts to undermine established international norms of behavior, and interfere with democratic governance. To that end, my Administration will be providing a report to Congress in the coming days about Russia's efforts to interfere in our election, as well as malicious cyber activity related to our election cycle in previous elections.[83]

In addition to these punitive actions, it is possible that the United States also engaged in classified or covert actions that were not publicly disclosed.[84] In particular, the United States reportedly launched a cyber-attack against the Russian government as a proportional countermeasure to the election interference.[85] But the United States was careful not to describe any of its responses as either countermeasures or retorsions. Although this refusal is somewhat perplexing, it may have been connected with Obama's general reluctance to declare Russian interference as "illegal" under international law.[86] Describing a punitive action as a countermeasure implies a conclusion both about the illegality of the offending conduct and also the illegality of the punitive measure under nonpunitive circumstances. The United States may have preferred to preserve maximum flexibility regarding its legal position on cyber-attacks. This may

---

[83] *See* The White House, Office of the Press Secretary, Statement by the President on Actions in Response to Russian Malicious Cyber Activity and Harassment (Dec. 29, 2016).

[84] When Obama stated that "[w]e will continue to take a variety of actions at a time and place of our choosing, some of which will not be publicized," most observers understood this as a reference to undisclosed cyber-attacks conducted by the United States against Russia.

[85] *See* Greg Miller, Ellen Nakashima and Adam Entous, *Obama's Secret Struggle to Punish Russia for Putin's Election Assault*, WASH. POST (June 23, 2017) (referring to a "cyber operation that was designed to be detected by Moscow but not cause significant damage" and "entailed implanting computer code in sensitive computer systems that Russia was bound to find . . . as a reminder to Moscow of the United States' cyber reach").

[86] Obama described Russia's interference as a violation of "established international norms of behavior," rather than as a violation of international law. *See* Press Release, The White House, Office of the Press Secretary, Statement by the President on Actions in Response to Russian Malicious Cyber Activity and Harassment (Dec. 29, 2016).

have contributed to the Obama Administration's relative silence on Russian inter-ference in the 2016 election.[87]

CONCLUSION

Russia's interference in the 2016 election may have violated international law, but it was neither an act of war nor was it the opening salvo in a cyber-war between the United States and Russia. But this is not to diminish its significance, or even to diminish its illegality under both U.S. and international law. It may still be illegal, and the sooner that the public recognizes that it does not trigger a right of kinetic response under article 51 of the UN Charter, the sooner a more nuanced discussion can open up about the range of permissible responses under international law, such as retorsions and countermeasures outside the context of the use of force.[88] Political leaders have a range of options at their disposal but selecting among them requires consideration of the vast tools for enforcing international law beyond the use of force.

To recap the argument presented in this chapter: The principles governing *jus in bello* and *jus ad bellum* apply with equal force in the realm of cyber-attacks. A cyber-attack that causes physical destruction may qualify as an armed attack triggering a right of self-defense under article 51 of the UN Charter, and a cyber-attack that causes physical destruction may constitute a resort to force that triggers the existence of an armed conflict and the application of IHL. But in the absence of physical destruction, cyber-attacks probably fall outside the scope of the laws of war.[89] Cyber-war is a real phenomenon, but in many cases, the "war" suffix is, legally speaking, a metaphor. In technical discussions, the term "war" is meant to convey the notion of an armed conflict pursued through sustained military engagements. In contrast, most cyber-attacks have more in common with the tools of statecraft than the tools of military science. Election interference falls in the category of statecraft, though it is important to remember that even statecraft is regulated by public international law.

---

[87] *See, e.g.*, Jack Crowe, *Rosenstein Calls Out Obama Admin For Failing to "Publicize" Russian Election Interference*, NATIONAL REVIEW (April 26, 2019).

[88] In this sense, Brown is absolutely right when he concludes that "[l]aw is a critical aspect of discussions about the cyber aspects of privacy rights, espionage, sovereignty, international norms of behavior, and more – but none of these things is within the realm of LOAC." Gary D. Brown, *International Law Applies to Cyber Warfare! Now What?*, 46 SW. L. REV. 355, 356 (2017).

[89] *See* Prescott, *supra* note 1, at 48 (asserting that "[b]elow the level of this use of force, cyber operations that result only in direct effects within cyberspace itself would not be considered uses of force regulated by LOAC, even though their indirect effects might have far-reaching and negative impacts upon the nation targeted."); Lubell, *supra* note 49, at 259 (concluding that "[t]here can be plenty of cyber operations that occur outside the context of an armed conflict, such as certain types of cyber espionage between supposedly friendly countries to which the law of armed conflict would not apply"). Lubell also argues that psychological operations (such as operations that have the goal of disseminating propaganda) "are not considered to be ones that cause direct harm to the civilian population and, as such, can be excluded from certain restrictions placed on attacks." *Id.* at 263.

Just because a tool of statecraft falls below the legal threshold for armed conflict does not necessarily mean that the tool is part of a state's exclusive discretion, or what international lawyers sometimes call its *domaine réservé*.

The next two chapters focus on two competing frameworks for regulating cyber-election interference. Chapter 3 analyzes whether "sovereignty" is the correct concept, such that cyber interference might be viewed as an illegal infringement of a state's sovereignty. Among international lawyers, this is the "preferred" framework or the "majority" approach, though there are significant drawbacks to the approach, and I count myself as a dissenting voice. Then, Chapter 4 analyzes whether "self-determination" is a more promising framework, so that cyber interference might be viewed as a violation of a people's collective right of self-determination. This is an uncommon approach not yet adopted by public international lawyers, though they should give this approach a second look. In addition to being doctrinally salient, the concept of self-determination dovetails with our commonsense intuition that election interference is harmful because of its corrosive effect on the machinery of core democratic institutions.

3

Limits of the Sovereignty Framework

INTRODUCTION

When international lawyers talk about election interference and whether it violates international law, they usually ask whether it violates the sovereignty of the target state. Under this approach, the legal question is whether a foreign state has inappropriately intervened in the domestic affairs of the state holding the election in a way that violates the target state's sovereignty. This sovereignty-based framework for evaluating election interference is by far the most common approach taken by mainstream international lawyers studying the issue. Although politicians and policy experts often jump to the cyber-war framework, which was discussed in Chapter 2, the first reaction among sophisticated international lawyers is to ask whether election interference violates the sovereignty of the state holding the election. It is the dominant approach in the literature and for obvious reasons. Sovereignty is arguably the cornerstone of the Westphalian international order; sovereignty is what makes states "states" under international law.[1] Indeed, as will be explored below, the Montevideo Convention, a treaty that purports to articulate criteria for statehood, announces that the sovereignty of each state, that is, its freedom from outside intervention, is a paramount protection afforded to each state, while leaving most of the other consequences of statehood unstated or unexplored in the Convention.[2] But the sovereignty of states, and their freedom from outside intervention, could not be left unsaid, because the sovereignty of states is such a central facet of their existence.[3] So, it is no surprise that international lawyers grab the sovereignty tool from the shelf when confronted with the problem of election interference.

[1] For a discussion of the history of the concept of sovereignty, see Sophie Clavier, *Contrasting Franco-American Perspectives on Sovereignty*, 14 ANN. SURV. INT'L & COMP. L. 1, 4 (2008).

[2] *See* Convention on the Rights and Duties of States (Montevideo Convention), Dec. 26, 1933, 165 L.N. T.S. 19 [hereinafter cited as "Montevideo Convention"].

[3] *See* Winston P. Nagan, FRSA and Craig Hammer, *The Changing Character of Sovereignty in International Law and International Relations*, 43 COLUM. J. TRANSNAT'L L. 141, 149 (2004) (noting that "the concept of sovereignty is used as an instrument by which to establish and maintain authority"); Thomas D. Grant, *Defining Statehood: The Montevideo Convention and Its Discontents*, 37 COLUM. J. TRANSNAT'L L. 403, 434 (1999).

As the following sections will demonstrate, however, the sovereignty framework is poorly suited to resolving the case of foreign election interference, for several reasons.[4] The doctrinal requirements for a violation of sovereignty require either a territorial intrusion of the type discussed in the prior chapter, the element of coercion, or the usurpation of an inherently governmental function. However, none of these requirements is satisfied by the types of election interference that were at issue in the 2016 election. (Interference that involves tampering with election machines or changing vote tallies might qualify, however.[5]) Since the facts of modern election interference do not fit with the doctrinal requirements for a sovereignty violation, one might be tempted to conclude that election interference is therefore lawful under international law. But this would be a myopic response. One can only say, with confidence, that election interference is lawful under international law if one has confidence that no other principle of international law, besides sovereignty, comes into play. As the next chapter demonstrates, however, the principle of self-determination is very much at issue in election interference, and once sovereignty is dismissed as a viable framework, the principle of self-determination can be examined.

But before that work of examining the principle of self-determination is performed in Chapter 4, we must focus first on the concept of sovereignty. Instead of demonstrating that election interference is lawful under international law, an examination of the doctrine merely confirms that sovereignty is irrelevant to the question of election interference's lawfulness. Sovereignty, that first impulse of every international lawyer, fails to capture the significant (and unique) harm of election interference. Election interference does not infringe the target state's control over its people and its territory; election interference infringes the target people's right to select their own political destiny, a right that is achieved through the electoral process.

Section 1 of this chapter will focus on the conceptual link between the concept of sovereignty and the principle of nonintervention; the latter is parasitic upon the former. Understanding this relationship helps to elucidate the doctrinal requirements for the principle of nonintervention. Section 2 will focus on interventions that violate the *political independence* of the target state; a seemingly promising doctrine but one that runs up against the wall of "coercion" as a required element.

---

[4] See Duncan B. Hollis, *Why States Need an International Law for Information Operations*, 11 LEWIS & CLARK L. REV. 1023, 1050 (2007) (arguing that current international legal doctrine proves inadequate for resolving the case of information operations conducted via cyber-attacks).

[5] See Rebecca Crootof, *International Cybertorts: Expanding State Accountability in Cyberspace*, 103 CORNELL L. REV. 565, 615–16 (2018) ("While the DNC hack may not have been itself unlawful, imagine if Russian actors instead hacked voting machines and altered individual votes. If such an action caused significant harm, it might be an international cybertort. But it would also be something more – unlawful interference."). *See also* Brian J. Egan, Legal Adviser, U.S. Dept. of State, *International Law and Stability in Cyberspace*, Speech at Berkeley Law School (Nov. 10, 2016) ("[A] cyber operation by a State that interferes with another country's ability to hold an election or that manipulates another country's election results would be a clear violation of the rule of non-intervention.").

Consequently, Section 3 will show why coercion is not present in cases of election interference. Finally, Section 4 will focus on "usurpation" as a distinct sovereignty violation (one that does not require a finding of coercion), but one that fails to accord with the foreign election interference that takes place on social media platforms and which was described in detail in Chapter 1. Consequently, the principle of sovereignty, while seemingly so attractive as a framework for describing foreign election interference, is surprisingly inapposite. A new conceptual framework is required.[6]

1. THE GENERAL PRINCIPLE OF NONINTERVENTION

Technically, the legal prohibition at issue is the principle of nonintervention, or the idea that states should not interfere inappropriately with the internal affairs of another state.[7] As will be clear, it is not always easy to distinguish between permissible and impermissible cases of interference. At some point, however, interference becomes so problematic that it violates the principle of nonintervention. The principle is ancient; most lawyers attribute the principle's first explicit articulation to Emmerich de Vattel,[8] who noted in Book I, Chapter III of his treatise that:

> In short, all these affairs being solely a national concern, no foreign power has a right to interfere in them, nor ought to intermeddle with them otherwise by its good offices, unless requested to do it, or induced by particular reasons. If any intrude into the domestic concerns of another nation, and attempt to put a constraint on its deliberations they do it an injury.[9]

The reference to "deliberations" is particularly striking – but ambiguous. Deliberations can refer to the deliberations of the government (i.e. the sovereign) in deciding which actions to take (its national policies). But deliberations can also refer to the political deliberations of the *people*, in deciding which individuals shall

---

[6] Other commentators have noted that current legal doctrines are inadequate for analyzing election interference. *See, e.g.*, Logan Hamilton, *Beyond Ballot-Stuffing: Current Gaps in International Law Regarding Foreign State Hacking to Influence A Foreign Election*, 35 Wis. Int'l L.J. 179, 204 (2017) ("A state affected by such a campaign would also have little recourse to governing international law, such as the UN Charter and customary international law. Such laws have few effective remedies for such behavior or are otherwise inapplicable due to various definitional requirements."). *Compare with* Catherine Lotrionte, *State Sovereignty and Self-Defense in Cyberspace: A Normative Framework for Balancing Legal Rights*, 26 Emory Int'l L. Rev. 825, 830 (2012) ("Cyber operations against another state's territorial infrastructure can violate a state's sovereignty.").

[7] *See* Maziar Jamnejad and Michael Wood, *The Principle of Non-Intervention*, 22 Leiden J. Int'l L. 345 (2009).

[8] *See* Michael Wood, *Non-Intervention (Non-interference in domestic affairs)*, Encyclopedia Princetoniensis.

[9] *See* Emmerich de Vattel, The Law of Nations; Or Principles of the Law of Nature, Applied to the Conduct and Affairs of Nations and Sovereigns 11 para. 37 (Joseph Chitty (ed.), Philadelphia, T. & J.W. Johnson, Law Booksellers, 1844) (1758).

occupy positions of power, a decision which in a democratic society ends with the holding of an election.

Modern commentators continue to echo Vattel's articulation of the principle of nonintervention.[10] Oppenheim's treatise states plainly, almost arrogantly: "That intervention is, as a rule, forbidden by international law there is no doubt."[11] Oppenheim notes that the ILC's Draft Declaration on Rights and Duties of States includes, in article 3, the statement that: "Every state has the duty to refrain from intervention in the internal or external affairs of any other State."[12] The most clear-cut statement of the principle of nonintervention came in the *Nicaragua* case before the International Court of Justice, and legal analyses of election interference usually start with that Court's articulation of the principle in that case. In *Nicaragua*, the United States was accused of violating international law by supporting the Contras, an anti-Communist rebel group that was seeking to overthrow the Communist-aligned government of Nicaragua. The government of Nicaragua also accused the United States of violating Nicaraguan sovereignty by placing mines in Nicaragua's harbors. In deciding that the United States had violated Nicaraguan sovereignty, the ICJ made the following statement about the principle of nonintervention:

> The principle of non-intervention involves the right of every sovereign State to conduct its affairs without outside interference; though examples of trespass against this principle are not infrequent, the Court considers that it is part and parcel of customary international law ... . Expressions of an opinio juris regarding the existence of the principle of non-intervention in customary international law are numerous and not difficult to find. Of course, statements whereby States avow their recognition of the principles of international law set forth in the United Nations Charter cannot strictly be interpreted as applying to the principle of non-intervention by States in the internal and external affairs of other States, since this principle is not, as such, spelt out in the Charter. But it was never intended that the Charter should embody written confirmation of every essential principle of international law in force. The existence in the opinio juris of States of the principle of non-intervention is backed by established and substantial practice.[13]

In the *Corfu Channel* case in 1949, the ICJ stressed that a principle of nonintervention was essential to protect weaker states from simply being railroaded into doing whatever powerful states wanted them to do – a state of affairs that would conflict

---

[10]   The intellectual debt to Vattel is so deep that at least one scholar has suggested that Westphalian sovereignty is better described as "Vattelian sovereignty." *See* Stephen D. Krasner, *The Hole in the Whole: Sovereignty, Shared Sovereignty, and International Law*, 25 MICH. J. INT'L L. 1075, 1077 (2004).

[11]   *See* LASSA OPPENHEIM, OPPENHEIM'S INTERNATIONAL LAW: LAW OF PEACE 428 (Robert Jennings and Arthur Watt (eds.), 9th edn., Oxford University Press, 1992).

[12]   *See* Draft Declaration on Rights and Duties of States with commentaries 1949, annex to G.A. Res. 375 (IV), Dec. 6, 1949.

[13]   Case Concerning Military & Paramilitary Activities in & Against Nicaragua (Nicaragua v. United States), 1986 I.C.J. 14, 106 (June 27).

with the very notion of sovereignty. Specifically, the Court noted in *Corfu Channel* that:

> [T]he alleged right of intervention as the manifestation of a policy of force, such as has, in the past, given rise to most serious abuses and such as cannot, whatever be the present defects in international organization, find a place in international law. Intervention is perhaps still less admissible in the particular form it would take here; for, from the nature of things, it would be reserved for the most powerful States, and might easily lead to perverting the administration of international justice itself.[14]

The Montevideo Convention goes even further, stating in article 8 that "[n]o state has the right to intervene in the internal or external affairs of another."[15] This prohibition is particularly striking since the Montevideo Convention purports to be an expression of the international legal criteria for recognizing states; it is, in other words, a work of meta-law, establishing criteria for the very entities (states) that will be both the subjects and objects of international law.[16] While international law imposes many regulations and prohibitions on states, the Montevideo Convention fails to outline most of them, leaving that task to other legal instruments.[17] So, why would the drafters have included article 8 in the Convention? Because the principle of nonintervention is, in a sense, constitutive of the notion of sovereignty and statehood.[18] Part of what it means to be a state is to be sovereign; what it means to be sovereign is to be free from outside interference (or at least some forms of egregious interference). Without this cluster of ideas, the international legal system would not exist in its current form.

The relationship between sovereignty and nonintervention is an ancient one, going back to both Kellogg-Briand and Westphalia. The Kellogg-Briand Pact of 1928 outlawed aggressive war and pledged that "the settlement or solution of all disputes or conflicts of whatever nature or of whatever origin they may be, which may arise among them, shall never be sought except by pacific means."[19] However, Kellogg-Briand was focused on military interventions, whereas the much older and broader

---

[14]   Corfu Channel Case, 1949 I.C.J. 4, 35 (April 9).

[15]   Montevideo Convention, *supra* note 2, art. 8.

[16]   States create international law by signing treaties and by engaging in state practice; in turn, states are subject to regulation by international law.

[17]   Indeed, the idea that the Montevideo Convention outlines the "rights and duties" of states, as its title suggests, is laughable since all of international law accomplishes this task, not this one legal instrument.

[18]   *See* Michael N. Schmitt, *"Virtual" Disenfranchisement: Cyber Election Meddling in the Grey Zones of International Law*, 19 CHI. J. INT'L L. 30, 40 (2018) ("As a principle, the concept denotes international law's acknowledgment that States are primarily responsible for what happens on their territory and that other States should respect said competence. On this basis, sovereignty is the fount from which various primary rules, like the prohibition on intervention into the internal affairs of other States, emerged.").

[19]   Treaty Between the United States and Other Powers Providing for the Renunciation of War as an Instrument of National Policy, Aug. 27, 1928, 46 Stat. 2343, 94 L.N.T.S. 57 (1929) [hereinafter cited as "Kellogg-Briand"].

Treaty of Westphalia required its contractors to pledge not to interfere with each other.[20] The cornerstone of the Westphalian system is a community of nation-states, each one enjoying the formal equality of sovereignty, and each one pledging to all the others to govern their internal affairs without external interference.

Of course, the difference between the "internal affairs" of a state and something that is legitimately the subject of international concern is far from clear. International lawyers often use the phrase *domaine réservé* to refer to that aspect of a state's existence that forms part of their sovereign discretion. But the mere use of a foreign phrase – and italics, no less – adds nothing more than the illusion of precision. Figuring out what counts as a state's *domaine réservé* requires additional conceptual content – some standard, norm, or principle that defines what counts as a state's sovereign discretion.

Prohibited interference is the easiest to determine in the case of violations of territorial integrity. The ICJ in *Nicaragua* clarified that the element of coercion, which often delimitates permissible from impermissible interferences, is "particularly obvious in the case of an intervention which uses force, either in the direct form of military action, or in the indirect form of support for subversive or terrorist armed activities within another State."[21] The reason why sovereignty violations are "particularly obvious" in these cases is because a state's sovereignty is at its highest when it is acting on its own territory; conversely, when a foreign state engages in a physical infringement of another state's territory, the infringement is more likely to be deemed an interference in a state's *domaine réservé*. Part of a state's *domaine réservé* is the right to govern its own territory. Absent some exceptional situation (a state of necessity, a state of self-defense), a state's control over its own territory is considered to be a presumptive aspect of its sovereign control.

The concept of territorial integrity makes the case of election interference particularly difficult. Most cases of election interference do not involve the type of offensive cyber-attacks that would be regulated by the laws of war. Those attacks are more likely to involve a territorial infringement that would violate the principle of nonintervention.[22] However, the election interference described in Chapter 1

---

[20]   *See* Treaty of Westphalia, article II: "That there shall be on the one side and the other a perpetual Oblivion, Amnesty, or Pardon of all that has been committed since the beginning of these Troubles, in what place, or what manner soever the Hostilitys have been practis'd, in such a manner, that no body, under any pretext whatsoever, shall practice any Acts of Hostility, entertain any Enmity, or cause any Trouble to each other; neither as to Persons, Effects and Securitys, neither of themselves or by others, neither privately nor openly, neither directly nor indirectly, neither under the colour of Right, nor by the way of Deed, either within or without the extent of the Empire, notwithstanding all Covenants made before to the contrary: That they shall not act, or permit to be acted, any wrong or injury to any whatsoever; but that all that has pass'd on the one side, and the other, as well before as during the War, in Words, Writings, and Outrageous Actions, in Violences, Hostilitys, Damages and Expences, without any respect to Persons or Things, shall be entirely abolish'd in such a manner that all that might be demanded of, or pretended to, by each other on that behalf, shall be bury'd in eternal Oblivion."

[21]   *Nicaragua, supra* note 13, at 108.

[22]   *See generally* Joshua E. Kastenberg, *Non-Intervention and Neutrality in Cyberspace: An Emerging Principle in the National Practice of International Law*, 64 A.F.L.R. 43, 45–7 (2009).

involved little to no violations of territorial integrity. No Russian tanks crossed American borders; no missiles flew into American airspace; no Russian submarines sailed in American waters. The most territorial infringement that occurred was Russian computer hacking of American computer accounts and servers, some of which were located on American territory. While this is certainly a territorial infringement, it probably does not rise to the level of territorial infringement of the type described in *Nicaragua*. Furthermore, the rest of the Russian interference in the election involved no territorial infringement whatsoever. Russian agents working in the St. Petersburg troll farms authored fraudulent social media posts that were viewed by American citizens located within the United States, thus altering the political discourse. These actions involved a violation that is best described as political rather than territorial.

The *Tallinn Manual 2.0* includes two related rules on sovereignty. The first, Rule 3, states that "[a] State is free to conduct cyber activities in its international relations, subject to any contrary rule of international law binding on it."[23] The second, Rule 4, states that "A State must not conduct cyber operations that violate the sovereignty of another State."[24] Synthesized together, these rules stand for the proposition that a state may use cyber-attacks or cyber-activities unless doing so would violate the sovereignty of another state. The question, of course, is when those cyber-activities would violate the sovereignty of another state. On that point, the Tallinn Manual notes that a state may "control access to its territory" as a part of its territorial integrity, though the Manual also notes that sovereignty violations may occur in other circumstances as well.[25] However, at least some experts believed that physical destruction resulting from the cyber-attack would be required before a finding of a sovereignty violation could be made. For example, the Manual states that "[t]o the extent that non-consensual physical presence on another State's territory to conduct cyber operations amounts to a violation of sovereignty, the Experts concurred that the causation of physical consequences by remote means on that territory likewise constitutes a violation of sovereignty."[26] However, the Manual also states that "no consensus could be achieved as to whether a cyber operation that results in neither physical damage nor the loss of functionality amounts to a violation of sovereignty."[27] The Manual goes on to note that among those experts who believed that a violation of sovereignty could occur without physical damage or loss of functionality, the following circumstances might qualify: "a cyber operation causing cyber infrastructure or programs to operate differently; altering or deleting data stored in cyber infrastructure without causing physical of functional consequences . . . ; emplacing malware into a system installing backdoors; and

---

[23] TALLINN MANUAL 2.0 ON THE INTERNATIONAL LAW APPLICABLE TO CYBER OPERATIONS 16 (Michael M. Schmitt and Liis Vihul (eds.), 2017) [hereinafter cited as "TALLINN MANUAL 2.0"].

[24] *Id.* at 17.

[25] *Id.* at 18.

[26] *Id.* at 20.

[27] *Id.* at 21.

causing a temporary, but significant, loss of functionality, as in the case of a major DDoS operation."[28]

What is striking is that even this list of potential sovereignty violations is contested and does not represent a scholarly consensus. But even if this list were widely or universally accepted, none of these examples would cover the type of troll farm activity that the Russian government engaged in during the 2016 presidential election.[29] The lack of physical damage, loss of functionality, or lack of other *physical* consequences makes the case of election interference via information operations (as opposed to disruption of voting machinery) a poor fit for the legal framework of sovereignty.

For this reason, it is unfortunate that most international lawyers – excellent ones – insist on analyzing election interference exclusively through the lens of sovereignty.[30] Of course, this tendency is natural because modern international law is built from the raw materials of sovereignty.[31] Consequently, it is no surprise that, for example, Schmitt would conclude that "[i]n the case of election meddling, the likeliest breach by a State of its international law obligations is violation of the target State's sovereignty."[32] Similarly, former State Department Legal Advisor Brian Egan referred to sovereignty as the key concept violated by illegal election interference.[33] Other scholars have suggested that the concept of sovereignty provides the foundation for prohibitions on foreign participation in elections.[34] Even

---

[28] *Id.*

[29] Several scholars have argued that a cyber-attack that shuts down a computer system could constitute a form of illegal intervention. *See, e.g.,* William Mattessich, *Digital Destruction: Applying the Principle of Non-Intervention to Distributed Denial of Service Attacks Manifesting No Physical Damage,* 54 COLUM. J. TRANSNAT'L L. 873, 890 (2016) ("Regardless of whether a specific policy goal is being pursued by the attacking state, DDoS attacks causing widespread disruption of communications and digital functionality violate international law.").

[30] *See* Michael N. Schmitt and Liis Vihul, *Sovereignty in Cyberspace: Lex Lata Vel Non?,* 111 AJIL UNBOUND 213, 213 (2017) ("Perhaps the most operationally relevant, and hence politically delicate, legal issue with respect to the cyber environment is the identification of criteria for determining when cyber operations directed against a state violate its sovereignty."). *But see* Ahmed Ghappour, *Tallinn, Hacking, and Customary International Law,* 111 AJIL UNBOUND 224, 225 (2017) ("That is, *Tallinn* indicates that sovereignty is a norm from which no derogation is permitted, raising the stakes for violation and the importance of understanding when a violation has occurred. Yet the principle is not defined in any primary international law source, and it is thus difficult to pin down a definition that is acceptable to all.").

[31] *See* Allison Denton, *Fake News: The Legality of the Russian 2016 Facebook Influence Campaign,* 37 B. U. INT'L L.J. 183, 202 (2019) (concluding that "[t]hus, the Facebook influence campaign likely does not constitute a violation of sovereignty.").

[32] *See* Schmitt, *supra* note 18, at 39.

[33] *See* Egan, *supra* note 5 (suggesting that some attacks against election infrastructure could violate American sovereignty). *See also* Ryan Goodman, *International Law and the US Response to Russian Election Interference,* JUST SECURITY (Jan. 5, 2017).

[34] *See* Zephyr Teachout, *Extraterritorial Electioneering and the Globalization of American Elections,* 27 BERKELEY J. INT'L L. 162, 187 (2009) ("On the whole, concerns about sovereignty, unlike concerns about self-government, will tend to militate against extraterritorial electioneering.").

the U.N. General Assembly has analyzed election interference through the lens of sovereignty.[35]

A few international lawyers have questioned whether sovereignty is so important in the context of cyber-attacks, although many of these arguments have been made with the goal of asserting that states enjoy wide legal discretion to conduct cyber-operations against foreign states.[36] Similarly, Barrie Sander, in an important article on election interference, considers sovereignty as the key legal concept for evaluating its compliance with international law but notes that the "status of sovereignty as an international legal obligation is currently contested."[37]

My contention here is that the literature's focus (and the public discourse) on sovereignty is misplaced.[38] Journalists and politicians have consistently described Russian election interference as an assault on American sovereignty.[39] In one sense, this reliance on the concept of sovereignty is fully reasonable and to be expected because sovereignty is a common lay concept for understanding a country's independence. The term is sometimes used in a legal sense but in other situations the word takes on a broader and less technical meaning. But international lawyers understand sovereignty in very particular ways, related to the prohibition on nonintervention, and its doctrinal requirements are a poor fit for evaluating election interference.

---

[35] *See* U.N.G.A. Res. 46/130 (Dec. 17, 1991) (noting that "respect for the principles of national sovereignty and non-interference in the internal affairs of states in their electoral processes"), *quoted in* Gabriel Shumba, *International Standards and the 2002 Presidential Election in Zimbabwe*, 10 ILSA J. Int'l & Comp. L. 95, 100 (2003).

[36] *See* Gary P. Corn and Robert Taylor, *Sovereignty in the Age of Cyber*, 111 AJIL Unbound 207, 208–09 (2017) ("law and state practice instead indicate that sovereignty serves as a principle of international law that guides state interactions, but is not itself a binding rule that dictates results under international law. While this principle of sovereignty, including territorial sovereignty, should factor into the conduct of every cyber operation, it does not establish an absolute bar against individual or collective state cyber operations that affect cyberinfrastructure within another state, provided that the effects do not rise to the level of an unlawful use of force or an unlawful intervention.").

[37] *See* Barrie Sander, *Democracy Under The Influence: Paradigms of State Responsibility for Cyber Influence Operations on Elections*, 18 Chinese J. Int'l L. 1 (2019) (canvassing the various legal norms that election interference might violate and concluding that problems exist with each one). However, it should be noted that Sander believes, as many do, that sovereignty and nonintervention are separate norms, whereas I think the better view is that nonintervention is the prohibition that flows from the principle of sovereignty.

[38] I have made this argument elsewhere. *See* Jens David Ohlin, *Did Russian Cyber Interference in the 2016 Election Violate International Law?*, 95 Tex. L. Rev. 1579, 1580 (2017) ("The lack of fit with the doctrinal requirements for an illegal intervention against another State's sovereignty is simply an indication that the notions of 'sovereignty' and 'intervention' – though mainstays of contemporary public international law doctrine – are poorly suited to analyzing the legality of the conduct in this case.").

[39] *See* Editorial Board, *How Do You Say 'Witch Hunt' in Russian?*, N.Y. Times (July 13, 2018) ("while Republicans in Congress spend their time fulminating not about the assault on American sovereignty, but about the private text messages of an F.B.I. agent investigating that attack"); *On the World Stage, Trump Goes Solo*, Star Tribune (Sept. 26, 2018) ("even though the president spent much of his speech emphasizing sovereignty, he did not criticize Russia for its interference in the 2016 U.S. election and the ongoing, online malice it spreads in Western democracies").

2. POLITICAL INDEPENDENCE

A more promising legal prong for seeing election interference as a violation of the principle of nonintervention is to view it as an attack against the political independence or integrity of the state that is targeted. This legal framework still falls within the general rubric of the principle of nonintervention, but in this case the intervention is a violation of sovereignty not because the acting state violates the territorial integrity of the target state but rather because it violates the political integrity of the state. Since the holding of an election is an important, arguably *the most* important, political institution in a democratic state, it is tempting to view election meddling as an intervention against a state's political interests.

Various statements from the International Court of Justice make clear that the principle of nonintervention applies to political as well as territorial infringements. For example, in the *Corfu Channel* case, the ICJ stated that: "Between independent States, respect for territorial sovereignty is an essential foundation of international relations,"[40] to which the ICJ in *Nicaragua* added the following addendum: "and international law requires political integrity also to be respected."[41] As for what counts as prohibited intervention, the ICJ also stated in *Nicaragua* that a "prohibited intervention must accordingly be one bearing on matters in which each State is permitted, by the principle of State sovereignty, to decide freely. One of these is the choice of a political, economic, social and cultural system, and the formulation of foreign policy ... "[42]

The idea that some political decisions of a state should be free from outside interference is one that comes much closer to the idea of election interference, though the types of interference (supporting an organized armed group, the Contras) is far different from the case of election interference. In *Nicaragua*, Judge Schwebel noted that "[t]he essence of that law long has been recognized to prohibit the *dictatorial* interference by one State in the affairs of the other."[43] This suggests that the key to the principle of nonintervention is the denial of the target state's freedom to decide matters on its own, rather than imposing the will of the intervening state.

The leading article on political interference was written by Lori Damrosch thirty years ago, long before the case of foreign election interference had established its current political currency.[44] Nonetheless, the politics of the 1980s was embroiled in another form of political interference, this one allegedly conducted by the United

---

[40] Corfu Channel Case, 1949 I.C.J. 35.

[41] *Nicaragua, supra* note 13, at para. 202.

[42] *Id.* After this quotation, the Court went on to analyze the requirement of coercion in cases of alleged intervention, which will be analyzed in Section 3 of this chapter.

[43] Dissenting Opinion of Judge Schwebel, Case Concerning Military & Paramilitary Activities in & Against Nicaragua, 1986 I.C.J. 14, 305–6, paras. 98–9 (June 27) [hereinafter cited as "Schwebel Dissenting Opinion"].

[44] See Lori Fisler Damrosch, *Politics Across Borders: Nonintervention and Nonforcible Influence over Domestic Affairs,* 83 AM. J. INT'L L. 1, 44 (1989).

States. At the time of Damrosch's study, the ICJ had decided, three years prior, that the United States had interfered in the fate of Nicaragua by seeking regime change through supporting the Contras, who were trying to overthrow the government of Nicaragua. And the notion of impermissible political interference was far from limited to Nicaragua. In the midst of the Cold War, American anti-Communist politicians were convinced that the security of the United States, and perhaps freedom itself, required that the United States intervene abroad to counter the encroachment of communism across the globe. Critics of the United States approach viewed these communist and socialist governments as the product of homegrown local decisions (communist revolutions), while the United States viewed them as the product of Soviet interference. Under the U.S. government view (under President Reagan), any U.S. interference was merely an attempt to counteract the effects of earlier Soviet interference in constructing client states across the globe. But the ICJ took a different view and considered the United States attempt at regime change in Nicaragua as an unjustified interference in the political integrity of Nicaragua. The concept of political interference in violation of international law was as urgent then as it is now.

Damrosch conceptualized the distinctive harm of political interference as a form of "distortion" of the "free choice of the polity."[45] This conceptualization is arguably implicit in the ICJ's *Nicaragua* opinion, although the language of distortion is genuinely novel and brings to life the underlying conceptual framework that the ICJ relied upon. As Damrosch states:

> The possibility is especially acute in the case of big-power attempts to influence the politics of small states; but it is not limited to that case, as small states may occasionally be able to achieve such distortion through covert or corrupt payments. Thus, target states that choose to bar foreign involvement in their elections, provided that they simultaneously ensure rights of political participation by the citizenry, can justifiably insist that other states honor that choice. Observance of these principles may also serve the state system value of preventing tension between influenced and influencing states that might otherwise develop into interstate conflict.[46]

This "political" conception of nonintervention begins to correctly identify the distinctive harm of election interference and why it might fall within the ambit of the principle of nonintervention.[47] Damrosch calls this a "distortion" interest.

In the context of political independence or political integrity, how does the law distinguish between permissible and impermissible forms of intervention? Some commentators have referred to "dictatorial interference" as being

[45] *Id.* at 44.
[46] *Id.*
[47] *Id.* at 5 (concluding that "there is a legally binding norm of nonintervention that reaches certain kinds of nonforcible political influence, but that the conduct it regulates is not as broad as is often assumed").

illegal.[48] This language of "dictating" terms was also picked up by Schwebel in its *Nicaragua* opinion, where he referred to "dictatorial interference by one State in the affairs of the other."[49] It is unclear what dictatorial means in this context, because our commonsense understanding of a dictator always takes place within a domestic context: a dictator who controls and imposes his or her will on domestic subjects without their consent. But what exactly does it mean for a state to impose its will on another state on the international stage? Translating the concept of a dictator from the domestic to the international context is not so simple, because the legal systems through which the dictation occurred are far different. Perhaps the unifying concept is power – the subjugation of will through forcible means (though not necessarily military), all in the service of domination.

Modern international lawyers have defined "dictatorial" interference as involving some type of "coercion" – as good as any other definition of dictatorial. The ICJ in *Nicaragua* noted that "[t]he element of coercion . . . defines, and indeed forms the very essence of, prohibited intervention."[50] Coercion "is particularly obvious in the case of an intervention which uses force, either in the direct form of military action, or in the indirect form of support for subversive or terrorist armed activities within another State."[51] This explains why, for example, the ICJ viewed the funding of the Contras as a form of coercion, since it involved support for subversive armed activities. But would other activities that do not involve the use of force also constitute coercion? In some circumstances yes, although there are many types of statecraft that would not involve a coercive aspect.

The legal element of coercion turns out to be the sticking point for the entire sovereignty framework.[52] Whether framed as an intervention against territorial or political integrity, the legal doctrine requires that the intervention involve some element of coercion.[53] Consequently, the success of the sovereignty framework will depend on whether modern election interference, in particular the hacking and releasing of emails, or social media troll farm activity, qualifies as coercive in some way. This topic will be explored in detail in Section 3. If we conclude that election interference does not include a coercive aspect, then we will be forced to conclude

---

[48] *See* OPPENHEIM, *supra* note 11, at 430 ("Although states often use the term 'intervention' loosely to cover such matters as criticism of another state's conduct, in international law it has a stricter meaning, according to which intervention is forcible or dictatorial interference by a state in the affairs of another state, calculated to impose certain conduct or consequences on that other state.").

[49] Schwebel Dissenting Opinion, *supra* note 43, at paras. 98–9.

[50] *Nicaragua*, *supra* note 13, at para. 205.

[51] *Id.*

[52] As Ido Kilovaty puts it, "it is immensely difficult to define the boundary between coercive and non-coercive actions." *See* Ido Kilovaty, *Doxfare: Politically Motivated Leaks and the Future of the Norm on Non-Intervention in the Era of Weaponized Information*, 9 HARV. NAT'L SEC. J. 146, 168 (2018).

[53] *See* Mattessich, *supra* note 29, at 891 ("Coercion can be present even if no physical damage occurs . . . .").

either that sovereignty is the wrong framing device or to conclude that election interference is consistent with international law.

3. A CLOSER LOOK AT COERCION

As noted above, the scholarly consensus is that a cyber-attack aimed at interfering in another state's election would only violate the principle of noninterference if the attack had some dictatorial or coercive quality.[54] Similarly, the Declaration on Principles of International Law concerning Friendly Relations states that "[n]o State may use or encourage the use of economic, political or any other type of measure to coerce another State in order to obtain from it the subordination of the exercise of its sovereign rights and to secure from it advantages of any kind."[55] As noted by the ICJ in *Nicaragua*, regarding the types of internal decisions that are protected by the principle of nonintervention: "One of these is the choice of a political, economic, social and cultural system, and the formulation of foreign policy. Intervention is wrongful when it uses methods of coercion in regard to such choices, which must remain free ones."[56] Others have noted that the element of coercion is the *sine qua non* of illegal intervention. It distinguishes which choices are protected as part of sovereignty's *domaine réservé* and which choices are outside exclusive sovereign discretion and part of the rough and tumble of international statecraft.

Although the international case law includes no specific standards for judging coercion, scholars have devised various guideposts to be used in evaluating coercion. Viewed in the most abstract, coercion stands at the intersection between "war" and "peace," in the sense that "this dichotomy is hardly a faithful reflection of the fluid and complex process of coercion in the contemporary world arena or of the equally complex process of legal authority."[57] A state of peace is, ideally, genuinely free from force and the threat of force, whereas a state of war is the ultimate example of a state of unfreedom, at least for the losing side of the armed conflict. Moments of coercion fall in between these two extremes; coercion is a liminal moment where a state is in one sense free to act as it wishes but in other respects is deeply constrained and not at liberty to select its own destiny. There must be some loss of freedom for the intervention to count as coercive. As the Tallinn Manual puts it, "coercion must be distinguished from persuasion, criticism, public diplomacy, propaganda ... retribution, mere maliciousness, and the like in the sense that, unlike coercion,

54 *See* Christopher C. Joyner, Coercion, MAX PLANCK ENCYCLOPEDIA OF PUB. INT'L L. (Oxford University Press, 2006).

55 *See* Declaration on Principles of International Law concerning Friendly Relations and Co-operation among States in accordance with the Charter of the United Nations, U.N. G.A. Res. 2625 (Oct. 24, 1970).

56 *Nicaragua, supra* note 13, at para. 205.

57 Myres S. McDougal and Florentino P. Feliciano, *International Coercion and World Public Order: The General Principles of the Law of War*, 67 YALE L.J. 771, 776 (1958).

such activities merely involve either influencing (as distinct from factually compelling) the voluntary actions of the target State, or seek no action on the part of the target State at all."[58] There must be a loss of freedom and a manipulation.

There are few academic studies of coercion. In the legal literature, McDougal and Feliciano argued in 1958 that some of the key variables for evaluating coercion included consequentiality, extension or conservation, relation to the public order of the organized community, and methods.[59] Whatever the intrinsic value of McDougal and Feliciano's typology, it has not been highly influential in influencing the legal landscape, although this abstract statement may have been proven prescient: "contemporary technology makes possible a concentration and application of naked force hitherto inconceivable even in megalomania's wildest dreams."[60] Nozick's philosophical study of coercion links coercion to conditional threats, that is, a threat to make someone worse off if that individual does or fails to do something.[61] One way of identifying conditional threats is the threatener's prior intention to make the threat to alter the target's behavior.[62] This is necessary to distinguish between a conditional threat from a conditional warning, wherein a warning is issued that a consequence will follow, but the warning is not issued with the goal of coercing the target into changing behavior. Distinguishing between conditional threats and conditional warnings (and therefore coercion from noncoercion) has been immensely tricky and philosophically controversial. Ironically, one of Nozick's examples of coercion involves an election: "[A]n election is about to be held in a factory to determine whether the employees will be represented by a labor union. The owner of the factory announces to his employees that if the union wins the election, he will close his factory and go out of business."[63] Nozick describes this as a conditional threat if the owner's intention is strategic and designed to alter the voting behavior of the employees. Although this example flows from the labor context rather than a national election, it does provide a telling conceptual structure for understanding electoral coercion. At the heart of this coercion is the deliberate intention to change voting patterns by threatening a negative outcome if the voters cast their ballots in a way that contravenes the desires or interest of the person issuing the threat.

While the Russian election interference of 2016 was clearly distortionary, it is unclear what exactly is coercive about it. The paradigm of coercion involves an

---

[58]   TALLINN MANUAL 2.0, *supra* note 23, at 318–19.
[59]   *See* Myres S. McDougal and Florentino P. Feliciano, *International Coercion and World Public Order: The General Principles of the Law of War*, 67 YALE L.J. 771 (1958). Most of their work was concerned with military coercion.
[60]   *Id.* at 843.
[61]   *See* Robert Nozick, *Coercion*, in Morgenbesser et al. (eds.), PHILOSOPHY, SCIENCE, AND METHOD: ESSAYS IN HONOR OF ERNEST NAGEL 440–72 (St. Martin's Press, 1969).
[62]   *Id.* Similarly, Greenawalt refers to "manipulative" threats. *See* Kent Greenawalt, *Criminal Coercion and Freedom of Speech*, 78 Nw. U. L. REV. 1081 (1983–1984).
[63]   *See* Nozick, *supra* note 61, at 453.

internal decision that is negatively affected by an external pressure, some threatening pressure, that extends the sovereign will of the intervening state over the state that is targeted by the threat. By using a threat, one state casts a shadow over another state that is so strong that the leaders of the second state make decisions that bow to the will of the first state.[64] With this paradigm in mind, it is clear why coercion was at issue in the forcible campaigns (direct and indirect) in the *Nicaragua* case. In the case of direct action, the United States mined the harbors of Nicaragua. This action allegedly coerced (or attempted to coerce) the Nicaraguans into not using their own harbor for navigation, whether for commercial or military traffic. This choice was not a free one but rather one that was imposed on them by coercion; sailing through the mined waters would have resulted in destructive consequences to personnel and ships. Through this behavior, the United States accomplished a result that altered a decision that should have been within the sovereign discretion of the Nicaraguan government, that is, whether to sail through its own harbors or not. The coercion is plain in this case.

Similarly, the coercive aspect of the support of the Contras is also clear, although in this case the coercion was attempted through indirect, rather than direct, means. The United States hoped to steer Nicaragua away from a communist form of government by supporting the Contras enough that the Contras either forcibly deposed Nicaragua's Soviet-allied government or that the Contras achieved enough military gain that they might coerce the Nicaraguan government into negotiating a change in government. Either way, the change in government in Nicaragua would not have been a local choice, but one that was forced upon them by the military campaign of the Contras, and indirectly by the United States if the United States was found to have supported the Contras enough to be responsible for the actions of the Contras.[65] Through the support of the Contras, the United States allegedly hoped to overthrow the government of Nicaragua or coerce it into adopting a new political system.

When this standard is applied to the context of election interference, it is hard to identify the coercive aspect of the Russian interference in the 2016 election. A couple of scholars have struggled to find a coercive aspect to the Russian intervention and have cast Russian activity in this light. The best arguments were put forward by Steve Barela, who has argued that:

> Of course, one might ask if disseminating true material can be considered coercion. Is this "manipulation ... of public opinion on the eve of elections?" While manipulation is especially relevant when it is patently unfair, an act of this kind essentially turns on skillfully influencing others to view something (a candidate in this case) in

---

[64] *See also* Benjamin Sachs, *Why Coercion is Wrong When It's Wrong*, 91 AUSTRALASIAN J. PHIL. 63 (2013).

[65] This issue hinges on whether the United States enjoyed effective control over the actions of the Contras, a legal standard that has been hotly debated in legal practice ever since. In various decisions, the International Criminal Tribunal for Yugoslavia has suggested an alternative standard, overall control, which does not require the same level of operational insight as effective control.

a certain manner. The fact that the material was shopped to different outlets and released piecemeal for maximum effect certainly speaks to the intent to manipulate.[66]

Although the argument has some intuitive appeal, the basic structure of the alleged coercion is still very hard to elucidate. True, the Russians sought to influence the outcome of the election and moreover they did so with deception. But deception is not the same thing as coercion. Indeed, it is quite different, because in cases of coercion one need not necessarily engage in acts of deception (though one might). When the Russians hacked into the email accounts of the DNC, the DCCC, and the Clinton campaign, and subsequently released those emails through Wikileaks and DCLeaks, the Russians were hoping to change the outcome of the election, but not through the method of coercion. Rather they were trying to induce a particular result, not by threatening an undesirable outcome, but rather by tampering with the deliberative process by introducing private information into the political sphere.

Similarly, Russia's troll farm activity, launched from the IRA center in St. Petersburg, used deception rather than coercion as its métier. Posts on Facebook and Twitter sparked and amplified divisive political issues, ultimately coarsening the political discourse and angering potential Trump supporters and encouraging them to vote against Hillary Clinton. Fake "grassroots" organizations were created on Facebook and street protests were organized. If someone was "coerced" it is unclear who that person would be.[67] Was Hillary Clinton coerced, and if so how? Did she engage in particular actions because she feared a particular outcome that Russia might impose? Arguably not. Or was the American public coerced? It is unclear how this could be so, because if members of the voting public voted in one way rather than the other, it is because their political opinions were sharpened by Russian troll farms, not because they were coerced into doing so in order to avoid an undesirable outcome. The problem with the Russian interference was its distortion rather than its coercion.

American lawmakers, law-enforcement officials, and intelligence agency analysts have not used the language of coercion in describing the Russian interference in the 2016 election. Although the language used by officials in these domains is not always selected for its legal significance, it is nonetheless telling that lay assessments have strayed from the coercion framework. Furthermore, the vast majority of scholars who have written about the issue have concluded that the Russian interference did not represent a form of impermissible coercion.

---

[66] See, e.g., Steven J. Barela, *Cross-Border Cyber Ops to Erode Legitimacy: An Act of Coercion*, JUST SECURITY (Jan. 12, 2017).

[67] For more on this argument, see Ohlin, *supra* note 38, at 1592 (asking but not ultimately dismissing the possible argument that "Russian intervention came with an implied threat to withhold benefits if Hillary Clinton were elected and that Russia would act in a more cooperative manner towards the United States if Trump were elected, perhaps in exchange for reciprocal considerations from a new Trump Administration"). This suggested argument is dismissed because it appears that Clinton neither changed her views on Russia nor did the American people vote for Trump over Clinton because they feared Russian retaliation.

For example, Michael Schmitt, the lead editor of the Tallinn Manual, has written elsewhere (not in the Tallinn Manual) that:

> Some election meddling certainly would reach this threshold. As Brian Egan noted while serving as Department of State Legal Adviser, "a cyber operation by a State that interferes with another country's ability to hold an election or that manipulates another country's election results would be a clear violation of the rule of non-intervention." Blocking voting by cyber means, such as by disabling election machinery or by conducting a distributed denial of service attack, would likewise be coercive. In both of these situations, the result of the election, which is the expression of the freedom of choice of the electorate, is being manipulated against the will of the electorate. At the other end of the spectrum are cyber operations designed to influence decisions in the target State without reaching the threshold of coercion.[68]

Schmitt gets it exactly right here. The use of information operations to influence an electoral outcome – though often devastating in result – does not satisfy the coercion requirement. This result is particularly surprising, or ironic, because information operations might be more significant in size, depth, and resources, when compared to coercive operations designed to produce similar outcomes. In other words, the legal requirement of coercion does not track the size of the operation or its result; it tracks the method used. A small and insignificant operation could satisfy the requirement of coercion, while at the same time a massive and devastating operation might fail to satisfy the coercion prong.

The drafters of the Tallinn Manual concluded that coercion, by itself, is not enough to generate a violation of the principle of nonintervention; the protected interest must be one that falls within the state's sovereign discretion, or *domaine réservé*. To understand how one could have coercion in a case that falls outside the target state's sovereign discretion, consider the following example: "[A] state … blocks the access of its citizens to another State's currency without violating any international law norms when doing so. The latter conducts cyber operations that severely hamper the former State's electronic trading in an effort to compel that State to reopen access."[69] A second example might involve a dispute between two states over media access.[70] The first state blocks its own citizens from viewing foreign websites, including websites originating from a second state. The second state then launches a cyber-attack against the first state with the goal of pressuring the first state to allow its citizens to access media from the second state. According to the Tallinn Manual, "the first State's control over cyber activities on its territory is generally considered a matter of internal concern (unless implicating an applicable

---

[68] Michael N. Schmitt, *"Virtual" Disenfranchisement: Cyber Election Meddling in the Grey Zones of International Law*, 19 CHI. J. INT'L L. 30, 50 (2018).

[69] TALLINN MANUAL 2.0, *supra* note 23, at 317–18.

[70] *Id.* at 318.

international human rights law norm to the contrary ...), and the second State has engaged in coercive cyber activities that intervene into the internal affairs of the first."[71]

In order to conclude that the principle of nonintervention has been violated, the offending state must have acted with coercion but also must intervene against a protected interest of the target state. In the case of email hacking and release, there is a violation of a protected interest but no coercive quality.[72] Similarly, in the case of social media troll farms, there may be a protected interest – the political interest in holding an election free from outside distortion – but there is no coercive aspect to the behavior. Because of the lack of coercion, the alleged violation of the principle of nonintervention seems to disappear.

This conclusion might be hard for some international lawyers to swallow, because many lawyers have a gut intuition that such extensive campaigns of disinformation must be illegal under international law. And it may be tempting to engage in a teleological, intuition-driven analysis: since election interference must be illegal, we should declare it "coercive," even in the absence of evidence or common sense.[73] However, this conclusion would be a hasty one. For example, when the experts working on the Tallinn Manual 2.0 considered the case of social media election interference, the majority concluded that "the activity is not coercive in nature and therefore does not constitute prohibited intervention" because "the coercive act must have the potential for compelling the target State to engage in an action that it would otherwise not take (or refrain from taking an action it would otherwise take."[74] But a minority of the Tallinn Manual's experts were unwilling to swallow this bitter pill and concluded that it is "impossible to prejudge whether an act constitutes intervention without knowing its specific context and consequences," because that context and consequences could mysteriously "raise it to that level" of coercion.[75]

The reasoning of the minority is fallacious (though the motivation is perhaps laudable). These information operations are not coercive simply because one hopes they are. The teleological reasoning here is symptomatic of a greater difficulty, which is the stranglehold that sovereignty and the principle of nonintervention have on contemporary legal discourse. Outside the context of a military intervention, too many legal analyses are focused exclusively around the framework of sovereignty and nonintervention. If there is illegality in the case of social media

---

[71] *Id.* at 318.

[72] Kilovaty has argued that "a cyber operation that simply exfiltrates information without using it to coerce the victim state to change the course of its internal or external affairs would not be considered in violation of the norm on nonintervention." *See* Ido Kilovaty, *Doxfare: Politically Motivated Leaks and the Future of the Norm on Non-Intervention in the Era of Weaponized Information*, 9 HARV. NAT'L SEC. J. 146, 169 (2018).

[73] For example, a lawyer could describe it as a form of "constructive" coercion – constructive being the old common-law term that jurists use whenever a requirement is legally required but factually absent.

[74] TALLINN MANUAL 2.0, *supra* note 23, at 319.

[75] *Id.* at 319.

operations, the legal analysis must get away from the requirement of coercion, which is ill-suited to understanding the situation.

It is noteworthy that the Tallinn Manual's example in the above-quoted paragraph involves a government spreading "critical" (i.e. negative) information over social media. This example is therefore distinct from the 2016 election interference in one crucial respect: the social media postings originating from the IRA troll farms were deceptive in both their content and their origin, in the sense that the posts were authored to sound like they were authored by American citizens and not the work of Russians. As will become clear in Chapter 4, the deceptive nature of the social media postings, particularly as to their origin, is the key factor in this new age of information operations – the "new normal" as Special Counsel Robert Mueller feared.[76] This is not the same thing as a foreign affairs department that issues a negative press release and pushes it out on its official social media channels. Once the deceptive nature of the IRA troll farm postings is fully digested, it will become clear that the Tallinn Manual minority was probably right but for the wrong reasons. Social media operations pose a distinct danger that may be illegal under international law, just not under the rubric of coercion and nonintervention. We must look elsewhere in the legal doctrine for the correct analysis.

4. USURPATION

There is one generally recognized exception to the requirement of coercion. If the intervening state has "usurped" an inherently governmental function, then there is no need to establish coercion.[77] In that case, by engaging in activity that is within the sovereign power of the target state, the intervening state has effectively sidelined the sovereign authority of the target state and replaced it with a foreign authority. In essence, the "target State enjoys the exclusive right to perform them [the inherently governmental functions], or to decide upon their performance."[78]

The usurpation argument is conceptually strong, though the legal evidence for its existence is a bit weak. It is not commonly used in contemporary discourse and has been mostly supplanted by the principle of nonintervention outlined in the *Nicaragua* case, including the signature requirement of coercion. However, there are echoes of the usurpation prong in older discussions of the principle of nonintervention, in particular in Vattel. In his treatise, Vattel argues that "no state has the smallest right to interfere in the government of another."[79] Or, as Winfield stated, "the object of intervention is, as a rule, not the infliction of a blow upon the

---

[76] Special Counsel Robert Mueller used this phrase during his congressional testimony in July of 2019.
[77] TALLINN MANUAL 2.0, *supra* note 23, at 21.
[78] *Id.* at 21–2. The Tallinn Manual clarifies that "it matters not whether physical damage, injury, or loss of functionality has resulted . . . ."
[79] *See* VATTEL, *supra* note 9, at 154 para. 54.

resources of a state, but the usurpation of some part of its powers of government."[80] The language of usurpation also appeared briefly in the Trail Smelter arbitration.[81]

The usurpation rule also helps explain why violations of the principle of non-intervention and the right of sovereignty are most obvious when there is some territorial infringement, rather than just a violation of a political interest. A state enjoys its greatest sovereign discretion on its own territory because it is assumed that sovereignty, whatever it means, includes the right to govern on one's territory. Of course, sovereignty does not entail absolute discretion when acting on home territory, nor is extraterritorial conduct excluded entirely from the domain of sovereign action. But the presumption of sovereign discretion is at its highest on home territory. A military intervention can also be understood in terms of usurpation, because the military forces usurp the target state's exclusive control over its territory.[82]

Likewise, if an intervening state has taken over a governmental function that the target state normally engages in on its own territory, it stands to reason that it is more likely to be labeled as an "inherently governmental function." So, for example, consider a hypothetical case where an intervening state used a cyber-attack to break into the computer systems of the IRS and steal tax funds that citizens had sent to the United States Treasury in fulfillment of their tax obligations. Let us also assume that the amount of money stolen is large – that is, valued at hundreds of millions or billions of dollars. This cyber-attack could be described as a simple cyber-theft, but it could also be described in more significant terms. The hypothetical theft interfered in the collection of taxes and it is clear that the levying and collecting of taxes is an inherently governmental function. Without taxes, a democratic government has no funds with which to operate; lack of funds can grind a government to a complete halt. By absconding with these funds, the theft interrupted this inherently governmental function and arguably constituted an illegal intervention against the victim state's sovereignty. There are also other examples of potential cyber-attacks that would qualify as illegal usurpations.[83]

---

[80] *See* P. N. Winfield, *The History of Intervention in International Law*, 3 Brit. Y.B. Int'l L. 130, 142 (1922–23) (noting that the "rule of non-interference, as stated by Vattel . . . forbids usurpation by one state of a part or the whole of the functions of government in another state").

[81] The arbitration panel quoted the following language from a Swiss Court: "This right (sovereignty) excludes. . . . not only the usurpation and exercise of sovereign rights (of another State). . . . but also an actual encroachment which might prejudice the natural use of the territory and the free movement of its inhabitants." *See* Trail Smelter Arbitration, III RIAA 1905, 1963.

[82] *See* C. H. M. Waldock, *The Regulation of the Use of Force by Individual States in International Law*, 81 Recueil des Cours 455, 467 (1952) ("The landing of forces without consent, being unmistakably a usurpation of political authority, is prima facie intervention. The question is whether it is an intervention which is justifiable as an exceptional measure of self-protection."), *cited in* Richard B. Lillich, *Intervention to Protect Human Rights*, 15 McGill L.J. 205, 209 n. 21 (1969).

[83] Also implicitly recognizing the concept of usurpation, see Ido Kilovaty, *The Elephant in the Room: Coercion*, 113 AJIL Unbound 87, 88 (2019); Dan Efrony and Yuval Shany, *A Rule Book on the Shelf? Tallinn Manual 2.0 on Cyberoperations and Subsequent State Practice*, 112 Am. J. Int'l L. 583, 653, 655–7 (2018).

When applied to the context of election interference, the outcome of the "usurpation" analysis would depend on what type of election interference is being conducted. If, for example, the intervening state used a cyber-attack to break into
election board computer servers, or election machines, and change vote tallies,
this would constitute an illegal usurpation of an inherently governmental function.
The holding of an election – setting up polling places, running voting machines,
counting ballots – is an inherently governmental function without which
a democratic regime cannot exist. While the election machinery could be out-
sourced to a private firm, it must always remain under the direction of the state, by
necessity. (A *purely* private government election is a contradiction in terms.) So, if
a foreign power were to intervene in an election and changed the vote tally, this
might count as usurpation, since the counting of votes after an election is an
inherently governmental function.[84] Similarly, if a foreign state were to interfere
in an election in order to disable voting machines or election computer systems, this
loss of functionality could be considered a usurpation of an inherently governmental
function. The intervening state would be usurping the power of the target state to
hold its election.[85]

In contrast, election interference that involves social media distortion would be
difficult to describe using the language of usurpation.[86] During the 2016 election,
there is no evidence that the Russian government actively changed vote tallies or
compromised election machines, although they may have laid the groundwork for
future operations with this aim. What the Russians did do is interfere with the
deliberations of the electorate – the give and take of opinions and reasons that is
the hallmark of deliberative democracy. This process was incredibly significant,
though it is hard to describe the deliberations of the electorate as a governmental
function. Rather, it is more accurate to say that the government convenes the
election while the electorate participates in it. The Russians interfered with citizen
participation in the election by deceiving the electorate about the nature of Russian

---

[84] See Michael N. Schmitt, *"Virtual" Disenfranchisement: Cyber Election Meddling in the Grey Zones of
International Law*, 19 CHI. J. INT'L L. 30, 46 (2018) ("While the usurpation criterion has little relevance
in the election meddling context, cyber operations may well be employed to interfere with another
State's elections. Certain operations would plainly qualify, as in the case of a cyber operation that
altered election data or a temporary distributed denial of service attack against election machinery
that rendered it impossible for voters in a particular district to cast their votes. In States with online
voting, the implantation of malware in private computers that blocks voting likewise would constitute
interference, as would using cyber operations to alter voter registration numbers.").

[85] This conclusion appears to be in accord with the Tallinn Manual, which states that usurpation would
involve "changing or deleting data such that it interferes with the delivery of social services, the
conduct of elections, the collection of taxes, the effective conduct of diplomacy, and the performance
of key national defence activities." *See* Tallinn Manual 2.0, *supra* note 23, at 22. The Tallinn Manual
is not more specific about what constitutes the conduct of elections. *See also* Ohlin, *supra* note 38, at
1594.

[86] *See* Schmitt, *supra* note 18, at 46 (concluding that "Russian operators succeeded by avoiding both
ends of this legal spectrum and instead operated adroitly in the legal grey zone lying between them").

foreign electioneering, but that probably should not be equated with interference in the government's convening of the election.

CONCLUSION

International lawyers are rightfully obsessed with sovereignty. It is the bedrock principle of the Westphalian international order. However, not all legal wrongs are best understood as violations of sovereignty or as violations of its companion concept, the principle of nonintervention.[87] The international legal order protects other legal interests. To state just the obvious, international human rights law protects the dignity of individual human beings. Not only is that individual dignity not reducible to state sovereignty, it is often in tension with it, since the international protection of individual rights often entails a constraint on state sovereignty. As Louis Henkin once suggested provocatively, "the sovereignty of states in international relations is essentially a mistake, an illegitimate offspring."[88] And there are other legal interests as well, including the collective right of self-determination, as will be explored in the next chapter.

Perhaps it is no surprise that international lawyers' thinking and writing about election interference should gravitate toward sovereignty and ignore the collective right of self-determination, since traditionally the two legal concepts have been conceived as polar opposites. The standard story is that the barrier to recognizing the collective right of self-determination, in many controversial cases, is the territorial sovereignty of existing states. So, for example, a people that wishes to fulfill its right of self-determination by seceding from an existing state runs into the obstacle that a forced separation, especially when supported or assisted by outside powers, would threaten or possibly violate the sovereignty of the parent state. In this way, sovereignty and self-determination are parallel universe concepts – neither existing in the same time and space as the other.

Unfortunately, as the next chapter will demonstrate, the concept of self-determination has much to offer as a conceptual framework for understanding election interference. The present chapter has demonstrated that the most salient harm of social media election interference is the infringement of a political interest, not a territorial interest, of the target state. The technical doctrinal requirements of the principle of nonintervention are more closely tied to the territorial interests of the state rather than its political interests, though the principle of nonintervention does recognize a political violation if coercion is present.

---

[87] Many scholars have remarked that the concept of sovereignty is conceptually underwhelming. *See* Stephen D. Krasner, *Pervasive Not Perverse: Semi-Sovereigns As the Global Norm*, 30 CORNELL INT'L L. J. 651 (1997) (concluding that "[t]he whole notion of sovereignty appears fragile, incorporeal, undefinable, and perhaps inconsequential for the modern world).

[88] *See* Louis Henkin, *That "S" Word: Sovereignty, and Globalization, and Human Rights, et Cetera*, 68 FORDHAM L. REV. 1, 2 (1999).

The forms of election interference that were used in 2016 involved neither coercion nor usurpation of inherently governmental functions – an alternative avenue for finding a violation of the principle of nonintervention. If there is a unique harm to election interference, it will not be found within the four corners of the concept of sovereignty.

4

The Promise of Self-Determination

INTRODUCTION

The concepts of sovereignty and nonintervention stand at the heart of the election interference discourse, but they are also a substantial shortcoming of that discourse. The scholarly literature needs to think more creatively about legal doctrines that can analyze election interference in an intuitive and compelling way. In the present chapter, I suggest that the answer lies in the long-ignored right of self-determination. Section 1 explains the right of self-determination and its undeniable status as a binding right under international law. Section 2 explains why election interference violates self-determination. Section 3 answers an obvious question: If self-determination is the key to understanding election interference, why have international lawyers so assiduously avoided this powerful legal category? Finally, Section 4 considers several objections to the self-determination framework, namely that: (i) self-determination applies before the creation of statehood but not after; (ii) there is insufficient state practice or *opinio juris* of states objecting to election interference on grounds of self-determination; (iii) election interference cannot be illegal under international law because so many states have engaged in it; and (iv) the right of self-determination might not apply when a state acts extraterritorially, as Russia did when it intervened in U.S. elections.

The argument in this chapter stands at the intersection of *lex lata* and *lex ferenda*. International lawyers use these terms to distinguish between the law as it currently stands (*lex lata*) and the law as it ought to be (*lex ferenda*). In one sense my argument is clearly *lex lata* because I argue that the law already recognizes self-determination as a preeminent collective right. However, there is a shadow of *lex ferenda* in the argument, but only in the following sense: international lawyers have failed to recognize the true significance of self-determination as a right of wide applicability and instead confine it to very limited circumstances. This strict relegation is a profound mistake. So, although my argument relies on existing legal norms, I am suggesting that most international lawyers fail to faithfully apply these norms appropriately. But it would be wrong to characterize the argument as completely or even mostly *de lege ferenda*, because this would suggest that I am advancing a vision for how the law should progress in the future. Rather, this chapter is steadfast in its conclusion that the right of self-determination *currently* protects a polity from foreign election interference; legal discourse has failed to recognize this application of self-determination because the doctrine takes an unnecessarily myopic view of self-determination. Once the collective right of self-determination is unburdened of these unwarranted restrictions, its scope and power will be unleashed. And the result is that international lawyers and policy experts working in the cyber-security and election spaces will have a powerful legal argument at their disposal. It is there for the taking; they just need to grab it.

1. THE COLLECTIVE RIGHT OF SELF-DETERMINATION

The right of self-determination is arguably the most fundamental right under international law, though it is often overlooked, and its full significance is often obscured in traditional legal accounts. In the post-World War II legal wellspring that produced the modern human rights movement, self-determination was given a privileged place not just as a legally binding human right but also as a preeminent right, arguably more significant and far more consequential than other, more subsidiary rights, that were codified in the relevant treaties and conventions and recognized by customary law.[1]

To see self-determination's preeminent place in the modern human rights law ecosystem, consider the following pieces of evidence. Article 1(2) of the U.N. Charter recognizes that one of the purposes of the United Nations is to "develop friendly relations among nations based on respect for the principle of equal rights and self-determination of peoples, and to take other appropriate measures to strengthen universal peace."[2] Similarly, article 55 of the Charter references the "creation of conditions of stability and well-being which are necessary for peaceful and friendly relations among nations based on respect for the principle of equal rights and self-determination of peoples."[3]

Although purely "aspirational," the Universal Declaration of Human Rights states that the "will of the people shall be the basis of the authority of government; this will shall be expressed in periodic and genuine elections which shall be by universal and equal suffrage and shall be held by secret vote or by equivalent free voting procedures."[4] Although this provision does not explicitly refer to self-determination, the content of the provision clearly tracks what other conventions refer to as the right of self-determination.

---

[1]   *See, e.g.,* ALLEN E. BUCHANAN, JUSTICE, LEGITIMACY, AND SELF-DETERMINATION: MORAL FOUNDATIONS FOR INTERNATIONAL LAW (Oxford University Press, 2003); KAREN KNOP, DIVERSITY AND SELF-DETERMINATION IN INTERNATIONAL LAW (Cambridge University Press, 2002).

[2]   *See* Charter of the United Nations, 59 STAT. 1031 (1945).

[3]   *Id.*

[4]   Universal Declaration of Human Rights, G.A. Res. 217A (III) U.N. Doc. A/RES/217(III), at art. 21(3).

Furthermore, the Universal Declaration arguably goes even further than traditional abstract invocations of the right of self-determination because the Universal Declaration explicitly links the right to participation in free elections, essentially connecting self-determination to *democratic* self-government, rather than some other form of government. As will be discussed below, there is an important connection between the collective right of self-determination and the basic democratic structure of the nation-states that are created to realize the right of self-determination. Although I will not go as far as other scholars in suggesting that self-determination logically entails a democratic structure, I will defend the more modest claim that self-determination entails that elections in a democratic system must be conducted in a manner that promotes or realizes the people's right to self-determination.

The rights articulated in the Universal Declaration were later codified in two foundational treaties that form an international "bill of rights" – the International Covenant on Civil and Political Rights (ICCPR) and the International Covenant on Economic, Social, and Cultural Rights (ICESCR). The right of self-determination retained its central place during the codification process. Specifically, article 1 of the ICCPR recognizes that: "All peoples have the right of self-determination. By virtue of that right they freely determine their political status and freely pursue their economic, social and cultural development."[5] Article 1 of the ICESCR contains the exact same provision.[6] Although it is not often described as such, one could describe it as "Common Article 1" because it is common to the ICCPR and the ICESCR, thus signaling its centrality to the human rights enterprise.[7] The centrality of these two conventions to the human rights regime cannot be overstated. The fact that among all human rights, the collective right of self-determination was mentioned as the very first right, in both conventions, is rather significant. Consequently, it would be impossible to contend that the right of self-determination is not protected by international law.[8]

Other legal instruments also recognize the collective right of self-determination. For example, article 20 of the African Charter on Human Rights states that "all peoples shall have the right to existence. They shall have the unquestionable and inalienable right to self- determination. They shall freely determine their political status and shall pursue their economic and social development according to the policy they have freely chosen."[9] The European Convention on Human Rights does

---

[5]   International Covenant on Civil and Political Rights, opened for signature Dec. 19, 1966, 999 U.N.T.S. 171, 173 (1976), art. 1.

[6]   International Covenant on Economic, Social and Cultural Rights, opened for signature Dec. 19, 1966, 993 U.N.T.S. 3, 5 (1976), art. 1.

[7]   This phrase would be similar to Common Article 3, which is the term used to refer to the article 3 provision that is repeated in all four Geneva Conventions, which is also sometimes referred to as the Geneva "mini-convention" that applies in noninternational armed conflicts.

[8]   *See* Antonio Cassese, Self-Determination of Peoples: A Legal Reappraisal (Cambridge University Press, 1995).

[9]   *See* African Charter on Human and Peoples' Rights, 21 I.L.M. 59 (1982).

not include a provision on self-determination and neither does the American Convention on Human Rights. However, the 1970 Declaration of Friendly Relations states:

> By virtue of the principle of equal rights and self-determination of peoples enshrined in the Charter of the United Nations, all peoples have the right freely to determine, without external interference, their political status and to pursue their economic, social and cultural development, and every State has the duty to respect this right in accordance with the provisions of the Charter.[10]

As for the content of self-determination, the most clear-cut consequence of self-determination is the right to secede, but only in some cases. In that vein, the collective right of self-determination stands in tension with a state's sovereignty and political integrity.[11] If the collective right of self-determination entails the breakup of a state, or the loss of significant territory, may the state resist calls for secession? In some cases, yes, in other cases, no, and international lawyers have struggled in vain to articulate the key factor that distinguishes permissible cases of secession from impermissible cases.

The best answer to this question came in the Supreme Court of Canada's Reference on the Secession of Quebec. In that decision, the Supreme Court distinguished between external and internal self-determination.[12] The Court suggested that all peoples have a right to self-determination, but the Court also confirmed that *external* self-determination is only triggered if a right of internal self-determination is stymied. Internal self-determination means that a people has sufficient access to domestic political (and possibly cultural) institutions in order to realize its right of self-determination.[13] Only if a people is denied this access, and therefore is prohibited from actualizing its self-determination through domestic institutions, does the people have the right to external self-determination, which potentially entails a right of remedial secession. In the case of Quebec, the Supreme Court looked to Quebecers' access to federal political office and the province of Quebec's control over matters pertaining to language and culture, and therefore

---

[10]   *See* Declaration on Principles of International Law concerning Friendly Relations and Co-operation among States in Accordance with the Charter of the United Nations ("Friendly Relations Declaration"), General Assembly ("UNGA") Resolution 2625 (XXV), Oct. 24, 1970.

[11]   *See* Angelina M. Sasich, *The Right to Self-Determination and Its Implication on the Sovereign Right of States: The Inconsistent Application of International Standards for Independence with Respect to Kosovo*, 20 MICH. ST. INT'L L. REV. 495, 496 (2012) ("The right of a sovereign state to exercise control is threatened by the right of self-determination. The two are forced to co-exist, however, not harmoniously.").

[12]   *See Reference re: Secession of Quebec* [1998] 2 S.C.R. 217 (Can.).

[13]   *See, e.g.*, Lee Seshagiri, *Democratic Disobedience: Reconceiving Self-Determination and Secession at International Law*, 51 HARV. INT'L L.J. 553, 555 (2010) ("a population within any particular state will have achieved a significant measure of internal self-determination when it implements five societal institutions that support democratic rule").

concluded that Quebecers could fulfill their right of self-determination through the Canadian federal arrangement.[14]

In other cases, though, participation in the federal arrangement might not be enough if, for example, that federal arrangement is discriminatory. Or, to take the most extreme example, if the minority people are oppressed by the majority in the domestic system, possibly through acts of violence, the arguments for external self-determination become that much more compelling.[15]

The ICJ was called upon to answer some of these questions in its Advisory Opinion on the Legality of Kosovo's Declaration of Independence.[16] Unfortunately, the ICJ refused to lay out the criteria for when external self-determination is warranted, instead limiting its opinion (controversially) to the rather esoteric question of whether Kosovo's *statement* of independence violated international law, without passing judgment on whether Kosovo's statement was legally effective in creating an independent Kosovar state, which was presumably what most international lawyers had wanted to hear from the ICJ.[17] In the face of ICJ passivity, then, the Canadian Supreme Court judgment is arguably the most authoritative statement on the issue.

It is clear then that the right of self-determination, in at least some cases, permits independence and the creation of a new state.[18] The argument in favor of statehood is most compelling in the context of decolonization, when the entity that seeks independence is not a geographically continuous province within a federal state but is rather a distant colony that was at some point in its history conquered by an imperial army or imperial settlers.[19] In that situation, almost every international lawyer agrees that self-determination entails independence if the colony so wishes. By now, though, the process of voluntary decolonization is virtually complete, so the complicated cases that remain are ones of geographically continuous units that seek independence – Quebec, Catalonia, Basque, etc.

---

[14] *Id.* at para. 136 (concluding that "The population of Quebec cannot plausibly be said to be denied access to government. Quebecers occupy prominent positions within the government of Canada. Residents of the province freely make political choices and pursue economic, social and cultural development within Quebec, across Canada, and throughout the world. The population of Quebec is equitably represented in legislative, executive and judicial institutions.").

[15] For example, Kosovo's argument for secession from Serbia included these arguments.

[16] Accordance with International Law of the Unilateral Declaration of Independence in Respect of Kosovo, 2010 I.C.J. 403 (July 22).

[17] *Id.* at para. 78.

[18] *See* Y. Frank Chiang, *State, Sovereignty, and Taiwan*, 23 FORDHAM INT'L L.J. 959, 1002 (2000) ("In its historical context, the doctrine of self-determination means determination by a group of people with the same social, ethnic, and cultural background inhabiting one area, or sometimes a group of people living in a territory within a state, of its own political future, including establishing a state of its own by a referendum or other methods.").

[19] *See, e.g.*, Laurence S. Hanauer, *The Irrelevance of Self-Determination Law to Ethno-National Conflict: A New Look at the Western Sahara Case*, 9 EMORY INT'L L. REV. 133, 133–4 (1995) (concluding that "[s]elf-determination, as it exists in international law, applies only to peoples living within the territorial boundaries of former European colonies; the concept has developed into a set of legal prescriptions specifically governing the decolonization of territory").

Beyond the creation of an independent state, does the right of self-determination entail anything about how the newly independent state will be governed after its creation? This question implicates the complex relationship between democracy and self-determination.[20] The concepts are intertwined in two important ways. Assuming that self-determination can be defined as a people selecting its own political destiny, then self-determination can be understood as requiring a referendum or plebiscite on the question of whether it should separate from a parent state. But secondly, there is the question of whether a newly independent state, courtesy of the right of self-determination, must be governed through a democratic system.[21] What if a newly independent state is controlled by a dictator, an oligarchy, or a military junta? Do these political arrangements violate the collective right of self-determination?[22]

Over the years, many scholars have suggested that self-determination entails a commitment to democratic self-government. One of the highest-profile arguments came from the international lawyer Thomas Franck, who famously wrote in 1992 that:

> Self-determination is the historic root from which the democratic entitlement grew. Its deep-rootedness continues to confer important elements of legitimacy on self-determination, as well as on the entitlement's two newer branches, freedom of expression and the electoral right.[23]

On the right to a democratic election as an outgrowth of the right of self-determination, Franck noted that:

> With the balance now heavily tilting toward the substantial new majority of states actually practicing a reasonably credible version of electoral democracy, the treaty-based legal entitlement also begins to approximate prevailing practice and thus may be said to be stating what is becoming a customary legal norm applicable to all.[24]

Of course, Franck is quick to concede that the right to self-determination and the right to participatory democracy are not the same.[25] The right of self-determination

---

[20] *See* Russell A. Miller, *Self-Determination in International Law and the Demise of Democracy?*, 41 COLUM. J. TRANSNAT'L L. 601, 612 (2003) (concluding that "[a]n examination of the democratic heritage of self-determination can be pursued through two defining schools, both of which recognize strong non-democratic dimensions that exist alongside the democratic tendencies of self-determination").

[21] *See* Ibrahim J. Gassama, *Ballots and Bullets: The Right to Democratic Governance in International Law After the Egyptian Coup*, 32 WIS. INT'L L.J. 621, 644 (2014) ("a democratic entitlement under international law . . . does exist").

[22] *See* Glen Anderson, *Unilateral Non-Colonial Secession and Internal Self-Determination: A Right of Newly Seceded Peoples to Democracy?*, 34 ARIZ. J. INT'L & COMP. L. 1, 51 (2017) ("A more controversial interpretation (which, on balance, may not have yet passed the threshold of lex lata) is that internal self-determination requires states to adhere to Western electoral democracy.").

[23] *See* Thomas M. Franck, *The Emerging Right to Democratic Governance*, 86 AM. J. INT'L L. 46, 52 (1992).

[24] *Id.*

[25] *See* Thomas M. Franck, *The Democratic Entitlement*, 29 U. RICH. L. REV. 1, 8–9 (1994) ("Participatory democracy is becoming such a common value of humanity and it is to this value that international law is already starting to respond.").

is a collective right that attaches to peoples, while the right to democracy is allegedly an individual right.[26] This strikes me as wrong, because there is no reason to think of the two rights diverging regarding their source. Either self-determination and the right to democratic self-government are both collective rights, or both are individual rights, and there is little reason to think that one is collective while the other is not.

In any event, the deeper question is why self-determination allegedly entails a right of democracy. One answer is that a neo-Kantian view of the community of states presumes that each state, in order to remain legitimate, has an internal procedure to validate the state's representation of its nationals on the world stage.[27] A similar idea is expressed in Rawls' conception of a second-round social-contract original position.[28] However, Rawls conceives of the international social contract as between liberal states and simply excludes, by fiat, nonliberal states from the law of peoples.[29] This definitional move is not available in the international *legal* system, which usually assumes that all peoples, not just liberal ones, are entitled to rights under the international legal system. A few other legal theorists have suggested that the right to self-determination only applies to peoples that have organized some element of democratic self-rule. Under this view, a people must first have sufficient internal organization to be able to express their own preferences, possibly through a referendum, before the right of external self-determination attaches. Then, presumably, those institutions of democratic expression can continue after independence.

Another argument for what theorists have called the "democratic entitlement" is that a people must not only use self-determination to justify the creation of their nation-state but must also use self-determination to continually justify the existence of their state in an ongoing fashion. Just as the plebiscite or referendum is used to justify the creation of the state, regularly held elections justify the continuation of the state as a legitimate representation of the people's will.[30] A state that fails to conduct

---

[26] *Id.* ("The right to self-determination is not identical to the right to democracy. One deals with 'peoples,' the other with 'persons.' One is a collective right, the other an individual one. Although the collective desire of a 'people' to self-determine their collective destiny differs from the desire of a person to participate individually in the shaping of that people's collective policy, the common thread is readily apparent: the desire for meaningful participation in a coherent socio-political process.").

[27] *See* Gerry J. Simpson, *The Diffusion of Sovereignty: Self-Determination in the Post-Colonial Age*, 32 STAN. J. INT'L L. 255, 279 (1996) ("The Kantian view, sympathetic to Franck, envisages a federation of sovereign states in which each state holds regular, public, universal, and free elections. In this way, each person is secured his or her right to personal political self-determination.").

[28] *See* JOHN RAWLS, THE LAW OF PEOPLES 61 (Harvard University Press, 1999).

[29] *Id.* at 10 (describing the second original position as producing an agreement between the representatives of liberal peoples).

[30] *See* Carol C. Gould, *Self-Determination beyond Sovereignty: Relating Transnational Democracy to Local Autonomy*, 37 J. SOCIAL PHIL. 44, 53 (2006) (recognizing the relationship between self-determination and democracy, because "democracy is currently phrased in terms of a right to take part in government directly or through representatives, and is specified in terms of free periodic elections").

regular elections violates this ongoing obligation to respect its own people's right of self-determination.

The problem is that positive international law has arguably failed to keep up with these theoretical statements. If democracy is implied by self-determination, it runs into the problem that a significant percentage of the world's states are illegitimate by that criterion. Martti Koskenniemi famously said that international law vacillates between apology and utopia.[31] If Koskenniemi's insight is true, then a rule of international law that declares half of the world's states as being fundamentally illegitimate would be seriously utopian, in the sense that it is unrealistic to declare illegal the very existence of every nondemocratic state in the world. For most international lawyers, raised on the state practice and *opinio juris* that provides the foundation for customary international law, this would be a bridge too far. Although it is a highly contested point, at least some lawyers would accept that there is a range of legally permissible political orders and that the consent of the governed could be demonstrated in ways other than periodic elections. In other words, some societies might be organized in nondemocratic arrangements that nonetheless manage to preserve the collective right of the people to self-government, free from imperial control or outside intervention.[32] For example, a highly religious society may be willing to accept rule by a religious entity, without periodic elections, provided that the population is similarly religious and wishes to be ruled in this way. This would provide a counterexample to the argument that self-determination entails democracy in every case.

Luckily, the argument in this chapter does not logically depend on the claim that the right of self-determination guarantees to each individual the right to live in a democratic order. So, there is no need for this chapter to argue that self-determination requires a democratic order. Rather, this chapter simply needs to show that *if* a state is organized as an electoral democracy, self-determination prohibits outside interference in that electoral process.[33] This, I submit, is a much lighter lift. The following section is devoted to making that argument.

2. ELECTION INTERFERENCE AS A VIOLATION OF SELF-DETERMINATION

Why does election interference violate self-determination? As we saw in the previous section, self-determination is connected to democracy, but the connection is

---

[31] *See generally* MARTTI KOSKENNIEMI, FROM APOLOGY TO UTOPIA: THE STRUCTURE OF INTERNATIONAL LEGAL ARGUMENT (Cambridge University Press, 1989).

[32] *See, e.g.,* Amy E. Eckert, *Free Determination or the Determination to Be Free? Self-Determination and the Democratic Entitlement*, 4 UCLA J. INT'L L. & FOREIGN AFF. 55, 57 (1999) (concluding that "the right to democracy is not equivalent to self-determination").

[33] For a supporting argument, see Russell A. Miller, *Collective Discursive Democracy As the Indigenous Right to Self-Determination*, 31 AM. INDIAN L. REV. 341, 357 (2007) ("an international law right to self-determination can be interpreted to require discourse and the procedures necessary to make discourse effective").

a subtle one.[34] In this section, I argue in favor of the conditional claim that elections – if they are the engine of deciding the popular will – must express the will of the people rather than the will of some other people.[35] Election integrity is legally protected by the *self* in self-determination.[36] I take no stand on the larger issue of whether self-determination entails a commitment to democracy in all instances. I neither support nor reject that argument but simply put it to the side to make this more modest argument.

Why would self-determination entail election integrity?[37] Consider the manner in which elections are conducted, regulated, and protected. As will be explored in greater depth in the next chapter, citizens are permitted to vote in elections whereas foreigners, even resident foreigners, are precluded from participation in American elections. The rationale for this line-drawing exercise is that only members of the polity are permitted to determine its present and future policies. Similarly, the United States has enacted campaign finance regulations that permit citizens, both individuals and corporations, to donate to political campaigns, while politicians are prohibited from accepting donations from foreigners. Again, the rationale is that the process of *electioneering*, not just the process of voting, should be limited to members of the polity. Finally, only citizens are permitted to run for elected office on the assumption that members of the polity may only choose from among themselves when they select a representative to engage in the process of governing.

Why do these regulatory regimes exist? And why is it so important to protect them? These regulations help to ensure that the election is an expression of the will of the American electorate. The goal of an election is for a polity to express its own decisions on policy matters and to select a future direction for the affairs of the polis. In this sense, the key process of the election is not just its voting but also the deliberation and debate that precedes it. In that deliberation, the polity begins

---

[34] *See* Cécile Vandewoude, *The Rise of Self-Determination Versus the Rise of Democracy*, 2 GROETTINGEN J. INT'L L. 981, 983 (2010).

[35] For a similar argument, see Samantha Besson, *Human Rights and Constitutional Law: Patterns of Mutual Validation and Legitimation*, in Rowan Cruft, et al. (eds.), PHILOSOPHICAL FOUNDATIONS OF HUMAN RIGHTS 279, 295 (Oxford University Press, 2015).

[36] *See, e.g.*, Ashley Fernandez, *The Arab Spring: A New Season for Self-Determination*, 47 N.Y.U. J. INT'L L. & POL. 647, 654 (2015) ("In contrast, true democracies meet the continuous application criterion by ascertaining the wishes of the people through periodic elections. This process provides the requisite constant appraisal and implementation of popular will. Accordingly, those who argue against the normative requirement of democracy fail to properly address the logistical implications necessary to sustain self-determination.").

[37] International lawyers have previously recognized the relationship between self-determination and elections although not in every context. *See* Melida N. Hodgson, *When to Accept, When to Abstain: A Framework for U.N. Election Monitoring*, 25 N.Y.U. J. INT'L L. & POL. 137, 137–8 (1992) ("At the outset, U.N. election monitoring activities were principally outgrowths of peacekeeping efforts, aimed at achieving world stability and the fulfillment of the United Nations decolonization principles. Today, however, the United Nations focuses on the promotion of self-determination. Consequently, there has been a corresponding shift in the types of elections that are monitored by the Organization away from decolonization referenda to national elections in independent states torn by civil strife.").

the process of debating its popular will, followed by a decision procedure (majority rule or some version of it) to decide among competing visions that are articulated by different members of the public. Through this deliberation and decision procedure, the American people decide on a vision that they wish to adopt as the popular will of the people.

Of course, the deliberative process is not perfect, even under ideal conditions without foreign interference. Most democratic societies do not have pure democracies based on majority rule, but rather complex institutional mechanisms with some democratic legitimacy. For example, voting for the United States President is based on the electoral college, which is not a pure one-person-one-vote democracy. And while representation in the House of Representatives is by individual, representation in the Senate is by state, thus fundamentally altering the balance of power among individuals and giving individuals in smaller states a greater voice in the political process than individuals in more populous states. Consequently, even a democratic state may have institutional features that are designed to blunt the sharp edge of the popular will. Some of these features are intentionally added into the design structure of a constitutional democracy and must be considered features rather than bugs.

Similarly, even under relatively ideal conditions, the deliberative process can function in ways that advance the popular will or frustrate it. Ideology might prevent members of the public from freely considering competing options because some options are dismissed, without sufficient consideration, simply because they conflict with an ideology or other core belief.[38] The idealized portrait of the deliberative democracy where every idea is considered and weighed, rationally, against every other competing proposal is not likely to occur in reality; political communities do not deliberate the way a chess-playing computer would, that is, neutrally evaluating every option without undue reliance on preconception, irrelevant aesthetic criteria, or emotional rhetoric. Even though the demands of rationality might suggest that communities *should* deliberate this way, the reality on the ground is messier and more complicated.

Deliberation does not occur in a vacuum but rather presupposes certain basic conditions for its free exercise. The first condition for successful deliberation is legally protected freedom of thought, without which citizens will feel compelled to adopt positions that they do not, in good conscience, actually support. A second condition is legally protected freedom of speech, without which citizens will not advocate or articulate the views that they actually hold. A third condition is legally protected freedom of the press, which creates a public forum through which citizen speech might occur.

---

[38] *See* William Lewis, *War, Manipulation of Consent, and Deliberative Democracy*, 22 J. SPECULATIVE PHIL. 266 (2009).

A fourth condition is unrestricted access to information, which gives individuals the evidence that they require to test hypotheses and evaluate competing policy proposals. The public's lack of information will obstruct efficient deliberation.[39] Deliberation will only express the popular will of the people if the people has access to the relevant information about the challenges that it faces and accurate information about the existing and potential policies that could be adopted to resolve those challenges. To the extent that the public has no access to the relevant information, or has access to fraudulent or corrupted information, the deliberation and decision-making processes will be compromised by the lack of information. Without access to a shared (i.e. public) "database" of information in the public domain, the electorate has no basis to inform its deliberations. When beliefs are thrown into doubt, they are tested against a set of beliefs that are not thrown into doubt; among the latter beliefs are pieces of information from the public database of information that the public has access to. If a society severely restricts the type of information that the public has access to, the "deliberations" of that public are severely compromised and fail to reflect the popular will of the people.

Scholars of propaganda have long understood this dynamic. By controlling the flow of information, or by corrupting that information, a government can influence or even control the deliberations of the public. The government can then claim that its elections are free, which in one sense they are because the public might go to the polls to cast ballots. But in another sense these fraudulent elections fail to accord with the popular will of the people because the deliberations are compromised by government-controlled propaganda that fail to give the public the type of objective knowledge that true deliberation requires. For anyone who doubts this conclusion, consider the case of North Korea, whose population appears to sincerely idolize its president. But when the public is barred from receiving access to the world's information (by internet firewalls), but instead is fed a steady diet of state-sponsored propaganda, the "deliberations" of the public fail to reflect the popular will of the public.

Applying these theoretical insights to the case of foreign interference in the 2016 election, there is substantial reason to conclude that the interference compromised the deliberations of the public. As explained in Chapter 1, the Russian troll farms distorted the social media landscape by authoring thousands and millions of posts (once retweets are considered) that deceived readers about their true origins. The posts not only circulated false information, but they also became *part* of the database of knowledge, insofar as the posts became evidence about what a large percentage of population believed. This created not just an echo chamber but also a false datapoint.

The Russian troll farms also used social media campaigns to increase public exposure to fringe, conspiratorial ideas that were damaging to Clinton and the

[39] See Lewis, *supra* note 38, at 271.

Democrats. As noted in Chapter 1, these false stories included a claim that DNC staffer Seth Rich was murdered by prominent Democrats because he leaked Hillary Clinton's emails (which he was not and did not) and the false and outlandish claim that Democrats were using a pizza parlor to run a major child abuse ring. And these are just two examples. Widely false and bizarre stories circulated on social media and their reach was strategically amplified by Russian troll farm activity. These operations introduced fraudulent information that fundamentally altered the political discourse during the 2016 election campaign by amplifying the level of hatred regarding certain candidates.

The Russian interference also included email hacking of Clinton and other DNC officials, and their release through the DCLeaks and Wikipedia to the media. At this point, one might object that the release of this information could not be considered depriving information to the public marketplace of ideas, because the emails involved *true* information. How could the release of *more* information (the emails) pose a problem for public deliberation? There are two important responses to this objection. The first is that the email hacking was not the only form of election interference, and even if the public release of hacked information did not compromise public deliberation, the circulation by troll farms of blatantly fraudulent stories on social media certainly did corrupt the public's deliberation. The second response is that the email releases, even if they included true information, corrupted public deliberation because they created an asymmetry of information. Because only Democratic email accounts were hacked by the Russians and released by Wikileaks, the public only received negative information about the Democrats but did not receive the same level of private information about Republican politicians or officials. This asymmetry, with positive information about one side, and negative information about the other, introduced an information asymmetry that fundamentally distorted the public's deliberations. And this release is precisely what was intended by the Russian information operation.

Under the account just developed, it is significant that the conduct (both the email hacking and the troll farm activity) involved foreign actors. If domestic individuals had hacked DNC email servers and released the information over the Internet, the hacking would have violated domestic criminal statutes regarding computer intrusion but arguably would not have violated the right of self-determination. Any corruption would have come from within the polity itself and therefore would not have displaced the people's will with the will of an outside actor. Similarly, social media activity conducted by American citizens would not have compromised the will of the American people, it would have expressed it. In contrast, Russian interference corrupted the political discourse precisely because it had a foreign source.

From the evidence outlined in this section, a compelling account emerges of the Russian interference as a violation of the collective right of self-determination. Although the right of self-determination does not entitle every people to a democratic regime, it does require some mechanism to ensure that the government represents the will of the people rather than the will of outside forces. In a democratic society, that mechanism is periodic elections. These elections must be conducted with integrity and free from outside interference that might distort the deliberations of the electorate.

The Russian interference in the 2016 election arguably distorted the deliberations leading up to the general election, even if the interference did not compromise the actual process of casting and counting ballots. But as the preceding analysis has demonstrated, the deliberations that precede election day are just as important as the casting of ballots on the final day of the election. An election whose deliberations are compromised or distorted will not reflect the will of the people, and we must remember that the whole point of an election is to represent the will of the people. If the election fails to accomplish this task, there is no point in having the election in the first place. In fact, having a compromised election may even be worse than holding no election at all, because a compromised election gives the patina of legitimacy, falsely suggesting that the right of self-determination is being respected, when in fact the outcome of the political process is that it represents the will of outsiders.

In order to comply with the right of self-determination, democratic regimes are required to protect elections, ensure their integrity, and foreclose the possibility of foreign influence. Although not every form of outside influence must be prohibited, there is a core set of concerns that flow from the right of self-determination. These concerns require policing the boundary between insiders and outsiders, ensuring that only insiders, that is, members of the polity, participate in the election. The most obvious requirement is the prohibition on foreign voting. To state the obvious, if Swedes were to allow everyone around the world to vote in their elections, the result of the election would not express the will of the Swedish people but would express the views of the world community. This result would make a mockery of the right of self-determination. It would substitute the "self" in self-determination for a form of global-determination.

Similarly, democratic regimes must protect the deliberative process to ensure that those who are outside the polity are not permitted to corrupt deliberations by introducing erroneous information into the process. Moreover, outsiders who would engage in this type of corruption are violating the right of self-determination. The outcome of this analysis is that Russia's interference in 2016 election violated the American people's collective right of self-determination, rather than violated the sovereignty of the United States or violated the principle of nonintervention. The self-determination framework turns out to be more intuitive, convincing, and legally accurate than the sovereignty framework.

Two final points. First, some commentators have asserted that Russian interference violated the popular sovereignty of the American people.[40] Although these

---

[40] *See, e.g.,* Claire Finkelstein, *How Democracy, in the Kremlin's Crosshairs, Can Fight Back*, ZOCALO PUBLIC SQUARE (May 11, 2017) (arguing that "[i]nstitutions that are dependent on the concept of

invocations refer to the language of sovereignty, it is my contention that these statements are better described by what lawyers mean by self-determination. The word "sovereignty" has many meanings and its usage does not always accord with what lawyers mean by the concept of sovereignty. The word sovereignty also has a political connotation, especially when it is connected to the word "popular," in that it denotes an electoral ideal.[41] The people of the United States express their popular sovereignty through elections, and in that sense it is exactly right to conclude that the Russian government violated the popular sovereignty of the American people. But in translating that point to legal discourse, the better translation is the concept of self-determination rather than the concept of sovereignty as that term is understood by public international lawyers.

Second, a few legal scholars have followed my lead in recognizing the significance of self-determination in the legal analysis of election interference, though they have included it as a sub-variant of the principle of nonintervention under the rubric of sovereignty. In prior chapters, I argued that sovereignty was a poor fit for understanding election interference and that the collective right of self-determination was a more promising framework. My view was that self-determination and sovereignty were *alternative* frameworks. However, at least a few scholars have tried to meld them together into a single argument; the violation of self-determination would be one way that a foreign state could violate the sovereignty of another state. Consider, for example, the view of Nicholas Tsagourias, who argues that:

> [T]he right to self-determination is broader and is not exclusively linked to the right of peoples to form their own State. Moreover it does not cease once a State has been created . . . . External interference through disinformation combined with identity falsification, for example, distorts, undermines or inverses this process and nullifies the genuine expression and authority and will by the people.[42]

This seems exactly right, though Tsagourias then links sovereignty and self-determination together and argues that by doing so the "domain and object of intervention shifts from the government, to the actual power holder, the people."[43]

---

    popular sovereignty are sitting ducks for foreign intervention carried out by cyberattack, cyber influence, and cyber manipulation").

[41] For example, the legal scholar Ciara Torres-Spelliscy has referred to foreign financing as a problem of "popular sovereignty." *See* Ciara Torres-Spelliscy, *Dark Money as a Political Sovereignty Problem*, 28 KINGS L.J. 239 (2017) (arguing that "[a] key factor to both sovereignty of the nation and the popular sovereignty of the American people is the soundness of the electoral process," noting that a "close corollary to sovereignty is the right of a people to self-determination," and concluding that "the concepts of sovereignty and self-determination are intertwined in a democracy, as the people in a given country decide their fate"). This reference to popular sovereignty is exactly right and the prior skepticism toward "sovereignty" discourse in the prior chapter does not apply in this instance, since the usage in this case more closely tracks the concept of self-determination.

[42] *See* Nicholas Tsagourias, Electoral Cyber Interference, Self-Determination and the Principle of Non-Intervention in Cyberspace, in Dennis Broeders and Bibi van Den Berg (eds.), GOVERNING CYBERSPACE: BEHAVIOUR, POWER AND DIPLOMACY (Rowman & Littlefield, 2020).

[43] *Id.*

The problem with this view is that it is unclear what is to be gained by locating the right of self-determination within the concept of sovereignty, rather than outside it. Self-determination is already legally protected by international law, as a collective right, so one does not need the concept of sovereignty and the principle of non-intervention to demonstrate that election interference is illegal. Its illegality is already determined once self-determination is brought into the picture; describing it as a violation of sovereignty does not make it any *more* illegal. Consequently, it is unclear what additional doctrinal payoff we receive once we link the two frameworks together. Moreover, it comes at some cost, since it is inconsistent with the prevailing view of sovereignty.

On the other hand, my approach comes with costs as well, since international lawyers are not accustomed to thinking of self-determination so robustly. In the end, this may be an intramural dispute of little consequence. Whether self-determination is viewed as an independent framework or as a doctrinal prong within the framework of sovereignty and the principle of nonintervention, the good news is that a few international lawyers have recognized that election interference is illegal because it violates – in some way – the right of self-determination.

3. WHY SELF-DETERMINATION IS OVERLOOKED

If self-determination is a more compelling framework than sovereignty for analyzing election interference, there is one obvious question: why have international lawyers failed to appreciate the significance of self-determination in this case? The answer, broadly speaking, is that self-determination is often overlooked in international law, so the diagnosis has more to do with self-determination than with election interference. As this section will demonstrate, international lawyers disfavor references to self-determination for at least four reasons, each of which will now be explored in greater depth: the category of "peoples" is frustratingly indeterminate; peoples are inconsistent with international law's prevailing methodology of positivism; self-determination's status as a collective right fits uncomfortably within the prevailing individualism that reigns in human rights law; and self-determination is falsely assumed to be limited to the process of decolonization.[44]

While most rights and entitlements under international law attach to states, the right of self-determination, by definition, cannot attach to states. There is a simple explanation for this impossibility. The right of self-determination often entails that a group is entitled to statehood and the creation of a state to fulfill its right of self-determination. Lawyers sometimes refer to this as external self-determination. In these cases where self-determination entails secession and statehood, the right of self-determination cannot attach to a state because it applies to an entity that is

---

[44] *See, e.g.,* Thomas D. Grant, *Extending Decolonization: How the United Nations Might Have Addressed Kosovo,* 28 Ga. J. Int'l & Comp. L. 9, 11 (1999) (noting that "self-determination has notoriously lacked concrete legal content").

seeking statehood and therefore is not yet a state. For the right to have any meaning or impact whatsoever, it must attach to some pre-state entity. Political philosophers sometimes refer to "nations" as the holders of this right, although "nationhood" is an ambiguous term that has different meanings in different contexts.[45] In contrast, international lawyers prefer to use the phrase "peoples" as the bearer of the right of self-determination, as in the phrase "all peoples have the right to self-determination." The language of "peoples" is reinforced by the codifications of the right that were outlined at the beginning of this chapter. The ICCPR, ICESCR, and other major instruments make clear that it is peoples who enjoy this particular right.

Modern international lawyers hate discussing "peoples" and hate that the outcome of any analysis of self-determination is dependent on whether an entity is a people or not. The problem is that international law has no defined criteria for what counts as a people. There are, however, defined criteria for what counts as a state, outlined in the Montevideo Convention, customary international law, and a rich body of scholarly literature on the topic.[46] In contrast, any determination of what counts as a people would require reference to disciplinary tools that are outside the field of legal study. Anthropologists, sociologists, and historians are more equipped than lawyers to determine whether a particular group counts as a "people." The question will be determined by cultural, religious, linguistic, and ethnic relationships among the individuals who make up the group, and how these relationships overlap or intersect with other groups. Individuals within a particular group will share some exclusive trait, whereas other traits, such as religion, might also be shared with individuals outside the group. So, for example, the province of Quebec is overwhelmingly francophone and Catholic, but they are not the only Catholics or francophones in the world. All of this makes the determination of who counts as a people messy and impossible to adjudicate using the tools (criteria) that international lawyers usually deploy.

There is a substantial likelihood that any debate about self-determination will get bogged down over disputes about whether the particular group is a people or not, and therefore whether they are entitled to self-determination. That fundamental indeterminacy is so frustrating for international lawyers that they have an incentive to confine self-determination to as narrow a range of cases as possible. While it may not be possible to deny self-determination a place in the international legal ecosystem, international lawyers can confine it to the shortest possible orbit, to limit its significance, and discourage reliance on it.

To take just the most obvious example, the prohibition on genocide is widely considered to be a peremptory norm of international law and a cornerstone of the post-World War II human rights regime. The prohibition on genocide protects

---

[45]   The term "nation" can sometimes be used as synonymous with statehood, especially in the phrase "nation-state."

[46]   Convention on the Rights and Duties of States (Montevideo Convention), Dec. 26, 1933, 165 L.N.T.S. 19.

a defined set of groups, including national, ethnical, racial, and religious groups. Consequently, one cannot understand the prohibition on genocide without reference to these groups, none of which are necessarily synonymous with statehood. These groupings are extralegal categories and through the prohibition on genocide the law protects membership in these groups. The law recognizes that when one of these groups is destroyed, the world is diminished. These groups have a legally recognized right to exist. What this means is that the law cannot reduce everything to statehood; there are other collective categories that are relevant rights-bearing entities.

In making these observations, I do not mean to suggest that the right of self-determination is relativistic and that there is no objective answer to which group counts as a people. This would be an overreaction. Rather, I am suggesting that the ground rules for making this objective determination require reference to evidence that international lawyers are not comfortable discussing, which is one reason why international lawyers prefer to avoid the collective right of self-determination, at almost any cost.

Second, and relatedly, the concept of "peoples" is inconsistent with international law's prevailing positivism.[47] International law has a rigorous theory of sources, which includes treaties and customary international law, and most international lawyers observe a strict separation between law and morality. The criteria for what we should count as international law is particularly strict, and most international lawyers zealously distinguish legal discourse from philosophy or ethics. The category of "states" fits comfortably within that positivistic worldview, because international law has clear criteria, in the Montevideo Convention and international custom, for determining what counts as a state. Figuring out what counts as a people strikes most international lawyers as an exercise in philosophy or some other humanistic enterprise – a noble effort but not one deserving the label of "law."[48]

The third reason for self-determination's subordinate status in international law is that it is collective, and human rights discourse is usually individualistic. Think of it this way. International law usually ascribes rights to either states or individual human beings. The former are state-based rights that are part of general public international law. The latter are individualistic rights that form the core of international human rights law. Collective rights that accrue to "peoples" fit uncomfortably within this scheme, at home in neither region. As noted at the beginning of this chapter, the collective right of self-determination is codified in both the ICCPR and the ICESCR, though its status as a collective right fits uncomfortably within the

---

[47] *See* Jean d'Aspremont, *Reductionist Legal Positivism in International Law*, 106 AM. SOC'Y INT'L L. PROC. 368, 368 (2012) (advocating for "a reductionist understanding of ILP construed as a theory of identification of international legal rules based on a theory of sources").

[48] *See* Ayelet Banai, *Territorial Conflict and Territorial Rights: The Crimean Question Reconsidered*, 16 GERMAN L.J. 608, 610 (2015) (referring to, but not endorsing, an "indeterminacy objection . . . that the idea of a people is too vague, whereby a plausible distinction and judgment about who is a people – so as to be a subject and right-holder of self-determination – is not possible").

ICCPR's structure as a protector of individualistic rights. There is an argument that it fits more squarely within the ICESCR, which protects more communal rights, though even its inclusion there is in some tension with the basic structure of international human rights law. Self-determination is the fish out of water in the field of human rights law.

The last reason that international lawyers limit their references to self-determination is that they consider it mostly confined to the decolonization context, meaning that it granted the right of colonies to separate from imperial powers but that once the process of voluntary decolonization was complete, self-determination automatically faded into irrelevance. While not every international lawyer subscribes to this view, it is common enough that self-determination has had a limited role to play outside the context of decolonization.[49]

However, it is wrong to think that self-determination is limited to the decolonization process. If it were, the codifications of the right would have said that it was so limited. It is important to distinguish between the inspiration for the codification for the right and its general applicability. Just because the impetus for recognizing the right was the problem of colonization does not entail that the right is strictly limited to that context. Rather, the right of self-determination applies to all peoples, and when it is violated it entails that peoples are entitled to a reorganization that protects that right. In theory and in reality, the right of self-determination is a general right that applies in a general way. If the right were simply limited to former colonies, the codified provisions would have said that colonized peoples have a right of self-determination, but this is not what the provisions say. Moreover, the problem of colonization was just one exemplar of denials of the right of self-determination. One can imagine others, such as a people that is dominated by a political arrangement that is not between an imperial power and a colony. The definition of a colony is very limited and there are plenty of situations where noncolonized peoples are denied the right to self-determination.

All of this is just to say that international lawyers are wrong to dismiss the significance of self-determination, both in general and in the particular case of election interference. International lawyers avoid the rights of peoples at their own risk. It is central to many other areas of international law which could not function without heavy reliance on the concept of a people or some other collective entity (other than the state). The stranglehold that the concept of statehood has on modern international law is unfortunate.

---

[49] *See* W. Michael Reisman, *The Struggle for the Falklands*, 93 YALE L.J. 287, 305 (1983) (noting that there "is a tendency to view self-determination and decolonization as synonymous" and that in many but not all cases, "self-determination claims and decolonization claims have been perfectly congruent"); Natsu Taylor Saito, *Decolonization, Development, and Denial*, 6 FLA. A & M U.L. REV. 1, 15 (2010) (suggesting that "self-determination is the heart and soul of decolonization; without it, decolonization is meaningless").

4. OBJECTIONS TO THE SELF-DETERMINATION FRAMEWORK

Applying a self-determination framework to election interference has already met with criticism from international lawyers. Typically, the objections fall into four categories. The first is that self-determination applies before statehood but not afterwards. The second is that there is insufficient state practice or *opinio juris* to support the theory. The third is that election interference cannot violate international law because so many states have engaged in, or continue to engage in, the practice. The fourth objection is that self-determination, like human rights generally, cannot be applied extraterritorially. I shall address each objection in this section.

The idea that self-determination applies before statehood but not afterwards flows from a certain conception of the relationship between self-determination and statehood. Under this view, "peoples" are recognized in contexts where they are denied statehood. So, only in situations where a people are denied its self-determination does the law need to step in and declare the existence of a people entitled to statehood. However, once the people's claim to statehood is accepted and a state is created, the right of self-determination allegedly fades into the background, with the state becoming the primary engine for its nationals to assert various claims under international law. At that moment, a legal discourse based on self-determination gives way to a legal discourse framed around the concept of sovereignty.[50] Under this view, that transition point is both significant and irreversible; once sovereignty becomes the primary framework for the state, one cannot go back and assert claims based on one's status as a people and the right of self-determination.[51] That opportunity has passed. If this view is correct, sovereignty must be the only framework for debating claims about election interference because these violations occur past the point in time when self-determination is relevant.[52]

This critique is wrong for one obvious reason: the right of self-determination continues to remain relevant, even after the state is created. There are several reasons for this. First, lawyers use the concept of internal self-determination all the time. The

---

[50] *See, e.g.,* Michael N. Schmitt, *"Virtual" Disenfranchisement: Cyber Election Meddling in the Grey Zones of International Law,* 19 CHI. J. INT'L L. 30, 55–6 (2018) (arguing that "self-determination is simply not meant to apply to a situation where the 'people' are all citizens of a State rather than a distinct group therein that is denied the right to govern itself, as in the case of colonialism, apartheid, alien subjugation, and perhaps occupation"); Duncan Hollis, *The Influence of War; the War for Influence,* 32 TEMP. INT'L & COMP. L.J. 31, 43 (2018) ("The history of self-determination has focused on peoples' rights in creating states, not in discourse about electing governments.").

[51] For example, Barrie Sander has written that "self-determination has traditionally been relied upon in the context of peoples attempting to create new States rather than the election of a new government in an already-existing State." *See* Barrie Sander, *Democracy Under the Influence: Paradigms of State Responsibility for Cyber Influence Operations on Elections,* 18 CHINESE J. INT'L L. 1, 43 (2019).

[52] Schmitt also appears to take this view when he states that "arguments based on self-determination typically appear when groups are trying to create a State, perhaps through succession, and that the will of the 'people' cannot be determined with any degree of certainty before an election." *See* Schmitt, *supra* note 50, at 55.

concept of internal self-determination applies when a people has its right to self-determination respected within a particular state. That discourse would be meaningless if self-determination disappears once a state is created. In this one context, international lawyers agree that self-determination remains relevant even after the creation of the state.

Of course, internal self-determination involves situations where a people arguably does not have its own, *exclusive* state, but participates in a multicultural state or a state that is the fulfillment of another people's right of self-determination. So, one might distinguish the case of internal self-determination on that basis. However, there is another answer to this objection. As noted earlier, even when a state is created, the right of self-determination still applies to *justify* the state's existence as a fulfillment of the people's right of self-determination. It is a fallacy to assume that a people need only refer to self-determination to justify the *creation* of a state; the continuing *existence* of the state is also subject to justification, and the right of self-determination must be continuously invoked in order to justify that existence – especially where that existence imposes costs on others (land, territory) that stand in need of justification.

The second objection to the self-determination paradigm is that there is insufficient evidence of customary support for the view. If indeed election interference violated the right of self-determination under international law, especially under customary law, one would expect to find state practice or *opinio juris* invoking this language. The fact that states have either not objected to election interference, or when they have objected to it they have objected to using the language of sovereignty, suggests that election interference cannot be a violation of self-determination under customary international law.[53]

This criticism is a common one in many international legal arguments. When a particular lawyer suggests that something is illegal under international law, other international lawyers say that the practice has not been objected to by other states, thus (allegedly) conclusively establishing that customary international law permits the practice. But this objection, both in the case of election interference but also in other contexts, confuses the requirements for establishing the legal norm and the requirements for applying that norm to a particular fact situation. Custom, as a source of international law, requires a finding of state practice and the associated *opinio juris*. However, this requirement, which stems from a theory of sources, including custom, applies to the identification of the legal norm itself, not to the application of that norm to a particular fact pattern. In other words, international law requires state practice to identify what counts as a rule, legal norm, or other law, in the abstract, not in the application of that norm to a particular fact pattern. The fact finder is tasked with looking to state practice and custom to determine whether

---

[53]   *See* Hollis, *supra* note 50, at 43 ("IOs have a long – and, some would say, successful – history of interfering with foreign national elections without self-determination complaints.").

something is a legal norm under international law, but then engages independent analysis to determine whether a particular state's conduct has run afoul of that legal norm.

In this case, one should look to state practice, *opinio juris*, and treaty codification, to determine whether the rule in question is a valid norm under international law. This means looking to state practice and treaty to determine whether the collective right of self-determination is a valid principle of international law. But in deciding whether a particular course of conduct violates self-determination, one must apply the norm to a set of facts, and that is the province of law-application-to-fact, not the identification of legal norms, the latter of which is governed by the theory of sources and the requirements of state practice and custom.

It is important to note that this is a frequent problem in international law – the overreliance on state practice and *opinio juris*, and the confusion between identification of legal norms and the application of those norms to particular facts. If we required state practice and *opinio juris* in every single case, then international law would be nothing more than what the world says it is at any one moment, and international law would be nothing more than an international plebiscite on state behavior. But that would be an impoverished view of international law. International law involves looking to defined sources to determine particular legal norms, but then the legal analysis must apply that norm to the facts of the case, judged by standards of reason and evidence.

Take an example from another area of international law. Say a state engages in the use of force and argues that its conduct was justified by self-defense. One looks to treaty interpretation and customary international law to figure out the requirements of self-defense. But then in applying that legal norm to the state's conduct, one engages in an independent legal analysis of whether the state's conduct violated the legal norm. One does not simply look to the world community to see whether other states have objected to the state's conduct. In the application of the legal norm to the facts, it is perfectly coherent to say that the state's conduct ran afoul of the law even though few – or no – states objected to the conduct. International lawyers make this methodological mistake all the time, and the existence of this mistake is one reason why Martti Koskenniemi (*supra*) complained that international law has an aspect of "apology." The application of international law might simply reinforce what the world community wants it to say. If that were the case, one should not be surprised when the content of the law matches exactly the interests of the major players of the world community. This chapter is a call to recognize a different methodology: one consults state practice to determine whether a particular rule exists, but one is then liberated from the shackles of state practice and *opinio juris* when it comes time to apply that norm. I submit that this is a more faithful adoption of the theory of sources, which was meant to carefully limit the identification of norms, not limit how they are applied in any particular scenario.

It should not matter that states have not connected election interference with the right of self-determination in their public statements. This is evidence of nothing more than the fact that ministries of foreign affairs have downgraded the right of self-determination just as much as academic lawyers have. It is also evidence of a failure of legal imagination. Almost every state on the planet recognizes the right of self-determination as a collective right protected by international law, and binding on all states. The fact that states have failed to recognize the import of this right is inapposite. It is always the case that states think of themselves as complying with international law; but sometimes they find out after the fact that their interpretations of the law are wrong. Russia may or may not believe that its operations complied with international law, but this is entirely consistent with a conclusion that its operations violated the self-determination of the American people. The task of determining whether a violation occurred is the province of objective legal analysis, not a plebiscite among the world's nations to see if they believe that it violated the right of self-determination.

The third objection is a general one pertaining to any argument that concludes that election interference violates international law (whether because of self-determination or some other principle). Many states have engaged in this behavior in the past, including the United States. How can election interference violate international law when so many states have engaged in the practice in the past?

To add urgency to this question, it is useful to make a brief detour through the history of information operations and so-called "active measures." Although certainly not the historical beginning of information operations broadly construed, which could include earlier examples of propaganda, many scholars point to the Soviet and Russian government's organized units dedicated to "active measures" during the 1920s up until the present day. These active measures were far broader than election interference and included efforts to influence the public opinion of domestic and foreign audiences.[54] These efforts included the creation of fake advocacy organizations, distribution of falsified or fraudulent information, or the use of *kompromat* to coerce targets into acting in ways contrary to their national interest.[55]

To take one historical example, the Russian government launched a campaign of active measures to influence French public opinion during the administration of Charles de Gaulle. The goal of the campaign was to increase public opinion of the

---

[54] See L. John Martin, *Disinformation: An Instrumentality in the Propaganda Arsenal*, 2 Pol. Communication 47 (1982); Herbert Romerstein, *Disinformation as a KGB Weapon in the Cold War*, 1 J. Intelligence Hist. 54 (2001).

[55] China also has engaged in substantial information operations. See Dean Cheng, Cyber Dragon: Inside China's Information Warfare and Cyber Operations (Praeger, 2017). Recent reports have suggested that China has used an extensive information operation to discredit and delegitimize the Hong Kong protests. See Steven Lee Myers and Paul Mozur, *China is Waging a Disinformation War Against Hong Kong Protestors*, N.Y. Times (Aug. 13, 2019) ("In China's version, a small, violent gang of protestors, unsupported by residents and provoked by foreign agents, is running rampant, calling for Kong Kong's independence and tearing China apart.").

Soviet Union, drive a wedge between the United States and France, and increase the possibility of a closer relationship between France and the Soviet Union.[56] The campaign involved multiple strands, including the creation of a news agency, a weekly newsletter, and relationships with established journalists.[57] Soviet agents also allegedly infiltrated the leftist newspaper *Le Monde* in order to encourage pro-communist and anti-American coverage, though to what extent *Le Monde's* coverage was "biased" is hotly debated.[58] According to Andrew and Mitrokhin, French public opinion of the Soviet Union increased during this time, while French public opinion of the United States decreased, though drawing a causal connection is hard to do.[59]

What is remarkable about this one historical example is how little has changed about the underlying structure of "active measures" campaigns, though the techno-logical engine has shifted dramatically. Instead of creating an entire news agency, the Russian government now uses a troll farm to harness the power of Twitter and Facebook. Instead of infiltrating *Le Monde* and other leftist periodicals with Soviet agents, the Russians now produce their own content that is directly consumed by the American public over social media platforms. While the strategic goals of these active measure campaigns are similar, technological change has increased the temperature, and the immediacy, of the interactions.

Similarly, it is undeniable that the United States, through the CIA and other intelligence agencies, has engaged in information operations in the past.[60] Arguably the heyday of these manipulations was the Cold War era, when U.S. intelligence agencies used disinformation campaigns to discourage the spread of communism and to achieve other strategic objectives.[61] These efforts involved supporting anti-communist movements, supporting anti-communist leaders, and even installing them in power through nondemocratic measures. Some of these efforts involved explicit disinforma-tion campaigns, such as the spreading of false rumors, or propaganda, to achieve these results.[62] The use of information operations is admittedly widespread in today's world.[63]

---

[56] *See* CHRISTOPHER ANDREW AND VASILI MITROKHIN, THE SWORD AND THE SHIELD 464 (Basic Books, 1999).

[57] *Id.* at 464–8.

[58] *Id.* at 470.

[59] *Id.* at 466.

[60] *See* ROGER C. MOLANDER, ANDREW RIDDILE, PETER A. WILSON, STEPHANIE WILLIAMSON, STRATEGIC INFORMATION WARFARE: A NEW FACE OF WAR (RAND Corporation, 1996) (noting that one of the defining features of information operations is "low entry cost"); DANIEL VENTRE, INFORMATION WARFARE (2nd edn., Wiley, 2016) (presumptively before the 2016 election noting that the term information warfare has fallen out of fashion).

[61] *See* Ladislav Bittman, *The Use of Disinformation by Democracies*, 4 J. INTELLIGENCE & COUNTERINTELLIGENCE 243 (1990).

[62] *See* Scott Shane, *Russia Isn't the Only One Meddling in Elections. We Do It, Too*, N.Y. TIMES (Feb. 17, 2018) (quoting Loch K. Johnson as saying: "We've been doing this kind of thing since the C.I.A. was created in 1947 . . . We've used posters, pamphlets, mailers, banners – you name it. We've planted false information in foreign newspapers. We've used what the British call 'King George's cavalry': suitcases of cash.").

[63] *See* SCOT MACDONALD, PROPAGANDA AND INFORMATION WARFARE IN THE TWENTY-FIRST CENTURY: ALTERED IMAGES AND DECEPTION OPERATIONS (Routledge, 2007) (referring to the United States as the "easiest mark").

Commentators and politicians have made two arguments about the U.S. past practice of information operations. The first argument is that the United States is hypocritical for complaining about Russian active measures given the U.S. history of using these tools of statecraft. The second argument is that the widespread use of these tools by the United States and other states shows that they cannot be illegal under international law.

It is certainly not the case that a practice is lawful just because states have engaged in it in the past. To take just the most obvious example, many states have engaged in violations of *jus ad bellum*, but this does not mean that the rules of *jus ad bellum* are illusory. Similarly, torture is undeniably a violation of international law – even a *jus cogens* violation – but many states have engaged in horrific instances of torture in the past. The fact that there are many violations of a rule is not evidence that the rule does not exist but rather evidence of the necessity for having the rule in the first place, that is, the existence of a social problem that requires regulation. If a rule was never violated there might not be the need to have the rule in the first place.

One might counter these objections of hypocrisy by suggesting that Russian active measures are different in degree or kind from what the United States has done in the past or is doing in the present.[64] I will not make that argument but will instead concede, just for the sake of argument, that election interference and information operations are established modes of statecraft for many states. With this concession, these complaints are symptomatic of the same argument that we discussed above. References to state practice are required for identifying the rule, not for figuring out the application of the rule to a particular set of facts. The rules in question are noninterference or self-determination (depending on whether you accept the argument in this chapter), not election interference specifically. To my mind, the objection is like saying that almost every state in the world discriminates against women in some way, so discrimination against women must be consistent with international human rights law. However, the scourge of discrimination is not evidence that human rights law permits discrimination against women. The better conclusion is that human rights law prohibits sex discrimination but that many states struggle to live up to the demands of the law.

Similarly, election interference is illegal under international law, but the world community has failed to adequately enforce the norm. There are multiple reasons for the world community's unwillingness or inability to enforce the prohibition against election interference. The biggest reason for the failure is the covert and clandestine nature of most information operations. States that engage in information

---

[64] For a description of American information operations in the present day, see Arturo Munoz, U.S. Military Information Operations in Afghanistan: Effectiveness of Psychological Operations, 2001–2010 120 (RAND Corporation, 2012) (discussing lack of integration of information operations and psychological operations with conventional "unit" operations); Thomas Rid and Marc Hecker, War 2.0: Irregular Warfare in the Information Age 2 (Praeger, 2009) (noting that information warfare gives irregular forces a strategic advantage).

operations rarely acknowledge their role in conducting the operations – certainly not close in time to the operation itself (they may admit it long after the fact). Information operations are usually conducted by the GRU, the CIA, or some other clandestine agency whose operations are rarely acknowledged by the state. Indeed, refusal to acknowledge responsibility for an information operation is part and parcel of these operations, because in many instances they involve falsifying the origins of the communications, so they appear to be authored by someone else rather than by a foreign intelligence agency. This is certainly the case with the social media operations conducted by the IRA troll farms supported by the GRU.[65]

A second and related reason for the world community's inability to enforce the prohibition against election interference is the attribution problem. The so-called attribution problem is a key feature of the scholarly literature and policy discussions about cyber-attacks and cyber-security. The idea is that it is very hard to stop a cyber-attack, or deter it beforehand, because the victim of the attack is often unable to identify the source or origin of the attack. The attribution problem also hinders efforts to hold the perpetrators legally responsible for the attack. But the attribution problem is not just a feature of cyber-attacks but is also a problem for information operations, even noncyber ones. If an intelligence agency carefully covers its tracks, it may be difficult to marshal evidence before the world community that a particular state is responsible for the information operations.[66] For these reasons, it is hard to bring election interference out of the shadows and into the harsh light of international law. But none of this means that election interference is necessarily lawful.

The final objection is that self-determination cannot be applied extraterritorially.[67] The debate about extraterritoriality goes to the heart of human rights law. Most of these debates focus on article 2(1) of the ICCPR, which states that: "[e]ach State Party to the present Covenant undertakes to respect and to ensure to all individuals within its territory and subject to its jurisdiction the rights recognized in the present Covenant . . . ." There are two ways of reading this provision. Under one interpretation, the territorial limitation ("within its territory and subject to its jurisdiction") applies to both the obligation to respect and to the obligation to ensure, so that the ICCPR imposes no obligations on a state when it engages in extraterritorial conduct. This was the interpretation that the United States government gave the ICCPR in 1995 and that interpretation has governed U.S. legal positions since then, although many states disagree with it. A second interpretation holds that the territorial limitation only applies to the obligation to "ensure" and that the obligation to "respect" is territorially unbounded and applies wherever the state

---

[65] *See* TODD C. HELMUS ET AL., RUSSIAN SOCIAL MEDIA INFLUENCE: UNDERSTANDING RUSSIAN PROPAGANDA IN EASTERN EUROPE 1 (RAND Corporation, 2018) (noting that the "Russian state's approach to social media appears to have become significantly more sophisticated following the antigovernment protests in 2011").

[66] *See generally* CHRISTOPHER PAUL, INFORMATION OPERATIONS: DOCTRINE AND PRACTICE (Praeger, 2008).

[67] This issue was first raised during online conversations with Barrie Sander.

is acting. State Department Legal Advisor Harold Koh favored this interpretation in his 2010 memorandum.[68] Koh noted that the obligation to respect is a negative right which does not logically require a state to have territorial control. In contrast, the obligation to ensure is a positive right and requires that the state enjoys territorial control, institutional structures, and government capacities. Consequently, it makes sense that the obligation to respect would be universal while the obligation to ensure would be territorially limited.

When applied to election interference, Russia could argue that its obligation to respect the right of self-determination would only apply to Russian territory and would not apply extraterritorially. If one accepts the Koh argument about the extraterritorial application of human rights obligations, then Russia would be wrong. Furthermore, the leading edge of human rights scholarship supports extra-territorial application of human rights.[69] Similarly, European case law has started to support extraterritorial application of the European Convention, albeit in the limited circumstance when a state enjoys "effective control," a criterion that might not be satisfied in the case of election interference over social media platforms.[70]

However, what happens if one does not agree with the general Koh position? Even if most human rights do not apply extraterritorially, there is a strong reason to treat the right to self-determination differently from the other rights identified in the ICCPR and other human rights treaties. Most human rights are individual rights and the individual stands in a particular subordinate relationship with his or her government – a relationship that is at its height on the territory of the state. In contrast, self-determination is a collective right and the same relationship between individual and government is not present. The conceptual structure of self-determination is completely different. It is designed to ensure that all peoples have access to a political arrangement that allows them to select their own destiny. Its inclusion in the ICCPR and ICESCR is somewhat anachronistic because self-determination appears to have more in common with general obligations under public international law, such as principles prohibiting the use of force or illegal interventions. These general obligations display the same collective structure as self-determination, in contradistinction to the human rights paradigm of protecting individuals from state authority. Just as the prohibition against committing genocide applies extraterritorially, so too the obligation to respect the collective right of self-determination should apply extraterritorially as well.

Self-determination's reach is arguably global because it was designed, originally, to deal with the scourge of empire, when imperial powers accumulated colonies in

[68] *See* Harold Koh, Office of Legal Advisor, State Department, Memorandum Opinion on the Geographic Scope of the International Covenant on Civil and Political Rights (Oct. 19, 2010).

[69] The most comprehensive analysis of this problem is contained in MARKO MILANOVIC, EXTRATERRITORIAL APPLICATION OF HUMAN RIGHTS TREATIES: LAW, PRINCIPLES, AND POLICY (Oxford University Press, 2011).

[70] *See, e.g.*, Al-Skeini and Others v. United Kingdom, App. No. 55721/07, 53 Eur. H.R. Rep. 589 (2011); Al-Saadoon and Mufdhi v. United Kingdom, App. No. 61498/08, 51 Eur. H.R. Rep. 212 (2010).

far flung locations. This provides some rationale for treating self-determination differently from individual human rights. The right of self-determination prohibits a state from engaging in action, in any location, that targets a protected group and frustrates its right to determine its own destiny. Consequently, it would be perfectly coherent to deny that human rights law generally applies extraterritorially, while insisting that self-determination operates as a global norm that constrains how a sovereign operates on the world stage. That would apply to election interference that is coordinated and conducted from computers in Russia, but which impacts the American electorate.[71]

CONCLUSION

International law protects the right of a people to select their own destiny; in a democratic society, that process is carried out through the holding of periodic elections. In order for elections to serve as a meaningful avenue for fulfilling a people's right of self-determination, the election must articulate the will of the people. The election serves as the expression of that will, so it is hard to state – logically – that the results of an election conflicted with the popular will. Making this statement would require independent, empirical access to the content of the popular will, which is impossible, since it is the election itself which is the only expression of the popular will.

However, if there are procedural deficits to an election, that provides an alternative avenue to questioning whether the results of an election accord with the popular will. There are many procedural elements to an election and not all of them would be of such a character that they would undermine confidence that an election was an expression of the popular will. Nonetheless, there are a class of procedural rules that are so fundamental that without them, an election cannot be said to express the popular will. These procedural rules are "boundary" rules, rules that distinguish between insiders and outsiders, between citizen participation and foreign participation, both with regard to voting but also spending and electioneering. When elections involve substantial foreign participation, the result of the election no longer expresses the will of the people, but a mixture of that will combined with the will of the foreigners who have infiltrated the election. This type of election interference violates the collective right of self-determination.

It is important to remember that this chapter has avoided the assertion that the right of self-determination requires a democratic form of government, preferring

---

[71] See Ido Kilovaty, *An Extraterritorial Human Right to Cybersecurity*, Notre Dame J. Int'l & Comp. L. (forthcoming) ("What is needed ... is an extraterritoriality standard for cyberspace that takes into account the negative effects experienced by victimized individuals. While the effective control standard looks at whether a state controls territory where violations have allegedly occurred, the standard for cyberspace should equally look at whether the state has control not over territory, but over the enjoyment of rights and the effects that individuals may experience should that state decide to carry out a cyber operation.").

instead the more modest – but equally relevant – claim that if a people has selected a democratic form of government, the right of self-determination protects the integrity of its elections. This "integrity" includes a protection against foreign involvement that would not only alter its vote, but also corrupt its deliberations in a way that prevents the election from expressing the will of the people. This "electoral integrity" conception of self-determination is built around the idea that elections are national affairs and cannot be globalized on pain of contradiction. An election is, by definition, limited to the polity that is conducting the election.

More importantly, the electoral integrity conception of self-determination is a better conceptual framework for understanding election interference than the concept of sovereignty. As this and the prior chapter have demonstrated, the concept of sovereignty is poorly suited for analyzing the core political interest that a state has in keeping its elections free from foreign involvement. The law of sovereignty and the principle of nonintervention fail to take seriously this interest. Also, from a purely lay perspective, sovereignty fails to articulate the real harm associated with election interference. The harm is political rather than territorial. A self-determination framework is a far more intuitive framework for understanding election interference.

One might object that as a legal framework, self-determination is ill-equipped to handle the case of election interference because self-determination plays almost no role in the contemporary legal doctrine. But that is only because international lawyers have unnecessarily relegated the doctrine to isolated pockets of the jurisprudence and have failed to appreciate the enduring significance of self-determination to contemporary political conflicts. If international lawyers were to revitalize the concept of self-determination and recognize its true doctrinal potential, problems of political integrity such as election interference could be confronted rather than ignored by international law, or worse yet shoehorned into more familiar but ultimately useless conceptual categories like sovereignty and nonintervention. This chapter has served as a mild corrective to reorient the legal discourse in more fruitful directions.

5

Foreign Electioneering and Transparency

INTRODUCTION

The distinguishing feature of the Russian interference of 2016 is that it violated the core "boundary" regulations involving election integrity: the prohibition on outside participation in elections. To see why this is the best way of understanding the Russian transgression, consider the following aspects of the Russian interference, each of which was noted in more detail in Chapter 1:

1. The Russians spent money on their 2016 election interference effort, in violation of a general norm prohibiting foreign spending in American elections.
2. The Russians purchased political advertisements on Facebook and other social media platforms, again in violation of the prohibition on foreign spending on American elections.
3. The Russians hacked into private email accounts and disclosed thousands of private messages belonging to Democratic candidates and operatives, while Republican candidates and operatives were not subject to the same treatment.
4. The Russians deployed assets who failed to register as agents of a foreign government, another "boundary" regulation.
5. The Russians spent money to operate a troll farm designed to generate and promote social media content that would spread false stories, conspiracy theorists, and extremist opinions, while concealing the foreign source of these social media accounts and posts.

The impact of the first two modalities on self-determination is rather straightforward. The prohibition on foreign spending is not a mere technical regulation created by bureaucrats; its underlying rationale and significance is quite profound. The prohibition on foreign spending is designed to ensure that outsiders do not engage in American electioneering, because if foreigners engage in this conduct, the outcome of the election will fail to express the popular will of the American people but will instead reflect the popular will of a broader constituency, including foreign actors. To allow this corruption of the political process would contradict the goals of self-determination. Instead of the American people deciding their own political destiny, that choice would be made by an overlapping collection of American and foreign actors. If that were to occur, self-determination would be replaced by what could only be described as "other-determination."

The third modality, email hacking and disclosure, also conflicts with self-determination for multiple reasons. First, the Russians spent money on the operation, which violates a general norm prohibiting foreign spending. Second, the operation was politically asymmetrical in the sense that it targeted only one side of the electoral contest and was designed to support one candidate and harm an opponent. The goal of the operation was to nudge the electorate in a direction that would benefit Russian strategic interests. Third, the operation concealed its foreign source because DCLeaks was not self-identified as a Russian entity, and Wikileaks was used for a similar reason, that is, to launder the information and release it to the public through a third-party organization. This effort again involved a substantial foreign participation in the American election, compromising the goal of an election which is to express the will of the American people.

The fourth and fifth modalities share a common theme: an attack on the ideal of transparency in electioneering. The Foreign Agent Registration Act (FARA) is designed to ensure that foreign governments, when acting in the United States, must disclose their identity, so that individuals acting on their behalf are understood for what they are: agents of a foreign power. This preserves the ideal of transparency so that the American polity understands (at least in theory) who is a member of the polity and who is an outside actor of a particular type: an agent representing the interests of a foreign government. At its heart, FARA is a transparency regime. When a FARA violation targets the political process, there is a potential for a violation of the collective right of self-determination.

Similarly, the social media posts that originated from the IRA troll farm were problematic because they violated a core requirement of transparency. By promoting false conspiracy theories and extremist opinions, the troll farms did more than allegedly alter the American political discourse. More importantly, the social media posts violated two core principles at the same time: transparency and boundary regulations. It is the *intersection* of the two principles that is especially problematic and dangerous. It would have been difficult enough if the troll farm posts had expressed American political opinions but done so transparently as Russian accounts. But the accounts pretended to be American in order to gain increased legitimacy within the political discourse. In that process, the troll farm managed to corrupt the political process by preventing the election from expressing the popular will of the American people. The deliberative process was corrupted by outside forces.

The goal of this chapter is to connect the existing prohibitions on foreign participation in elections, that is, to demonstrate that the familiar regulations – prohibitions on foreign voting and spending, as well as registration statutes – should be viewed as methods to protect the collective entity's exercise of its right of self-determination. Then, once these regulations are understood in this light, a conceptual space opens up to ask whether additional boundary regulations might be enacted in order to secure electoral integrity in the face of foreign election interference.[1] Specifically, this chapter will end with a discussion of transparency regimes that might help identify electioneering that originates from foreign sources. The existing regulations target noncitizen voting and foreign spending, but, as the Special Counsel indictment against the IRA demonstrated, it is often hard to enforce these regulations against foreign actors located outside the United States. For this reason, it is important to consider other methods of signaling to the public that election speech, such as social media posts, have originated from outside the polity.

1. THE PROHIBITION ON FOREIGN VOTING

The prohibition on foreign voting is the core boundary rule of election regulation. Elections are designed to express the will of the polity and, for that reason, outsiders need to be barred from the election. Polities have different methods of determining and defining membership, with citizenship and residency as the major categories. These categories, in turn, require their own definitions, since different polities have different criteria for citizenship based on either blood relations (*jus sanguinis*) or place of birth (*jus soli*). For example, one state might determine that lawful residents are eligible to apply for citizenship after five years of residency, another state might require ten, and another state might prohibit immigrants from receiving citizenship under any condition. Similarly, residency as a criterion for voting might take on different definitions, with different classes of residents entitled to different levels of participation in foreign elections.

The academic literature and the policy debate on noncitizen voting have focused on extending the franchise to noncitizen residents. Currently, noncitizen residents are prohibited from voting in U.S. elections, though historically the tolerance for noncitizen voting has waxed and waned.[2] During some periods, noncitizen voting has been permitted, only to be later prohibited, particularly during periods of

---

[1] *See, e.g.*, Celeste M. Murphy, *Searching for A Coherent National Policy: The Problem of Foreign Money in United States Politics*, 3 Buff. J. Int'l L. 541, 569 (1997) ("The United States regulations on foreign participation in U.S. political processes is a necessary and important part of the economic policy of the United States. These sovereign controls, exercised in the national legislation, safeguard national economic and political interests within the United States.").

[2] Virginia Harper-Ho, *Noncitizen Voting Rights: The History, the Law and Current Prospects for Change*, 18 Law & Ineq. 271, 282 (2000) (noting that "[b]efore alien suffrage officially ended in 1928, noncitizens had been voting for national Congressmen in various United States' territories for 70 years, but by the turn of the century alien suffrage had been gradually disappearing as anti-foreigner sentiment increased").

hostility towards foreigners and immigrants.[3] It is important to remember that our present "citizens-only" scheme for voting was not always the case.[4]

Even in this current era of strong anti-immigrant sentiment in which noncitizen voting is prohibited, the discourse is particularly significant, and much can be learned from it. Political and legal arguments in favor of noncitizen voting inevitably rely on a conception of membership in the polity. In other words, the arguments assert that noncitizen residents are closely connected enough with the affairs of the political community that they deserve a share in democratic decision-making as embodied in national or local elections.[5] Although this argument pushes against citizenship as the exclusive criterion for voting, the more important point is to recognize the assumptions that these arguments rely on, that is, that voting presupposes a sufficiently close relationship to the political community. Standing behind the particular claim that residency is enough to establish that relationship is the assumption that *some* relationship, a particularly close relationship, is a necessary prerequisite for participation in the democratic process.[6]

There are several insights that can be gleaned from this analysis. The first is that states are entitled to define, for themselves, criteria for membership in their own communities and then to enact regulations to enforce these criteria.[7] The second insight is that a close connection between the polity and the individual is required for membership to attach.[8] For citizens, this connection is obvious.[9] For lawful permanent residents, the connection is less obvious, though there is a compelling argument that permanent residents are sufficiently connected to the political community in order to enjoy a share in its decisions, especially since the policies of the

---

[3] *See* Gabriela Evia, *Consent by All the Governed: Reenfranchising Noncitizens As Partners in America's Democracy*, 77 S. Cal. L. Rev. 151, 155 (2003) (noting that "[t]he War of 1812 directly contributed to a decline in the support of noncitizen voting in the states" but then "[t]he post-War of 1812 trend away from noncitizen suffrage was countered in the mid-nineteenth century by the need and desire for immigration").

[4] *See, e.g.*, Jamin B. Raskin, *Legal Aliens, Local Citizens: The Historical, Constitutional, and Theoretical Meanings of Alien Suffrage*, 141 U. Pa. L. Rev. 1391, 1393 (1993); Bryant Yuan Fu Yang, *Fighting for an Equal Voice: Past and Present Struggle for Noncitizen Enfranchisement*, 13 Asian Am. L.J. 57, 89 (2006).

[5] *See* Stanley A. Renshon, Noncitizen Voting and American Democracy (Rowman & Littlefield, 2009).

[6] *See* Gerald M. Rosberg, *Aliens and Equal Protection: Why Not the Right to Vote?*, 75 Mich. L. Rev. 1092 (1977).

[7] *See, e.g.*, Foley v. Connelie, 435 U.S. 291, 295 (1978) (referring to the "sovereign's obligation 'to preserve the basic conception of a political community'").

[8] Bluman v. Fed. Election Comm'n, 800 F. Supp. 2d 281, 287 (D.D.C. 2011), *aff'd*, 565 U.S. 1104 (2012) ("But we also know from Supreme Court case law that foreign citizens may be denied certain rights and privileges that U.S. citizens possess. For example, the Court has ruled that government may bar foreign citizens from voting, serving as jurors, working as police or probation officers, or working as public school teachers.").

[9] *See* Sugarman v. Dougall, 413 U.S. 634, 648 (1973) (referring to "a State's historical power to exclude aliens from participation in its democratic political institutions" and noting that "implicit in many of this Court's voting rights decisions is the notion that citizenship is a permissible criterion for limiting such rights").

government will have a strong and direct impact on the lives of permanent residents.[10] To take just the most elementary examples, policies regarding education, health care, economic opportunities, and taxes will all impact permanent residents.

In contrast, these proposals never suggest that noncitizen-nonresidents should be entitled to vote.[11] The noncitizen-nonresident represents the paradigmatic outsider – an individual who falls outside the political community and therefore should have no participatory rights in the democratic order.

Nonresidents who are outside the community will no doubt be impacted by the actions of the government. The long arm of the government is not limited by territory. The government may engage in economic, diplomatic, and military initiatives that impact foreigners – sometimes with deadly effects. For example, a government might launch a war of aggression against another state, with devastating results for foreigners located in places where the state takes military action. But this is not enough to allow nonresidents to participate in the democratic system. Sovereign action, particularly for a major world power, will impact millions of people abroad.

What truly distinguishes and defines members of the political community is that the state is acting on their behalf, engaging in the process of government with the authority of the people. In a sense, this means that the state is acting on behalf of the individual, making the individual responsible as a member of the collective which is acting. As Francis Lieber once wrote,[12] the soldier and the state "advance and retrograde" together on the battlefield – an image that could apply equally between the people and the civilian government that acts on its behalf. The fact that the government acts on behalf of these individuals makes them members of the political community. When the military of a state bombs an enemy city, there is no sense in which the military acts on behalf of its victims; the military acts on behalf of its own population. This relationship helps to define membership in a political community.

This conceptual apparatus is tied to the concept of self-determination because the collective right only makes sense once one has a conception of the political community or the people whose will is "determined" by the political process. In a multiethnic state, the boundaries of the political community and the people might not be the same. To return to the example of Quebec, the people of Quebec participate in the Canadian political community, which involves a diverse group of peoples, including nonQuebecers but also many First Nations,

---

[10]   *See* Sanford Levinson, *Suffrage and Community: Who Should Vote?*, 41 FLA. L. REV. 545 (1989).

[11]   *See, e.g.*, Paul David Meyer, *Citizens, Residents, and the Body Politic*, 102 CAL. L. REV. 465, 467 (2014) ("Yet for more than a century, citizenship has been commonly described as a necessary marker of the body politic, defining the boundary of who may partake in our democracy and on what terms. Blanket prohibitions on noncitizen voting remain largely unchallenged in the courts without any great controversy or scholarly scrutiny.").

[12]   Francis Lieber, Instructions for the Government of Armies of the United States in the Field, General Order No. 100, art. 20 (Apr. 24, 1863).

each of which could be described as a people. Each of these peoples is accommodated in the political structure of Canada.

The proper response is that in a multiethnic state, the political arrangement helps the sharing of power among the peoples of the state, but, at the same time, the political arrangement also polices the boundaries of that political arrangement, ensuring that some peoples are given access to that political arrangement, while outsiders are kept outside the democratic framework. Immigration, the power to live in the political community, is one such regulation, and if it includes a pathway to citizenship, immigration is the avenue by which some individuals will join the political community as full-fledged members. The existence of elections highlights the need for regulations that police the requirements for participation in the political process.

Even assuming that the United States were to shift back to noncitizen voting, nonresident-noncitizen voting would still clearly be prohibited, otherwise everyone in the world would be permitted to vote in American elections. Although no one seriously suggests that nonresident-noncitizens should be entitled to vote, there is a question about the level of participation they should be permitted. Should they be permitted to contribute to campaigns, either through direct financial gifts or in-kind assistance? Should they be permitted to participate in elections by speaking out in favor of one candidate over another? Adding these two issues together yields the following combined question: Should they be allowed to engage in this speech if this speech involves financial expenditure? The next section starts this inquiry by analyzing the prohibition on foreign spending.

2. PROHIBITION ON FOREIGN CONTRIBUTIONS AND SPENDING

In 1976, Congress passed a statute that prohibited, among other things, foreign persons from spending on electioneering communications in federal elections.[13] The rules regarding local elections are more diverse and depend on the regulations in each state.[14] Some states permit spending by foreign persons (by lack of an applicable regulation) while others have passed statutes to prohibit it.[15] The

---

[13] *See* 52 U.S.C. § 30121 ("It shall be unlawful for – (1) a foreign national, directly or indirectly, to make – (A) a contribution or donation of money or other thing of value, or to make an express or implied promise to make a contribution or donation, in connection with a Federal, State, or local election; (B) a contribution or donation to a committee of a political party; or (C) an expenditure, independent expenditure, or disbursement for an electioneering communication (within the meaning of section 30104(f)(3) of this title) . . . .").

[14] *See Election Law-Limits on Political Spending by Foreign Entities-Alaska Prohibits Spending on Local Elections by Foreign-Influenced Corporations.-Alaska Stat. S 15.13.068 (2018)*, 132 HARV. L. REV. 2402 (2019).

[15] For example, Alaska law states that "(a) A foreign-influenced corporation or foreign national may not, directly or indirectly, in connection with an election under this chapter, make a contribution or expenditure or make an express or implied promise to make a contribution or expenditure." *See* Alaska Stat. Ann. § 15.13.068.

motivation behind the federal prohibition was relatively simple: the election spending of American persons (including corporations) would be substantially regulated while the election spending of foreign persons would be mostly prohibited. The regulations also included a prohibition of donating anything of value, not just a prohibition on monetary contributions. According to the Federal Election Commission (FEC), something can have value "even where the value of a good or service 'may be nominal or difficult to ascertain.'"[16] Independent expenditures by foreigners were prohibited if they were for an "electioneering communication."

The regulations include two major exceptions. The first is an exception for volunteering.[17] The second is an exception for media corporations which are permitted to spend money on covering political campaigns and elections.[18] The purpose of the media exception is to clarify that a media company does not improperly spend money on an election simply by allocating resources to covering an election through print, radio, TV, or internet dispatches.

The goal of this regulatory scheme is to ensure that foreign interests do not infiltrate American elections. The concern underlying this regulatory scheme does not relate to voting or voting security, but rather to preserving the integrity of the deliberative process leading up to the election. Underlying these regulations is nothing less than an assumption that the political deliberations of a democratic order must be fundamentally "internal" to the polity and that outside spending could corrupt those deliberations.[19]

That status quo was upended in 2010 when the Supreme Court handed down its *Citizens United* decision.[20] That decision struck down a law that limited the amount

[16] *See* Ellen L. Weintraub, Memorandum Re: Draft Interpretive Rule Concerning Prohibited Activities Involving Foreign Nationals, at 6 (Sept. 26, 2019), *citing* Advisory Opinion 2007–22, at 6, *citing* Regulations on Contribution Limitations and Prohibitions, 67 FR 69928, 69940 (Nov. 19, 2002).

[17] *See* FEC Advisory Op. 2007–22 (Dec. 3, 2007) (concluding that a Canadian citizen could provide volunteer services to a political campaign).

[18] The media exception for foreign contributions is codified at 11 C.F.R. § 100.73 ("Any cost incurred in covering or carrying a news story, commentary, or editorial by any broadcasting station (including a cable television operator, programmer or producer), Web site, newspaper, magazine, or other periodical publication, including any Internet or electronic publication, is not a contribution unless the facility is owned or controlled by any political party, political committee, or candidate . . . "). The corollate media exception for foreign expenditures is codified at 11 C.F.R. § 100.132.

[19] The Justice Department adroitly summarized this interest in its indictment against former Giuliani associates Lev Parnas, Igor Fruman, David Correia, and Andrey Kukushkin: "Through its election laws, Congress prohibits foreign nations from making contributions, donations, and certain expenditures in connection with federal, State, and local elections, and prohibits anyone from making contributions in the name of another. Congress further requires public reporting through the Federal Election Commission (the "FEC") of the sources and amounts of contributions and expenditures made in connection with federal elections. A purpose of these laws, taken together, is to protect the United States electoral system from illegal foreign financial influence, and to further inform all candidates, their campaign committees, federal regulators, and the public of (i) the true sources of contributions to candidates for federal office; and (ii) any effort by foreign nationals to influence federal, State, or local elections with foreign money." *See* Sealed Indictment, United States v. Parnas, Fruman, Correia, and Kukushkin (S.D.N.Y. 2019).

[20] *See* Citizens United v. Federal Election Commission, 558 U.S. 310 (2010).

of spending by corporations. Relying chiefly on a distinction between election "spending" and campaign contributions that was introduced in *Buckley v. Valeo*, the Supreme Court concluded that Congress could, consistent with a legitimate plan to regulate campaign financing, limit the amount of donations that any person, including a corporation, could give to a political campaign.[21] At the same time, however, Congress could not limit the amount of political "spending" by corporations because this spending was integral to political speech protected by the First Amendment.[22] In practical terms, this meant that a corporation could be prohibited from donating large sums of money to a presidential candidate, but a corporation could spend as much as it liked on, for example, television advertisements with a political theme, as long as the advertisements were not purchased in coordination with a political campaign. (This proviso was necessary to prevent the categories of political spending and contributions from collapsing into each other.)

The *Citizens United* decision created uncertainty over the prohibition on foreign spending. Although the Supreme Court was quick to bracket the question of foreign corporations as outside its holding, the decision at the very least opened up a question about the status of foreign spending.[23] But many assumed that the prohibition on foreign spending would soon fall if the Court decided to extend *Citizens United* in a future case. Indeed, President Obama worried during his State of the Union address that *Citizens United* would "open the floodgates for special interests – including foreign corporations – to spend without limit in our elections."[24] Justice John Paul Stevens expressed similar concerns.[25] Obama and Stevens feared what some others have hoped, that *Citizens United* would open the door to foreign corporations spending money on our elections. This would be a catastrophe. If allowed, it would fundamentally undermine the ideal of self-determination, since outsiders who are not members of the political community would be entitled to participate, through financial support, in an election designed to express a popular will that is not theirs. Presumably, the Supreme Court will have to return to the issue of foreign corporate spending in a future case to clarify the implications of *Citizens United*.

I will not address the underlying merits of the First Amendment claim first articulated in *Citizens United* and how it relates to foreigners; this will be the task of the next chapter. For our purposes here, the point is to explore the relationship

---

[21] In *Buckley v. Valeo*, 424 U.S. 1 (1976) (per curiam), the Supreme Court concluded that Congress can limit contributions but cannot limit expenditures.

[22] *Citizens United*, 558 U.S. at 337 ("These prohibitions are classic examples of censorship.").

[23] *Citizens United*, 558 U.S. at 362 ("We need not reach the question whether the Government has a compelling interest in preventing foreign individuals or associations from influencing our Nation's political process.").

[24] Perhaps the Court's statement bracketing the case of foreign corporations is one reason why Justice Alito famously shook his head and mouthed "not true" during the speech.

[25] *See* Bill Mears, *Former Justice Stevens Criticizes Court Over Campaign Spending Rules*, CNN (May 31, 2012).

between the prohibition on foreign financial participation and its underlying conceptual rationale. The goal is to show that although the current doctrinal debate has focused on the Supreme Court's abandonment of the anti-distortion rationale, the animating impulse behind regulations against foreign financial participation boil down to a desire to protect the collective right of self-determination of the American people.

In the case of foreign financial contributions, the impact on the right of self-determination is relatively clear and obvious. Financial contributions create a relationship between candidates and donors. The donation of money makes it more likely that the candidate will win the election because the candidate will have, all other things being equal, more financial resources than political opponents. In this way, donations influence outcomes in ways that respond to the interests of the foreign donors. Furthermore, candidates may seek to increase donations from foreign sources by adopting policy positions that are likely to be financially supported by foreign donors. The result is that foreign financial contributions influence the course of political deliberations in favor of outside forces rather than members of the polity.

The best way of understanding the problem with allowing outside political contributors to distort political deliberations is to couch these claims as infringing the collective right of self-determination. If outside contributions are allowed to influence the deliberative process, the result of the election will express the will of the outside funders rather than the will of the political insiders. One might object that no distortion will occur as long as voting is limited to insiders, that is, citizens and/or permanent residents, and that prohibiting outsider funding does nothing but infringe the rights of candidates who seek to raise money from foreign sources. But this objection fails to appreciate the fact that elections have two major components: deliberation and voting. While the process of voting may not be impacted by the use of foreign donations, the process of democratic deliberation and policymaking will be impacted by encouraging or forcing politicians to respond more to the concerns of foreigners than domestic audiences in order to build the financial resources necessary to win an election campaign.

The situation with foreign independent expenditures is slightly more complicated.[26] In that case, the connection between the candidate and the foreigner is less developed. Although there is still the possibility that the candidate might tailor their views to align with foreigners who are engaging in direct expenditures on the campaign, the greater risk is the corrosive impact that the expenditure will have on the deliberative process. As noted above, election campaigns involve both voting and deliberation, and the introduction of foreign spending into the deliberative process

---

[26] Of course, there remain controversial questions about what counts as election spending. *See* Zachary J. Piaker, *Can "Love" Be A Crime? The Scope of the Foreign National Spending Ban in Campaign Finance Law*, 118 COLUM. L. REV. 1857, 1879 (2018) ("'Political [o]pposition [r]esearch' – what Trump, Jr. believed he was being offered – is a resource-intensive product that campaigns regularly pay for.").

amplifies some views and voices at the expense of others. This point is nothing more than the recognition that foreign spending has an effect – an uncontroversial point because if foreign spending had no effect whatsoever then foreigners would not do it.

Foreign expenditures run the risk of compromising the right of self-determination because the deliberative process should be internal to the polity rather than including outside individuals. In order for an election to express the will of the people, the people need to deliberate among themselves about future policy directions and then have a voting procedure for selecting the desired direction. The deliberation is the crucial element because it structures the decision making; it is when the decisions get made, as opposed to the voting, which is when the decisions get expressed and recorded. In a sense, the voting is a pure ministerial act; the democratic ideal is vindicated by the deliberations that precede it. Deliberations with outsiders compromise the right of self-determination because the entity that directs the political direction of the community is broader than the community itself. For self-determination to be respected, there must be a one-to-one correspondence between the entity making the determinations and the entity whose future is decided.

Unfortunately, some scholars have failed to appreciate the significance of foreign expenditures and have concluded that the ban on foreign expenditures should be explicitly disallowed by the Supreme Court. For example, James Ianelli has written that the "ban on foreign independent expenditures deserves to be struck down for the same reason [as the ban on domestic corporate expenditures]: a foreign source does not increase the risk of quid-pro-quo corruption any more than a domestic source."[27] Unfortunately, this conclusion is wrong because it assumes, falsely, that the underlying rationale for banning foreign expenditures would be an anti-corruption rationale. To be sure, this assumption is understandable, since *Citizens United* relied on an anti-corruption rationale. Specifically, the Supreme Court concluded that "this Court now concludes that independent expenditures, including those made by corporations, do not give rise to corruption or the appearance of corruption. That speakers may have influence over or access to elected officials does not mean that those officials are corrupt. And the appearance of influence or access will not cause the electorate to lose faith in this democracy."[28]

This anti-corruption ideal was at the heart of *Buckley v. Valeo*'s distinction between contributions and expenditures; regulation of contributions was justified by the concern over corruption, whereas expenditures could not be so regulated because they did not give rise to the same concerns over quid-pro-quo corruption. This has led some to suggest that foreign expenditures are similarly unproblematic because they too do not raise concerns over quid-pro-quo corruption.

The problem with this line of reasoning is that it fails to take seriously the foreign source of independent expenditures and the potential problems that the foreign

---

[27] *See* James Ianelli, *Noncitizens and Citizens United*, 56 Loy. L. Rev. 869, 873 (2010).
[28] 558 U.S. 310 (2010) (syllabus).

source might cause. There might be wholly unrelated reasons to regulate or ban foreign expenditures that have nothing to do with corruption. And this is precisely why the Supreme Court in *Citizens United* bracketed the issue of foreign expenditures, which were not at issue in that case, because the Court recognized that foreign expenditures implicate a unique set of concerns.

The rationale for prohibiting foreign expenditures is not anti-corruption but anti-distortion.[29] Allowing foreign participation in elections, even if it is just expenditures, risks distorting the political process in a way that makes the political process more about the foreigners than domestic constituents.[30] This has nothing to do with corruption and represents a distinct rationale from anti-corruption. The need to keep the political process free from distortion animates all of the boundary regulations explored in this chapter: articulating standards and definitions for membership in the political community and enforcing those definitions. Allowing the political process to be distorted by foreigners transforms what would otherwise be an act of self-determination into a political process that has little to do with the polity holding the election.[31] Self-determination entails, by definition, a prohibition from outside participation.[32]

It is easy to claim "anti-distortion" as a rationale or justification for many regulations but it will only be legitimate in some cases. One can claim that almost anything "distorts" the political process. In many cases these allegations are hard to back up, because other than referring to the results of the election, it is hard to establish

---

[29] *See* David Solan, *In the Wake of Citizens United, Do Foreign Politics Still Stop at the Water's Edge?*, 19 TUL. J. INT'L & COMP. L. 281, 298 (2010) (suggesting that the prohibition on foreign contributions is required to "protect the integrity of the government's decision-making process from foreign influences" because "corporate loyalty is determined by the nationality of a corporation's home country, not its host country").

[30] *See* Sean J. Wright, *Reexamining Criminal Prosecutions Under the Foreign Nationals Ban*, 32 NOTRE DAME J.L. ETHICS & PUB. POL'Y 563, 566 (2018) (noting that the "current prohibitions on foreign national contributions are rooted in the long-standing goal to limit foreign influence in U.S. elections").

[31] Some scholars have noted the connection between self-determination and preventing foreign financial participation in elections. *See, e.g.*, Matt A. Vega, *The First Amendment Lost in Translation: Preventing Foreign Influence in U.S. Elections After Citizens United v. FEC*, 44 LOY. L.A. L. REV. 951, 955 (2011) (noting that "[t]he growing political influence of foreign corporations poses a very real threat to our nation's sovereignty and to our right to political self-determination" and concluding that "foreign corporations, through their American subsidiaries, stand to gain even more influence over the body politic").

[32] One reason why self-determination entails a prohibition on outside participation is that self-determination (or popular sovereignty) is located with the people itself, which would be negated if outsiders were allowed to participate in elections. *See* David Solan, *In the Wake of Citizens United, Do Foreign Politics Still Stop at the Water's Edge?*, 19 TUL. J. INT'L & COMP. L. 281, 297 (2010) ("'We the people' represented a profound revolutionary assertion of popular sovereignty by virtue of language that boldly asserted a foundational principle of the nation: that the ultimate power of the state rests with the members of the community, comprised of people who control their own destiny. American citizens are the intended beneficiaries of the blessings of liberty. Of course, noncitizen residents and illegal aliens are afforded many constitutional rights, but these protections do not apply to direct participation in the political process.").

a baseline against which to judge whether something counts as a distortion or not. But the case of foreign participation is different. One does not need to demonstrate an effect in order to prove distortion. The distortion flows simply from the fact that foreigners are participating in the election.[33]

Although the Supreme Court has not explicitly used the term "anti-distortion" in this context, its pronouncements regarding foreign participation all point in this direction. For example, in *Bluman v. FEC*, a federal district court noted that, "[i]t is fundamental to the definition of our national political community that foreign citizens do not have a constitutional right to participate in, and thus may be excluded from, activities of democratic self-government."[34] The concern is an ancient one going back to the founding of the republic.[35] The Supreme Court has long argued that the government has an essential interest in preventing outsiders from participating in the political process and financial participation is no different. Prior to being displaced by *Citizens United*, several Supreme Court cases referred to an anti-distortion rationale and considered it a compelling government interest.[36]

There are two possible responses to the Supreme Court's recent rejection, in *Citizens United*, of the anti-distortion rationale. The first is that it represented a wrong turn in the Court's jurisprudence of campaign financial regulations.[37] Indeed, Justice Stevens argued in dissent that the Court's rejection of the anti-distortion rationale was a mistake because it was fundamentally indistinguishable from its newer anti-corruption model of campaign finance regulation.[38] But the more plausible objection is that *Citizens United* did not deal with foreigners at all, and that the door is wide open for the court to recognize, in the foreign context, the anti-distortion rationale that it rejected in the domestic context. Although the Supreme Court in *Citizens United* rejected the idea that unlimited corporate spending would distort the democratic process, it can and should accept the idea that foreign spending does distort the democratic process because democratic

---

[33]   See Solan, *supra* note 32 at 297–8 (arguing that "foreign meddling risks undermining the citizenry's political rights, including the right to make political choices free from distortion").

[34]   800 F. Supp. 2d 281, 288 (D.D.C. 2011), *aff'd*, 565 U.S. 1104 (2012).

[35]   See Piaker, *supra* note 26, at 1863 (noting that "[a] distrust of foreign interference in elections was present in the American constitutional design at the Founding").

[36]   Austin v. Michigan Chamber of Commerce, 494 U.S. 652, 659–60 (1990) ("Michigan's regulation aims at a different type of corruption in the political arena: the corrosive and *distorting* effects of immense aggregations of wealth that are accumulated with the help of the corporate form and that have little or no correlation to the public's support for the corporation's political ideas.") (emphasis added). For a good discussion, see Kevin R. Huguelet, *Death by A Thousand Cuts: How the Supreme Court Has Effectively Killed Campaign Finance Regulation by Its Limited Recognition of Compelling State Interests*, 70 U. MIAMI L. REV. 348, 357 (2015).

[37]   See Richard L. Hasen, *Citizens United and the Orphaned Antidistortion Rationale*, 27 GA. ST. U. L. REV. 989, 1002 (2011).

[38]   See Citizens United v. Fed. Election Comm'n, 558 U.S. 310, 448 (2010) (Stevens, J., dissenting) ("Corruption operates along a spectrum, and the majority's apparent belief that quid pro quo arrangements can be neatly demarcated from other improper influences does not accord with the theory or reality of politics.").

elections are designed for insiders of a political community to decide their own destiny.

In this era of internet technology, the significance of foreign election spending has increased. In the past, problematic foreign spending might have included a foreigner purchasing television or radio advertisements – a costly exercise. Less expensive foreign expenditures would have had little effect. In today's world, how-ever, the "cost" of speech has radically declined.[39] With a relatively modest outlay of cash, a foreigner can build a social media presence that has a huge impact. A small number of dedicated employees who understand the mechanics of social media can introduce and amplify whatever narratives the purchaser wishes to promote. Furthermore, skillful use of algorithms and software solutions would allow the purchaser to engage in speech, or amplify a message on social media, with relatively few (or even no) employees. The result of these force multipliers is that the barriers for entry have been reduced and the possible frequency and impact of foreign electioneering has radically increased. Older generations, and older cases, may have viewed foreign spending as an isolated and mild irritant rather than the pervasive risk that it is today.[40] In other words, prior generations may not have appreciated the risk to self-determination posed by foreign speech.[41]

3. FOREIGN AGENT REGISTRATION AS TRANSPARENCY AND DISCLOSURE

In the prior section, we focused mostly on the prohibitions surrounding foreign financial participation in elections. However, campaign finance regulations also involve a transparency and disclosure regime; candidates are required to list all donations so that the public is aware of how the candidate has financed their campaign. Independent expenditures are largely immune from these candidate disclosure requirements, as long as they are truly independent (no coordination). The theory behind the lack of disclosure requirement is that independent expendi-tures do not run the same risk of corruption as direct campaign contributions which

---

[39] For an argument along these lines, see Richard L. Hasen, *Cheap Speech and What It Has Done (to American Democracy)*, 16 FIRST AMEND. L. REV. 200, 210 (2017).

[40] *See* Bruce D. Brown, *Alien Donors: The Participation of Non-Citizens in the U.S. Campaign Finance System*, 15 YALE L. & POL'Y REV. 503, 504 (1997) (concluding that "the controls on campaign spend-ing by non-citizens have received little empirical or theoretical attention"). Brown's statement was probably true in 1997 but doubtful today, now that many scholars and politicians have grown concerned about financial participation by foreign contributions.

[41] Lawmakers have responded with a set of bills designed to extend some reporting requirements to digital advertisements on social media platforms. *See* H.R. 4077, 115th Cong., 1st Sess., § 6 (introduced by Rep. Kilmer and Rep. Coffman, Oct. 19, 2017) (digital advertising on Facebook, etc.). This is a good start but not nearly enough. The current reporting requirements are outlined in 52 U.S.C. § 30104 (defining "electioneering communication" as referring to "any broadcast, cable, or satellite communication").

could give rise to a quid-pro-quo arrangement. Arguably, sunlight is the best disinfectant for reducing the possibility of "buying" political favors in this manner.

However, there are other areas where disclosure and transparency regimes are used to monitor foreign involvement in elections. For example, the Foreign Agent Registration Act (FARA) requires agents of a foreign power to register with the federal government. This requirement applies regardless of whether the foreign power is engaging in activities that might be considered electioneering or not. Any form of lobbying or similar work on behalf of a foreign power may give rise to the reporting requirements of FARA. By statute, the FARA regime applies to the following activity categories:

- political activities for or in the interests of such foreign principal
- public relations counsel, publicity agent, information-service employee or political consultant for or in the interests of such foreign principal
- solicits, collects, disburses, or dispenses contributions, loans, money, or other things of value for or in the interest of such foreign principal
- represents the interests of such foreign principal before any agency or official of the Government of the United States.[42]

The goal of the FARA regime is to impose transparency in an area – representation of foreign governments – that might otherwise be shrouded in clandestine or covert relationships. The law was passed in 1938; it is no accident that the law was enacted on the eve of World War II, when government officials were deeply concerned about the prospect of domestic actors acting in complicity with foreign powers.[43] At times, this concern has bordered on irrational hysteria, as demonstrated by the internment of U.S. citizens and permanent residents with Japanese heritage, or a decade later the McCarthy hearings into communist activities in key public and private industries. But in more sanguine times, the FARA registration statute has served an important purpose to force foreign governments into disclosing individuals who are acting on their behalf in the United States. The Justice Department maintains a publicly searchable online database of FARA reports.

Agents who fail to file FARA reports are subject to criminal prosecution and punishment. Over the years, the Justice Department's efforts to prosecute FARA violations have waxed and waned.[44] During World War II, FARA prosecutions

---

[42]   22 U.S.C. §§ 611–621.

[43]   *See* Mark B. Baker, *Updating the Foreign Agents Registration Act to Meet the Current Economic Threat to National Security*, 25 Tex. Int'l L.J. 23, 40 (1990) ("By enacting FARA, Congress sought to require disclosure of those foreign agents who promoted disunity within the nation, attempted to subvert the democratic process, or sought to direct the country's foreign policy in the furtherance of foreign agendas.").

[44]   *See* Philip J. Perry, *Recently Proposed Reforms to the Foreign Agents Registration Act*, 23 Cornell Int'l L.J. 133, 144 (1990) (noting that "FARA administrators ... rarely use the Act's criminal penalties because of the difficulty of proving intent"); Jahad Atieh, *Foreign Agents: Updating Fara to Protect American Democracy*, 31 U. Pa. J. Int'l L. 1051, 1062 (2010) ("FARA is essentially self-policed, such that

focused on fascist propaganda efforts. For some time, the federal government used the FARA statute as a justification for intercepting and destroying foreign source mail.[45] (A different version of this program was ultimately declared a violation of the First Amendment by the Supreme Court.[46]) In more recent decades, however, FARA enforcement has been relatively lax and many lawyers and lobbyists (even at large corporate firms) who worked for foreign governments failed to file the required FARA paperwork with no discernible consequences.[47]

The 2016 election changed all of that. Former Trump campaign chairman Paul Manafort was charged with, among other things, failing to register as a foreign agent, based on his extensive dealings with the Ukrainian government of Viktor Yanukovych.[48] Manafort was eventually convicted of these charges. Similarly, former White House Counsel Gregory Craig was charged, but ultimately acquitted, for lying to federal investigators during a FARA investigation. Maria Butina also was charged with operating as an unregistered agent in violation of FARA. In response to these prosecution efforts, lawyers and lobbyists working in Washington, D.C. have filed FARA paperwork with new-found diligence. These indictments suggest that the Justice Department has reinvigorated the FARA statute as a prosecutorial tool.

One might wonder what value the FARA scheme has, given that it is a pure reporting and transparency regime; by its own terms, it does not restrict the types of behavior that foreign agents can engage in, though other statutes certainly restrict their behavior. The goal of FARA is somewhat unclear, though at least one scholar has suggested that the goal of FARA should be to create transparency regarding: "(1) foreign lobbying; (2) foreign electioneering activity; and (3) foreign disinformation."[49] There is also a concern that corporations, particularly U.S. subsidiaries of foreign crown corporations, might act, indirectly, as agents for a foreign government.[50]

---

it requires the lobbyists themselves to take the initiative to learn which types of activities necessitate disclosures and when disclosures must be filed.").

[45] *See Government Exclusion of Foreign Political Propaganda*, 68 HARV. L. REV. 1393, 1395 (1955) ("The Attorney General was of the opinion that such exclusion was legally authorized, on the basis of the combined operation of the FARA and two sections of the Espionage Act of 1917, now sections 957 and 1717 of the Criminal Code."). *See also* Murray L. Schwartz and James C. N. Paul, *Foreign Communist Propaganda in the Mails: A Report on Some Problems of Federal Censorship*, 107 U. PENN. L. REV. 621 (1959).

[46] Lamont v. Postmaster General, 381 U.S. 301 (1965). For a discussion, see Nick Robinson, "Foreign Agents" in an Interconnected World: FARA and the Weaponization of Transparency, DUKE L.J. (forthcoming).

[47] *See* Baker, *supra* note 43, at 40 (noting the low level of compliance with the FARA in the period leading up to 1980).

[48] Yanukovych was the pro-Russian leader of the Ukrainian government until he was ousted during a popular uprising. Yanukovych's departure from Ukraine represented a shift in Ukraine's policy towards Russia. After Yanukovych's departure, the new Ukrainian government viewed Russia as a strategic threat. Military tensions between the two countries were sparked by Russia's annexation of Crimea in 2014 and Russia's covert support of pro-Russian rebels in Eastern Ukraine.

[49] *See* Robinson, *supra* note 46, at 55 (draft pagination).

[50] *See* David Solan, *In the Wake of Citizens United, Do Foreign Politics Still Stop at the Water's Edge?*, 19 TUL. J. INT'L & COMP. L. 281, 303 (2010) ("Even more alarming is the possibility that a domestic

But what goal does a transparency statute have in these contexts?[51] There are several possible answers, all of which are important. First, the registration and transparency requirements act as a cautionary element that might disincentivize foreign states from interfering in the domestic affairs of the United States. There are some strategic behaviors that a foreign state is going to engage in no matter the costs, but a state might forgo some behaviors if it is forced to acknowledge them as its own. At the very least, requiring transparency will increase the costs of a foreign state acting to influence the U.S. political system. States contemplating action within the United States will need to integrate these predicted consequences into their decision calculus.

Second, and perhaps most importantly, transparency and registration statutes give the public the information that it requires in order to properly identify the source of certain activities and certain communications that flow from a foreign source.[52] This gives the public an opportunity to understand the communication or the behavior in its true light.[53] For some people, knowing that an individual is working or lobbying for a foreign power will change their assessment of the person's behavior or speech and cast it in a new (truer) light. Motivations will become clearer. Ideas that were once advisable might become more suspect if their true origin were understood. For an example, an individual who argues in favor of a particular trade policy change might be viewed differently if the listener knows that the individual works for a foreign government and that government will be advantaged by the policy change. The listener can then evaluate for themselves whether the source of the viewpoint causes them to have more or less skepticism of the argument.

One might object that the First Amendment, or the Constitution generally, permits communications or actions to remain anonymous. Although a full answer to this objection must be deferred until the next chapter, it is sufficient to note for the

---

subsidiary of a foreign corporation that is controlled by a foreign government could slip through a legal loophole and influence U.S. elections. In this instance, there is a heightened fear that a domestic subsidiary may be operating as an agent of a foreign government when a foreign government has an ownership stake in the corporation.").

51 As Senator Heinz once stated in reference to FARA: "Now it appears we have met the enemy, and he sounds like one of us, but we have no idea who he really is." *See* 134 CONG. REC. S14,925 (daily ed. Oct. 6, 1988), *cited in* Philip J. Perry, *Recently Proposed Reforms to the Foreign Agents Registration Act*, 23 CORNELL INT'L L.J. 133 (1990).

52 *See* Charles Lawson, *Shining the "Spotlight of Pitiless Publicity" on Foreign Lobbyists? Evaluating the Impact of the Lobbying Disclosure Act of 1995 on the Foreign Agents Registration Act*, 29 VAND. J. TRANSNAT'L L. 1151, 1157 (1996) ("It was only through shining this "spotlight of pitiless publicity" that the people of the United States could identify those "engaged in . . . spread[ing] doctrines alien to our democratic form of government" and act in an informed manner to mitigate the "pernicious" nature of their actions."), *quoting* H.R. Rep. No. 75-1381, at 2 (1937).

53 *See* 88 CONG. REC. 802 (1942) (stating what FARA gives: the "government and the people of the United States may be informed of the identity of such persons and may appraise their statements and actions in the light of their associations and activities"), *cited in* Karim G. Lynn, *Unconstitutional Inhibitions: "Political Propaganda" and the Foreign Agents Registration Act*, 33 N.Y.L. SCH. L. REV. 345, 346 (1988).

moment that it is unlikely that the Constitution would afford to foreign governments a right to communicate anonymously in the United States without disclosing their connection to their agent's behavior. In this vein, it is important to remember that FARA is limited entirely to "agents" of foreign governments, so that if there is a restriction being imposed by FARA, it is a restriction being imposed on foreign governments and those acting directly on their behalf.

There are at least two problems that limit the effectiveness of FARA. The first is that FARA violations are only prosecuted against the individual violator, rather than the state on whose behalf the agent is working. This imposes an externality in the sense that the state may view the individual agent as dispensable and not worry whether the agent suffers unfortunate consequences for failing to register. Of course, the State Department might impose other consequences against a violating state, such as countermeasures or retorsions, including economic sanctions or expelling diplomatic personnel. For example, Obama imposed retorsions (and possibly covert countermeasures) against Russia in response to its interference in the election of 2016 – an effort that included FARA violations. But these larger consequences are not always imposed, or, if they are, they are often insignificant when compared with the greater advantages to be gained from using unregistered agents in the United States as an instrument of statecraft.

The second limitation on FARA is that it only applies to conduct within the territory of the United States. So, in theory, electioneering activity by a foreign agent that occurs within the United States can be prosecuted as a FARA violation, as was the case with Maria Butina. For example, the FARA statute requires that foreign agents must register with the Attorney General copies of any "informational materials" that they distribute, but this requirement only applies to a "person within the United States."[54] Similar provisions were upheld by the Supreme Court.[55]

But technological innovations have limited the need for direct presence on the territory of the United States. For sure, lobbying efforts and legal representation require in-person appearances and cannot be done remotely (if they are to be effective). However, electioneering activity can occur virtually over the Internet. The troll farm activity spearheaded by the IRA influenced the political discourse during the 2016 election, but because the individuals involved were outside the

---

[54] See 22 U.S.C. § 614 ("Every person within the United States who is an agent of a foreign principal and required to register under the provisions of this subchapter and who transmits or causes to be transmitted in the United States mails or by any means or instrumentality of interstate or foreign commerce any informational materials for or in the interests of such foreign principal (i) in the form of prints, or (ii) in any other form which is reasonably adapted to being, or which he believes will be, or which he intends to be, disseminated or circulated among two or more persons shall, not later than forty-eight hours after the beginning of the transmittal thereof, file with the Attorney General two copies thereof.").

[55] In *Meese v. Keene*, 481 U.S. 465, 480 (1987), the Supreme Court concluded that the provision simply provided additional information to the public because "Congress simply required the disseminators of such material to make additional disclosures that would better enable the public to evaluate the import of the propaganda."

United States, FARA did not apply. As social media has become more and more important in political discourse, FARA has evaporated as a meaningful tool for responding to the threat of foreign electioneering.[56] And the major reason for this evaporation is the incongruity of FARA's territorial requirement in a world where social media crosses boundaries. In this new world of social media electioneering, FARA is the past, not the future.[57]

The question is whether FARA can be used as a conceptual template for a new form of regulation that could respond to social media electioneering that crosses territorial boundaries. The idea would be to take what works for FARA – transparency or registration – and see how that might be applied extraterritorially with regard to foreign political behavior that is consumed in the United States on social media platforms. Of course, it would not be feasible to require everyone who posts a political view on the Internet to register as an agent of a foreign power; this is not the correct analogy. Rather, the idea is to think more creatively about a transparency-based regime that could respond to the problem of foreign electioneering and make clear to readers the foreign source of the material.[58] The next section will explore this idea, and its possible effectiveness, in greater detail.

4. TRANSPARENCY REGIMES ON THE INTERNET

The Foreign Agent Registration Act is but one example of a transparency regime. This section is devoted to a brainstorming exercise of sorts. Are other transparency regimes possible? Could a new transparency respond to the problem of foreign electioneering on the Internet? For example, a report on election interference from Stanford University recommended that "greater transparency is needed to ensure

---

[56] See Brittany Morgan Albaugh, *Two Paths to Preventing Foreign Influence: Reforming Campaign Finance and Lobbying Law*, 13 J. INT'L BUS. & L. 283, 285 (2014) (arguing that "Congress should pass a law that bans foreign influence in the U.S.'s political process by implementing campaign finance and lobbying restrictions").

[57] Some scholars and policy experts have argued that FARA should be amended to increase its regulatory reach. For example, Jahad Atieh argued that Congress should "update FARA by changing several of its provisions to allow the public more advance notice of lobbyist intent, before any actual lobbying activity has taken place." Jahad Atieh, *Foreign Agents: Updating Fara to Protect American Democracy*, 31 U. PA. J. INT'L L. 1051, 1053 (2010). While some of these reforms are advisable, they do not seek to address or resolve foreign electioneering over social media. In contrast, others have suggested limiting FARA's broad scope. See Baker, *supra* note 43, at 40 (concluding that "FARA should be restructured to eliminate the purpose, and the correspondingly charged language, of requiring the fomenters of political subversion to register" and that "[i]f any concern for this danger remains, it should be dealt with in other legislation addressing the dangers presented by political subversives").

[58] FARA already includes a labeling requirement for an identification statement for communications from an agent of a foreign principal. See 22 U.S.C. § 614 (requiring "a conspicuous statement that the materials are distributed by the agent on behalf of the foreign principal, and that additional information is on file with the Department of Justice" and that "[t]he Attorney General may by rule define what constitutes a conspicuous statement for the purposes of this subsection"). Again, however, the requirement only applies to agents who are "within the United States." *Id.* By definition, this provision cannot apply to social media communications originating outside the territory of the United States.

that voters will be able to make informed decisions for themselves about the appropriateness of these contacts and business deals with foreigners."[59] Similarly, Facebook announced in October 2019 that it would increase "transparency" on its platform.[60]

The legal literature on transparency and disclosure regimes within the context of election law focuses mainly on the issue of campaign finance.[61] The example of campaign finance regulations, when combined with FARA, helps to sketch out the outer contours of disclosure and transparency regimes in the context of elections. The question is whether these tools might be combined in new and innovative ways to tackle foreign election speech that could maximize and promote the collective right of self-determination that stands at the core of our ideal of election integrity.[62]

Prior chapters have identified the core problem of foreign speech masquerading as domestic speech, especially over the Internet. Prior chapters have also established that it is perfectly acceptable, even mandatory, for a state to enact boundary regulations to prohibit that foreign participation in democratic elections. Could a new boundary regulation deal with the problem of foreign speech on social media platforms?

It would not be necessary to ban or block foreign political communications from being posted online; this would arguably be overbroad and unconstitutional. Rather, a more modest regulation would simply seek to label social media postings that have a foreign origin. If foreign social media postings with a foreign origin could be labeled as such, then the American audience could consume that political speech with full knowledge that it originates from outside the polity.

One might object that the federal government does not have the resources to scan and label all social media postings that have a foreign origin. This much is true. However, a regulation could impose an obligation on social media companies to label foreign accounts as foreign accounts. The regulation would, in effect, require social media companies to spend considerable resources, both with regard to computer algorithms and human capital, to label accounts, whether on Twitter, Facebook, or other platforms, that have a foreign origin.

---

[59] *See* Michael McFaul, Andrew Grotto, and Alex Stamos, *Enhancing Transparency about Foreign Involvement in U.S. Elections*, in Michael McFaul (ed.), SECURING AMERICAN ELECTIONS: PRESCRIPTIONS FOR ENHANCING THE INTEGRITY AND INDEPENDENCE OF THE 2020 U.S. PRESIDENTIAL ELECTION AND BEYOND 53, 55 (Stanford University, 2019).

[60] *See Helping to Protect the 2020 US Elections*, FACEBOOK (Oct. 21, 2019) (announcing that it would be "Making Pages more transparent, including showing the confirmed owner of a Page; Labeling state-controlled media on their Page and in our Ad Library; [and] Making it easier to understand political ads, including a new US presidential candidate spend tracker.")

[61] *See generally* MICHAEL J. MALBIN AND THOMAS L. FAIS, THE DAY AFTER REFORM: SOBERING CAMPAIGN FINANCE LESSONS FROM THE AMERICAN STATES (Rockefeller Institute Press, 1998) (discussing disclosure regimes).

[62] *See* Katherine Shaw, *Taking Disclosure Seriously*, YALE L. & POL'Y REV. INTER ALIA (Apr. 3, 2016) (discussing the "electoral integrity" interest).

One issue with this proposal is the attribution problem. Troll farms such as the one operated by the IRA in St. Petersburg deployed technology to hide their foreign origin. Because of the possibility of this technology, there might be a technological barrier that would prevent a social media company from guaranteeing complete success in correctly identifying foreign accounts. Furthermore, as Facebook and Twitter deploy more sophisticated resources for complying with this regulation, social media users might increase their efforts with new technology to masquerade as American accounts and defeat whatever manual or automated efforts that the social media company has at its disposal. One might conclude, therefore, that in this technological war, the social media company (and by extension the state seeking to protect the integrity of its political deliberations) will never be able to declare total and complete victory.

This defeatist argument should be rejected; in most other contexts this defeatism is a bad look and it is equally inappropriate here. For example, the technological advances of cyber-criminals make it very difficult for companies to keep private information on their computer systems free from criminal hacking. As companies develop more and more techniques to make their systems impenetrable, criminals find new and ingenious ways to penetrate them. With each new technological innovation that one side deploys, the other side finds a new technology to defeat it. As such, one can never completely guarantee that a company's information will be completely safe. But it would be absurd to conclude on this basis that companies should not even *try* to secure their computer systems from outside attack. Of course they should, because imperfect cyber-security is better than no cyber-security at all.

The same goes for the proposed remedy here: labeling foreign social media accounts as foreign. To demonstrate that this proposal is at least prima facie plausible, consider the fact that both the social media companies and the U.S. intelligence agencies were able to link particular social media accounts with the IRA troll farm. Indeed, Twitter released a huge cache of tweets that the company identified as flowing from this troll farm. This release was only possible because Twitter was able to identify the source of the tweets – not just as foreign in nature but in fact coming from a very particular source. Furthermore, Facebook has already introduced an initiative to combat fake news that launches a dialogue box when questionable links are widely shared; the dialogue box indicates that the original post is a source of controversy and notes that other media sources have examined the claims in the original story. The dialogue box then points the user in the direction of the reputable news stories. This initiative is designed to be used in real time rather than simply as a historical tool. If Facebook is capable of labeling fake news as such, it ought to be able to label accounts and posts that have a foreign origin. And the same goes for Twitter.

Attribution can be accomplished in one of two ways. First, attribution can be accomplished "directly" through digital forensic analysis of IP addresses and similar markers.[63] In theory, direct attribution can be accomplished by algorithm or some other automatic function. The problem is that sophisticated troll farms, such as the IRA troll farm, can obfuscate their origin and frustrate attempts at direct attribution. However, this still leaves the option of "indirect" attribution which analyzes content and patterns of online activity to flag suspected foreign accounts.[64] Even if a Russian troll farm were able to hide its foreign origin from an automated detection system that looks for direct attribution, it would be more difficult to hide its foreign origin from a semantic analysis that performs indirect attribution – either through a complex automated analysis or through human analysis.[65] Obviously, the latter (semantic analysis using human researchers) would be more labor-intensive and would also introduce a sizeable time gap between the posting of the information and the attribution determination (and thus the labeling). While the time gap might frustrate the goal of the labeling regime (to give users information about the source of the social media post at the time that they are reading it), the time gap would not necessarily be fatal. It would be better to have a delayed labeling system rather than no labeling system at all. To be sure, it is important to concede that there would be technical barriers to a perfect labeling system, but even an imperfect labeling system could have tremendous value to the culture of political discourse on social media platforms. However, social media firms would need to devote substantial financial resources, and human resources, to make it happen.

One might argue that the proposed transparency regime under consideration – labeling foreign social media accounts as foreign – stands in tension with, and undermines, the culture of the Internet. Much of internet-based communication was built on the ethics of anonymity. Users meet in virtual worlds and cloak themselves in anonymity; this feature has had both salutary and dangerous consequences. It fosters free communications, especially about uncomfortable topics for marginalized communities, but it also facilitates criminal behavior. For that reason, internet companies – and their users – might chafe at the idea that they need to clearly label foreign social media posts.

The answer to this objection is twofold. First, the culture of anonymity on the Internet is not so absolute. Anonymity is not complete and total. There are clear exceptions to it because the degree of permissible anonymity goes up and down depending on the context. For example, Facebook built its social media platform

---

[63] Joshua R. Fattal, *FARA on Facebook: Modernizing the Foreign Agents Registration Act to Address Propagandists on Social Media*, 21 N.Y.U. J. Legis. & Pub. Pol'y 903, 932 (2019) (noting that "researchers have a number of tools at their disposal to make plausible inferences about an account's origin, and are working to improve their efforts" but concluding that "accurate identifications can be made with any degree of confidence only through direct attribution efforts like those evidenced by the U.S. government . . . and through work done by the social media companies themselves").

[64] Fattal distinguishes between direct and indirect attribution and argues that indirect attribution may be accomplished by "research experts who do not have access to identifying information like IP addresses or payments" but can compare "social media identities across platforms" and watch for "common themes." *Id.*

[65] *Id.*

based on the principle that only real people, using their real names, can create a Facebook account. The assumption was based on the idea that other Facebook users could only decide whether to accept a friend request from another user if the requester used their legitimate name. Of course, Facebook will only go so far to ensure that a Facebook user opens their account under a legitimate name, but the point is that pure anonymity is already inconsistent with a social media platform that is designed to network friends together. Facebook is not simply a chatroom of anonymous speakers; it is a social network for creating and building connections between people for which pure anonymity would be incompatible. In comparison, Twitter is not based on the same notion of building a network of friends, but rather is based on a social media feed that the user personally "curates" in order to create a list of messages from accounts that the user wishes to subscribe to, for lack of a better term. This might suggest that Twitter is more consistent with anonymity, because a Twitter user might wish to subscribe to a particular account based simply on a wish to read the postings from that anonymous user. However, it is important to remember that Twitter has expended great efforts to verify social media accounts of well-known individuals in order to prevent fraud. (The result of the verification process is a blue checkmark which is easily identifiable to Twitter users.) This initiative seems to recognize that there is something deeply pernicious about anonymous users creating fake accounts and using those accounts to masquerade as famous or noteworthy individuals. Even if there is no financial fraud involved, the risk that other users will be duped into thinking that the fake account is legitimate is problematic enough for Twitter to take action. Given these examples from Facebook and Twitter, it seems clear that social media platforms are capable of, and comfortable with, disclosure regimes. Labeling foreign accounts as foreign would go a long way to signaling to users that they may be reading foreign electioneering efforts.

The second answer to the objection about the culture of anonymity on the Internet is that social culture can be changed. Just because social media companies and their users act in particular ways does not mean that behavior cannot be subtly redirected based on new regulations. The idea that users are addicted to anonymous content runs the risk of falling victim to the naturalistic fallacy. Just because the Internet works one way today does not mean that it should work that way or that it is incapable of changing. In any event, change is not as difficult as one might think given that social media platforms already have a distaste for anonymity based on their status as social networks – a concept that entails some degree of transparency in interpersonal relations.

Anonymity is already disfavored in the political process and total anonymity is not legally protected.[66] Much of the existing regulatory landscape is based on the

---

[66] See P. Karlan, *The "Ambiguous Giving Out": The Complicated Roles of Disclosure and Anonymity in Political Activity*, 27 J.L. & POL. 655 (2012).

assumption that political participation in the form of campaign finance donations cannot, and should not, be anonymous.[67] Although voting is anonymous in the sense that one's voting decision is not publicly released, other aspects of voting are publicly available, such as whether one voted in a particular election or not. And whether one donated to a particular political campaign also is a matter of public record.[68] Existing election regulations are designed to limit anonymity in order to give the voting public access to relevant information about the political process.[69] Although a lack of anonymity may discourage some individuals from participating in the political process, this is an acceptable cost to pay when balanced against the public's need for access to relevant information to protect the integrity of the political process.[70] Disclosure regimes are perfectly compatible with democratic ideals; arguably, disclosure regimes enhance and protect these ideals.[71]

The regulation of foreign electioneering on social media platforms would simply be an extension of these efforts – efforts that seek to prevent users of the platform from confusing or lying to other users regarding *identity*.[72] As noted in prior chapters, the most pernicious aspect of the Russian interference was the use of social media platforms to spread foreign electioneering communications that masqueraded as American speech. Individuals at the IRA troll farm in St. Petersburg created fake Facebook and Twitter accounts to spread political messages and amplify divisive

---

[67] For a discussion of secrecy in the political context, see Helen Norton, *Secrets, Lies & Disclosure*, 27 J.L. & POL. 641, 641 (2012). Norton argues that there is a reason to prohibit people from keeping their identity a secret in the political or electoral context.

[68] For an argument that this information should not be publicly searchable, see Bruce Cain, *Shade from the Glare: The Case for Semi-Disclosure*, CATO UNBOUND (Nov. 8, 2010) (arguing that campaign finance information should be treated as confidential information and disclosed to government but not the public).

[69] *See* Jennifer A. Heerwig and Katherine Shaw, *Through A Glass, Darkly: The Rhetoric and Reality of Campaign Finance Disclosure*, 102 GEO. L.J. 1443, 1476 (2014) (noting that "[i]n a political environment saturated with conflicting messages of often-dubious quality, political institutions (like the FEC) may aid voters by helping them assess speakers and their messages" and "effective disclosure regimes must offer information users easily accessible, easily comprehensible, actionable, and credible information").

[70] *See* Raymond J. La Raja, *Does Transparency of Political Activity Have a Chilling Effect on Participation?*, MPSA Annual Conference (2011) (conceding that "[t]ransparency in politics is universally touted as salutary for democracy" but also noting the "potentially dampening effect of disclosure costs on political participation" because "divulging personal information about political activity might cause some to withdraw from politics"). This potential withdrawal of participation is a feature, not a bug, of this chapter's proposed transparency regime regarding social media electioneering, because prohibiting foreign participation in American elections is precisely what the government can and should achieve.

[71] Anthony Johnstone, *A Madisonian Case for Disclosure*, 19 GEO. MASON L. REV. 413 (2012).

[72] *See id.* at 646 (arguing that "policy prescriptions and doctrinal analysis distinguish a speaker's interest in keeping her identity secret because she is vulnerable to abuse by power from a speaker's interest in keeping her identity secret to better wield her own power to shape others' choices"). This is exactly the situation when a foreign state uses social media platforms for election interference. Troll farms seek to hide their identity, as foreigners, in order to "better wield" their own power to convince Americans of their views or to amplify existing views. Being perceived truthfully as outsiders would dilute or eliminate the persuasive power of their speech.

messages from other accounts in order to create an echo chamber. A key element of these efforts was that the accounts did not identify as Russian because American users would not have listened to Russian opinions on matters of American social policy. A transparency regime implemented by social media platforms could place a dent in this practice although it probably would not be able to eliminate it entirely. Speech would not be suppressed, prohibited, or censured – simply labeled for what it is, foreign speech. Just as Twitter "verifies" the accounts of noteworthy individuals with a blue checkmark, so too Twitter could label foreign accounts with a similarly prominent visual designation. The goal of the regulation would be to combat dishonesty (and lying) regarding the foreign source of election speech.[73]

There is an extensive academic literature on whether transparency and disclosure regimes will change people's behavior. The evidence is mixed, with some studies indicating a change in behavior and other studies failing to find a change in behavior. Some researchers have found changes in behavior based on required campaign finance disclosures.[74] Prominent examples of disclosure regimes in the health context include mandatory disclosures on cigarette packages or mandatory disclosure of calorie counts on restaurant menus. It is unclear whether these disclosures spur diners to select healthier options while eating out, though the disclosures may have spurred restaurants into preemptively reducing their calorie counts.[75] On the other hand, mandatory disclosures of health inspection violations certainly have a result in how many diners are likely to patronize a restaurant. This in turn gives restaurants a greater incentive to work harder to avoid violations because business will suffer if they are forced to post in their window a low grade from the inspection.

In the political system, the greatest example of a disclosure regime is campaign finance regulations. The goal of the system is to reduce anonymous donations and force campaigns to disclose the names of contributors. The argument in favor of this approach is that it reduces the likelihood of quid-pro-quo corruption because

---

[73] *See* Joshua S. Sellers, *Legislating Against Lying in Campaigns and Elections*, 71 Okla. L. Rev. 141, 144 (2018) (arguing that "narrowly drawn campaign and election speech restrictions are doctrinally defensible" especially with regard to foreigners, and "given the severe distortion in our democratic discourse, and, again, in light of recent foreign interference in our elections, laws of this sort could be defended as a corollary to proposed legislation aimed at eliminating foreign influence by way of the internet").

[74] *See* Abby K. Wood and Douglas M. Spencer, *In the Shadows of Sunlight: The Effects of Transparency on State Political Campaigns*, 15 Election L.J. 302 (2016) (finding that "contributors to state-level campaigns opt out to a very small degree in the wake of increased contribution visibility" and that "contributors are about 2–3 percentage points less likely to contribute in subsequent elections in states that increase the public visibility of campaign contributions, relative to contributors in states that do not change their disclosure laws or practices over the same time period").

[75] *See* Michael D. Guttentag, *Evolutionary Analysis in Law: On Disclosure Regulation*, 48 Ariz. St. L.J. 963, 986 (2016) (noting that "[c]alorie labeling requirements proved useful in reducing the caloric content of foods offered at restaurants not because consumers changed their behavior in light of the new information, but rather because restaurants chose to reduce the caloric content of the foods they offered in response to the new disclosure requirements").

candidates will be unlikely to reach corrupt deals with donors if the campaign is forced to reveal the names of the donors. On the other hand, some theorists have hypothesized that corruption actually requires a minimal level of publicity, though these claims are speculative at best.[76] In any event, it is probably the case that campaign finance disclosures have not eliminated the scourge of corruption in American politics.

However, none of the disclosure regimes just described is on all fours with the disclosure regime proposed in this chapter, that is, the labeling of foreign social media accounts. The goal of this regime is not to change people's behavior – such as getting people to smoke less – but rather is simply designed to prevent the possibility of confusion, that is, people thinking that a communication is American in origin when in fact it comes from Russia. The question is whether the transparency regime will have the desired effect. Will it give people pause when reading social media posts from a foreign account?

There is empirical evidence that additional information can help change people's assessments of the views that they are exposed to. For example, Conor Dowling and Amber Wichowsky conducted a study that found that study participants viewed the target of an attack advertisement more favorably if the participants were given information about the donors who funded the group that launched the attack campaign.[77] The only change between the control and experimental groups was the extra information regarding the funding source for the attack ad. It is a bit unclear why the addition of information about the funding source changed the experimental group's view of the target of the attack ad, although one can hypothesize an answer. Learning about the funding source for the attack throws into sharp relief the self-interested motivations that some individuals would have for financing the advertisement's creation and distribution. In other words, the financial disclosure brings to the forefront that a particular communication is not an objective, disinterested, or nonpartisan statement from, say, a scholar, but rather is a piece of advocacy pushed by a group of individuals with not only a point of view but also strategic interests that align with that point of view. The receipt of this information introduces a dose of skepticism into the consumer of the information, sparking renewed scrutiny and a critical reflection on the campaign communication.[78]

---

[76]   See, e.g., Michael D. Gilbert, *Transparency and Corruption: A General Analysis*, 2018 U. CHI. LEGAL F. 117 (2018) ("transparency in government causes the very corruption it aims to prevent, and the problem is universal" and "the CEO is more likely to buy the senator's vote if he can watch her cast it").

[77]   See Conor M. Dowling and Amber Wichowsky, *Does It Matter Who's Behind the Curtain? Anonymity in Political Advertising and the Effects of Campaign Finance Disclosure*, 41 AM. POL. RES. 965, 973–4 (2013) (reporting results of an empirical study).

[78]   See Richard L. Hasen, *Chill Out: A Qualified Defense of Campaign Finance Disclosure Laws in the Internet Age*, 27 J.L. & POL. 557, 560 (2012) ("As for the information interest, campaign finance data, especially when included on the face of campaign advertising, provides an important heuristic cue helping busy voters decide how to vote").

One should distinguish between required disclosures that are attached to a particular communication and a disclosure regime that is separated from the communication that is being regulated. Although this sounds like a trivial or inconsequential distinction, the Dowling and Wichowsky study involved a disclosure that took place at the same time that the consumer was receiving the communication. Other examples of this type of immediate disclosure include a calorie count which the diner reads on the menu at the very moment in time when the diner is deciding what to order. Another example would be a required disclosure included in a television political advertisement that says that the advertisement was paid for and approved by a particular political candidate. On the other end of the spectrum are campaign finance disclosure laws that require the public release of donor names and amounts; this information, collected and released *en masse*, is not consumed by the public at the same time that the public consumes campaign communications. So, for example, a member of the public could, in theory, watch a candidate advertisement one week but not learn about the candidate's campaign donors until the next week; or the consumer might never learn about the campaign donors at all because the information constitutes a "data dump."

The proposal in this chapter would ideally involve the labeling of foreign social media accounts so that the information can be digested by the public *as they view the accounts*. Simply publishing a list of suspected foreign social media accounts, or troll farm-connected accounts, might not change people's assessments of the information or opinions expressed in those accounts. Indeed, social media users may never connect up the bulk information they receive about foreign accounts with the content of those tweets – if the two sources of information are released at different points in time and in different locations. What makes the calorie count regulation so powerful is that the disclosure is presented to the consumer at the time and place when the consumer is making the relevant decision. An analogous regulation would require social media companies to place an indicator – similar to Twitter's blue checkmark – for foreign-based social media accounts, so that social media users can distinguish between political views expressed by insiders and political views expressed by outsiders. Technical limitations would prevent instantaneous effect, but social media firms should seek solutions that provide the information to users sooner rather than later.

Although the success of this particular disclosure regime would need to be empirically tested, it is clearly the case that disclosure regimes in general can change people's attitudes about the information they receive, making them less or more likely to be receptive to that information, depending on how that information is presented and whether it is accompanied by a required disclosure.[79] It stands to

---

[79] *See* Lear Jiang, *Disclosure's Last Stand? The Need to Clarify the "Informational Interest" Advanced by Campaign Finance Disclosure*, 119 COLUM. L. REV. 487, 490 (2019) (arguing that "placing a greater

reason that an American viewer would be less receptive to an election communication that is identified as being foreign in nature. An empirical study could be designed to consider a control group that sees a large number of tweets without any disclosure, while an experimental group would receive the same tweets but with a disclosure icon indicating the foreign source of the tweet. Both groups would be asked to rate the tweets along a variety of metrics, including their degree of agreement with the views expressed in the tweets.

Of course, it is theoretically possible that the disclosures would do nothing to dampen the user's enthusiasm for messages that accord with the user's predetermined ideological worldview. Perhaps users will simply like some content and not care about its source. But even if this is true, the goal of election integrity will be enhanced if users are given information about the source of the communication. Unlike a calorie count regulation that is specifically designed with the goal of changing consumer behavior (in favor of healthier choices), a social media disclosure regime would not be grounded by a desire to change people's behavior. If the American people want to consume information from abroad, and vote in accordance with those viewpoints, so be it. But the American people should at least have the relevant information, that is, to distinguish between statements from members of the political community and outsiders.[80]

If one is wondering why it is so important for Americans to have this information, the rationale flows from the underlying principle that animates the democratic enterprise: the right of self-determination. As articulated in prior chapters, the right of self-determination requires that in democratic societies, elections allow members of the political community to make decisions about the polity's future. In order for an election to be a meaningful exercise in self-government, the polity is entitled to enact boundary regulations and membership criteria in order to clarify which individuals are entitled to participate in the election. In addition to voting requirements, the process of political deliberation requires protection from outside forces that would distort the deliberative process. Although it would be too much to ban users from receiving foreign communications, the proposed regulation articulated in this chapter stakes out a far more modest proposal, a middle ground position

emphasis on disclosure's ability to generate increased political discourse can provide a more robust defense of future reforms"); Daniel R. Ortiz, *The Informational Interest*, 27 J.L. & Pol. 663, 665–6 (2012). The "informational interest" argument was most prominently articulated in *Buckley v. Valeo*, 424 U.S. 1 (1976).

[80]   Other proposed regulations have merit, though most of them fail to directly address the foreign nature of social media campaigning. *See, e.g.*, Honest Ads Act (proposing to make online advertisements subject to same disclaimer regime as television and radio election advertisements); Prevention of Foreign Interference with Elections Act of 2019 (proposing five-year imprisonment for the crime of conspiring "with an individual, while having knowledge or reasonable cause to believe such individual is a foreign national, to prevent, obstruct, impede, interfere with, promote, support, or oppose the nomination or the election of any candidate for any Federal, State, or local office, or any ballot measure, initiative, or referendum … "); Corporate Duty to Report Act of 2019 (proposing that corporations be required to disclose attempts by foreigners to purchase political advertisements).

that is neither an outright ban on foreign electoral communications over social media nor a blanket acceptance of them. The regulation simply requires that foreign communications over social media be identified as such so that outsiders are not permitted to masquerade as insiders and distort the political process on that basis.

CONCLUSION

The goal of this chapter was to show how the principle of self-determination is translated in practice into a set of regulations that protect the integrity of the political process and to argue that these regulations should be extended in some way to the landscape of social media. We are already accustomed to a panoply of regulations that protect the integrity of elections.[81] As we have seen in this chapter, these regulations fit into a number of categories. There are direct prohibitions on foreign participation, including prohibitions on foreign voting and prohibitions on foreign campaign contributions. Then there are transparency regimes, such as FARA, that are designed to ensure that activities conducted on behalf of foreign sovereigns are publicly acknowledged in a way that makes clear the connection between individual agents and the foreign principals on whose behalf they operate. Taking these regulations as a family resemblance concept, one can extrapolate other regulatory regimes that might extend the underlying goals of these regulations to the social media context. The result is an argument for a proposed regulation requiring social media companies to label social media accounts with a foreign source. The regulation avoids the potentially sticky question of banning or prohibiting foreign political speech altogether. As noted above, there might be technological obstacles that limit the effectiveness of the regulation, but the fact that some sophisticated users might circumvent the regulation is not a good argument for avoiding the problem altogether. A conceptually sound regulatory regime is a good idea even if compliance is not universal and even if the government remains one step behind the most sophisticated outsiders who seek to side-step the regulations.

Of course, one question has remained unexamined in this chapter: the degree to which the First Amendment might restrict the government's authority to regulate political activity. The Supreme Court has often overturned, on First Amendment grounds, statutory regulations designed to ensure the integrity of the electoral process. Most of these cases involved campaign finance regulations. In addition to the arguments already considered, the regulations in this chapter might be vulnerable to attack if the Constitution protects the rights of

---

[81] See Corey R. Sparks, *Foreigners United: Foreign Influence in American Elections After Citizens United v. Federal Election Commission*, 62 CLEV. ST. L. REV. 245, 253–4 (2014) ("Disclosure has long been a method for the government to ensure transparency and integrity in the electoral process, and many other tax-exempt organizations that spend money to influence elections, even in unlimited amounts, must adhere to disclosure requirements . . . .").

foreigners to participate in American elections, or if the Constitution protects the rights of Americans to receive foreign assistance or foreign electioneering. Answering this question requires a deeper dive into the relationship between the First Amendment and the concept of electoral integrity. That is the task of the next chapter.

6

Free Speech and Elections

INTRODUCTION

The prior chapter focused on the existence of boundary and transparency regulations that promote the right of self-determination. One issue that was mentioned but ultimately bracketed was the question of whether these regulations are ultimately compliant with the First Amendment. That question must now be attacked head on. In particular, this chapter uses the example of social media labeling as a test case for determining whether the First Amendment will be a barrier to implementing some legislative solutions for securing election integrity. These solutions are not the cyber-security initiatives that others have proposed, but rather social media regulations designed to deal with the most salient problem of election interference: foreign social media posts that are deceptive about their true source.

The goal of this chapter is simply to decide whether free speech is a knock-down constraint on social media labeling, not whether social media labeling is a good idea as an all-things-considered judgment. A number of considerations go into that latter determination and most of them will remain unaddressed in this study. The sole goal of this book is to suggest directions for future regulation based on the lodestar of self-determination. Then, we address the most trenchant objection to that regulation – the right to free speech. To that task we now turn.

This chapter addresses the following questions in sequence. First, are foreigners protected by the First Amendment? Second, if foreigners are not protected by the First Amendment, do Americans have a First Amendment right to receive or consume foreign speech? Third, are labeling and disclosure regimes consistent with the First Amendment, especially since they might compromise the core value of anonymity? Labeling and disclosure are common methods of regulation and are relatively uncontroversial in the commercial context. In contrast, labeling and disclosure regimes in the political context are far more controversial and demand a more searching level of constitutional scrutiny. Finally, the last question is whether international law or European human rights law might impose constraints on social media regulation. This last question is particularly important since election interference is a global problem and any solutions would need to be implemented by several nations. For that global constituency, the key constraint is not the U.S. Constitution but rather the international protection of free speech. The international protection of free expression is slightly different than the American jurisprudence, so it requires separate consideration.

1. FOREIGNERS AND THE FIRST AMENDMENT

Determining the extraterritorial reach of the Constitution is a difficult question. Some provisions apply extraterritorially while others do not. For example, in *United States v. Verdugo-Urquidez*, the Supreme Court concluded that the Fourth Amendment did not prohibit the government from performing a search of the defendant's residence in Mexico.[1] (The defendant was a Mexican citizen.) The Court noted that the Fourth Amendment, by its express text, was limited to the "right of the people" to be "secure in their persons, houses, papers, and effects, against unreasonable searches and seizures." The Court interpreted the Fourth Amendment's reference to the "right of the people" to refer to people within the United States and to police searches "which might be conducted by the United States in domestic matters."[2]

On the other hand, the Supreme Court concluded in *Reid v. Covert*, in 1956, that the defendant, the spouse of a military serviceman stationed in Britain, retained the right to a civilian jury trial, despite the fact that she was located outside the country and the crime occurred abroad. (The terms of the United States agreement with Britain called for crimes on the base to be prosecuted by military court martial pursuant to the UCMJ.) Indeed, the court waxed poetic about Paul's historical assertion of rights protected by Rome even while Paul was outside Roman territory.[3]

What explains why some of the protections of the Constitution are applicable outside the territory of the United States, while others are not?[4] Some constitutional constraints "follow the flag" when the United States and its agents act abroad, but not all of them. Apparently, when agents of the United States search a residence abroad, the Fourth Amendment does not follow the flag, but when the United States conducts a criminal trial (of a U.S. citizen) abroad, the Fifth Amendment follows the flag. In each of these cases, though, the litigants asserting an extraterritorial constitutional right were American citizens living or residing abroad, making the relationship between the individual and the American polity that much stronger. Foreigners located abroad do not enjoy the same constitutional protections, otherwise the U.S. Constitution would become a global document guaranteeing universal protection.

---

[1]   494 U.S. 259 (1990).

[2]   *Id.* at 266.

[3]   *See* Reid v. Covert, 354 U.S. 1, 6 (1957) ("This is not a novel concept. To the contrary, it is as old as government. It was recognized long before Paul successfully invoked his right as a Roman citizen to be tried in strict accordance with Roman law.").

[4]   For a discussion of this controversy, see Gerald L. Neuman, *Extraterritorial Rights and Constitutional Methodology After* Rasul v. Bush, 153 U. Pa. L. Rev. 2073 (2005).

The area where this can be seen most clearly is in the constitutional protections that regulate immigration law.[5] Immigrants located within the territory of the United States enjoy certain constitutional protections prior to their removal by the executive branch, though those protections do not require a criminal trial prior to deportation – nor do they even require a hearing before an Article III judge. Instead, immigrants are subject to removal after a hearing before an Article II Immigration Law Judge. Although the Supreme Court has recognized that immigrants located on the territory of the United States are not entitled to the same procedural protections as, for example, someone facing criminal punishment, the Supreme Court has recognized the applicability of due process in this context, precisely because the government is operating on domestic territory.[6] Similarly, although a border inspection falls under the special needs administrative exception and is therefore not a search for purposes of the Fourth Amendment, this is not to suggest that every action of the border patrol in every circumstance is immune from constitutional scrutiny.

However, immigrants located outside the territory of the United States (who by definition are not facing removal because they are not located on the territory of the United States) are not subject to any constitutional protection. Although immigration policy in this area can and should be regulated by statute, it is not constrained by the protections of the Constitution. No immigrant located outside the United States has a constitutional right to enter the United States, though a statutory scheme establishes criteria and procedures for the granting of visas.[7] If the Constitution were to apply extraterritorially in the immigration law context, every potential immigrant in the United States would be a potential litigant in a constitutional case. This would be untenable.

Similarly, foreigners located outside the United States do not, and should not, have a First Amendment right to participate in American elections, either through speech or financial participation.[8] Indeed, federal courts have generally held that the First Amendment does not apply at all to extraterritorial foreigners.[9] While it is one thing for *Citizens United* to conclude that domestic corporations have a First

---

[5] For a critical discussion of the application of constitutional norms to immigration law, see GERALD L. NEUMAN, STRANGERS TO THE CONSTITUTION: IMMIGRANTS, BORDERS, AND FUNDAMENTAL LAW (Princeton University Press, 1996).

[6] *See* Molina v. Whitaker, 910 F.3d 1056, 1060 (8th Cir. 2018) (holding, inter alia, that a removal proceeding must be a "fundamentally fair hearing").

[7] *See, e.g.,* Lleshi v. Kerry, 127 F. Supp. 3d 196, 200 (S.D.N.Y. 2015) (noting that "[c]onsular officials are vested by statute with the exclusive power to issue or deny visas").

[8] *See* Joshua S. Sellers, *Legislating Against Lying in Campaigns and Elections*, 71 OKLA. L. REV. 141, 144 (2018) (noting that "[t]he rights of foreign nationals to participate in campaigns and elections have been considered by courts in the campaign finance context" and predicting that the "regulations upheld in that context suggest that the regulation of foreign nationals' campaign and election speech might be sustained on similar grounds").

[9] *See* DKT Mem'l Fund Ltd. v. Agency for Int'l Dev., 887 F.2d 275, 285 (D.C. Cir. 1989) ("no First Amendment protection to aliens beyond the borders of the United States not within the custody or control of the United States").

Amendment right to engage in unlimited election spending free from burdensome campaign finance limits, it would be a heavy lift to extend this holding to foreign persons (whether corporations or individuals) located outside the territory of the United States.[10] By express limitation, the Supreme Court refused to apply its holding extraterritorially and with good reason – it would be a monumental shift in constitutional jurisprudence to confer First Amendment protections to foreigners located abroad.[11] Prior cases before *Citizens United* recognized that foreign corporations did not have a right to contribute to political campaigns, but at least some lawyers have argued that these cases are no longer good law in light of the arguments outlined in *Citizens United*.[12]

If the Supreme Court were to decide to extend the protections of the First Amendment to foreigners located outside the territory of the United States, the entire machinery of election regulations would be at risk.[13] As noted in prior chapters, election regulations are designed to ensure that outsiders are restricted from participating in foreign elections, including the purchasing of political advertisements.[14] If the First Amendment applied to foreign corporations and individuals, it is unclear how Congress could prevent foreigners from either donating to political campaigns or spending money on political speech designed to support them.[15]

For some free speech purists, this tectonic result would be a welcome development. Under a maximalist conception of free speech, all regulations on election

[10]   James Ianelli, *Noncitizens and* Citizens United, 56 LOY. L. REV. 869, 869–70 (2010) (asking whether the First Amendment will "give refuge to a foreigner who buys a thirty-second television advertisement lauding the virtues of a particular candidate a few days before an election?").

[11]   Citizens United v. Fed. Election Comm'n, 558 U.S. 310, 362 (2010) ("We need not reach the question whether the Government has a compelling interest in preventing foreign individuals or associations from influencing our Nation's political process.").

[12]   For example, consider *First Nat. Bank of Bos. v. Bellotti*, 435 U.S. 765, 788 n.26 (1978) (stating that "our consideration of a corporation's right to speak on issues of general public interest implies no comparable right in the quite different context of participation in a political campaign for election to public office" and concluding that "Congress might well be able to demonstrate the existence of a danger of real or apparent corruption in independent expenditures by corporations to influence candidate elections"). In *Citizens United*, the Supreme Court apparently viewed this footnote in *Bellotti* as "leav[ing] the question open."

[13]   *See* Helen Norton, *(At Least) Thirteen Ways of Looking at Election Lies*, 71 OKLA. L. REV. 117, 121 (2018) (concluding that "foreign speakers may not have any autonomy interests protected by the First Amendment" because "the Supreme Court has held that at least some constitutional guarantees do not extend to noncitizens overseas").

[14]   For an argument along these lines, see Matt A. Vega, *The First Amendment Lost in Translation: Preventing Foreign Influence in U.S. Elections After* Citizens United v. FEC, 44 LOY. L.A. L. REV. 951, 958–9 (2011) (concluding that "financial participation by foreign corporations in U.S. elections should be categorized as wholly unprotected speech under the First Amendment and lawfully banned").

[15]   *See* Richard Briffault, *The Uncertain Future of the Corporate Contribution Ban*, 49 VAL. U. L. REV. 397, 437 (2015); Richard L. Hasen, *Cheap Speech and What It Has Done (to American Democracy)*, 16 FIRST AMEND. L. REV. 200, 201 (2017) ("the Court's doctrine and accompanying libertarian ethos may stymie efforts to limit foreign money flowing into elections, including money being spent to propagate 'fake news'").

speech, including election spending, are suspect and should be prohibited under the First Amendment. The old adage is that the solution for bad speech is more (corrective) speech, and the government should not be in the business of regulating political speech at all. If this entails that foreigners participate in American elections by purchasing political advertisements or making campaign donations, so be it.[16] The American marketplace of ideas remains wide open for all to enter, including foreigners. As Toni Massaro has expressed the point, foreign nationals could be entitled to participate in American elections because none of the justifications articulated in *Citizens United* justify prohibiting foreign participation:

> The following arguments for restrictions on electoral expression therefore should not satisfy the Court's test, if the forgoing analytical, theoretical, and rhetorical moves of *Citizens United* are taken seriously: arguments that corporate speakers should be treated differently from individual speakers, arguments that foreign nationals may possess vast wealth that may skew political debates, arguments that PACs or other complicated or burdensome alternatives to use of general treasury funds for electoral expression eliminate any First Amendment concerns, arguments that independent expenditures (in contrast to quid-pro-quo contributions) may corrupt American officials, or arguments that the American public may be misled by foreign national electoral expression in ways that justify governmental intervention. Nothing about the foreign source of independent expenditures logically should revive any of these rejected bases for government restrictions on such expenditures.[17]

But, as Massaro notes, there are other rationales, not explored in *Citizens United*, that might justify treating foreign nationals as different for purposes of the First Amendment. For example, Massaro argues that:

> No law currently restricts a foreign national natural person from engaging in political expression in a public forum any more than it restricts a domestic speaker in the same public forum. For example, if a foreign national wishes to broadcast his or her political views on the sidewalk in front of the White House, no police officer may remove the speaker simply because he or she is not a United States citizen or a lawful permanent resident. Such speech may well be aimed at influencing an election, but it cannot be restricted for this reason alone.[18]

While this may be true, the same cannot be said of extraterritorial foreigners.[19] Although the First Amendment refers to "persons" rather than to "citizens," the best

---

[16] For example, consider James Ianelli who argues in *Noncitizens and* Citizens United, 56 Loy. L. Rev. 869, 873–4 (2010), that "the plain language of the First Amendment gives Congress no foothold with which to distinguish between foreign and domestic speakers."

[17] *See* Toni M. Massaro, *Foreign Nationals, Electoral Spending, and the First Amendment*, 34 Harv. J.L. & Pub. Pol'y 663, 675 (2011).

[18] *Id.* at 681–2.

[19] For a discussion of this issue, see Corey R. Sparks, *Foreigners United: Foreign Influence in American Elections After Citizens United v. Federal Election Commission*, 62 Clev. St. L. Rev. 245, 247 (2014)

view is that the relevant persons for purposes of the analysis are those located on the territory of the United States or who are otherwise connected to the polity through some relationship such as citizenship. To see why this is the case, consider the following example. Say the United States launches a cyber-attack against North Korea as a countermeasure (or retorsion) responding to a prior cyber-attack by North Korea. The United States cyber-attack involves shutting down the Internet in North Korea for a period of 72 hours. During that period, no one in North Korea has any access to the Internet through conventional land-based services (e.g. excluding satellite phones). As a consequence, no one in North Korea can post anything to Twitter, Facebook, or indeed any online service whatever. During this period, not only are the North Korean media prevented from reaching an outside audience, but in fact the entire population of North Korea is prevented from reaching a similar audience through online postings. If the First Amendment applied to extraterritorial foreigners, the action by the U.S. government would probably be an unconstitutional restriction of the free speech rights of the North Koreans. The attack infringed on their power to articulate their views on the platforms of their choosing. Moreover, although the federal government may have had a compelling interest in pursuing the attack, the prevailing absolutism that governs free speech doctrine would give the federal government little room to justify the infringement in this case. But that would be an absurd result, at least under the U.S. Constitution. To suggest that the citizens of North Korea could demand protection under the First Amendment would be to globalize the First Amendment in a way not anticipated either by the framers or by prior Supreme Court precedents.

The view that the First Amendment applies to extraterritorial foreigners does not hold water, though its insistence on free speech absolutism earns points for conceptual simplicity. The view is wrongheaded – and not just because of the importance of protecting the right of self-determination articulated in prior chapters. The view is also wrong because the First Amendment cannot protect foreigners located abroad who have no connection to the United States other than their desire to influence American elections.[20] The First Amendment was designed to protect open discourse within the United States, and any attempt to unmoor that protection from the territory of the United States would entail that every foreigner located outside the United States has equal access to the American political system.[21] It would be hard to

---

("*Citizens United* allows foreign nationals to circumvent the Congressional ban on influencing American elections, and ... should be reconsidered in light of this fact, as well as the compelling government interest in preventing such circumvention, and preserving the integrity of the electoral process").

[20] See Joseph Thai, *The Right to Receive Foreign Speech*, 71 OKLA. L. REV. 269, 318 (2018) (concluding that "foreign nations themselves do not possess any First Amendment interests").

[21] See Timothy Zick, *The First Amendment in Trans-Border Perspective: Toward A More Cosmopolitan Orientation*, 52 B.C. L. REV. 941, 944 (2011) (noting that "[a]s far as alien speakers and audiences are concerned, there appears to be little support for applying the First Amendment extraterritorially").

square this result with the denial of voting rights for foreigners. It would fundamentally alter the nature of American political campaigns.

In addition to being normatively undesirable, it is clear that this view of the First Amendment is not consistent with the Court's First Amendment jurisprudence. The First Amendment as currently understood by the Court would not be a barrier to the proposal discussed in the prior chapter: a regulation requiring social media companies to label foreign political speech as having a foreign origin. To the extent that foreigners using social media platforms objected to this regulation, they would not be entitled to successfully raise a First Amendment challenge before a federal court.

In *Bluman v. FEC*, a federal court explicitly recognized that the First Amendment permits the federal government to limit the participation of foreigners in order to protect the political process.[22] As other scholars have noted, *Bluman* is consistent with the idea that the First Amendment permits the government to regulate the political speech of foreigners.[23] Some scholars have argued that the federal government could prohibit "intentionally false lies containing express advocacy."[24] Although this is a worthwhile suggestion, one should separate out the foreign speech component from the intentional lie. Although the principles of self-determination and the integrity of the democratic process require distinguishing between domestic and foreign speakers, allowing the government to get into the business of distinguishing between truth and fiction in the *political* context is especially hazardous. In many other contexts the government does make those distinctions (such as health and welfare regulations), but in the context of political speech, the otherwise unproblematic enterprise becomes especially dangerous. Moreover, it is unclear why one should view the expression of lies by foreigners as any more corrosive to the political system than the expression of pure opinion by foreigners. As noted in prior chapters, what made the participation of foreign actors so corrosive in the 2016 election was not just the content of the social media postings but the fact that the opinions were made by Russians pretending to be Americans. The most salient characteristic of the deception was not deception in the content of the statements but rather deception regarding the identity of the speaker. This suggests that it is unnecessary to craft a government regulation, consistent with the First Amendment, that specifically targets deliberate lies. Rather, the proper response is to craft

---

[22] *See* Bluman v. Fed. Election Comm'n, 800 F. Supp. 2d 281, 288 (D.D.C. 2011), *aff'd*, 565 U.S. 1104 (2012) ("It follows, therefore, that the United States has a compelling interest for purposes of First Amendment analysis in limiting the participation of foreign citizens in activities of American democratic self-government, and in thereby preventing foreign influence over the U.S. political process.").

[23] Joshua S. Sellers, *Legislating Against Lying in Campaigns and Elections*, 71 Okla. L. Rev. 141, 157 (2018) (noting that "foreign nationals are prohibited from making contributions and expenditures," so "it naturally follows that their right to engage in intentionally false speech expressly advocating for or against the election of a candidate may be similarly regulated").

[24] *Id.*

a government regulation that goes after the identity of the speaker and requires disclosure of the foreign source of the speaker.

The most prominent example of a First Amendment case that discussed a government regulation designed to target deliberate falsehoods is *United States v. Alvarez*, which struck down the Stolen Valor Act.[25] In that case, the Court concluded that Congress could not penalize individuals who falsely claim to have been the recipients of military medals or honors.[26] Although the fractured set of opinions left uncertain the fate of the proposition that deliberate lies are not subject to special First Amendment protection, the plurality opinion noted that the court has held that falsehoods interfere with "the truth-seeking function of the market-place of ideas," but only when criminal falsehoods (e.g. perjury or the like) involved speech that involve a "legally cognizable harm."[27] In response to the Court's decision, Congress amended the Stolen Valor Act to limit the crime to cases that involved "obtaining money, property, or other tangible benefit" – the legally cogniz-able harm that the Court identified as key in *Alvarez*. When this criterion is applied to election speech, it seems clear that targeting election speech that contains deliberate falsehoods would only raise the specter of First Amendment scrutiny. The better solution is to design a regulation that is narrowly tailored to identifying and labeling foreign political speech rather than prohibiting deceptive political speech.

2. THE RIGHT TO RECEIVE FOREIGN SPEECH

The more plausible avenue for constitutional protection for foreign political speech involves focusing on the *recipient* of the political message. Even if a foreigner located outside the United States does not have a First Amendment right to engage in political speech, perhaps individuals within the United States have a First Amendment right to receive or consume that extraterritorial speech.[28] With this change in perspective, the constitutional protection comes not from speaking but

---

[25] 567 U.S. 709 (2012).

[26] For a discussion of the First Amendment protection of deliberate deception, see Jonathan D. Varat, *Truth, Courage, and Other Human Dispositions: Reflections on Falsehoods and the First Amendment*, 71 Okla. L. Rev. 35, 39 (2018) (noting that "until 2012 the Supreme Court had not extended First Amendment protection to lies").

[27] For more discussion of the implication of Alvarez for prohibiting deceptive political speech, see Thai, *supra* note 20, at 304 (concluding that the First Amendment might permit "narrow regulations of false political speech, including fake news and other misleading speech from abroad, to prevent the public in general and voters in particular from being misled" but also conceding that "the needle would – and should – be especially difficult to thread given the risk of censorship").

[28] See Zick, *supra* note 21, at 949–50 (noting that "Supreme Court and lower court precedents ... indicate that citizens enjoy only limited cross-border expressive and religious liberties"). Zick sum-marizes the rights that have been formally recognized by federal courts: "(1) a right to receive foreign political propaganda that is addressed to them so long as it has made it into the hands of U.S. postal officials, (2) a limited right to distribute foreign political propaganda inside the United States, (3) no First Amendment right to travel abroad even for expressive purposes, (4) limited rights of access and

from listening, as it were, on the theory that the right to consume particular speech is just as important to democracy as the right to engage in speech in the first place. Speech is a two-way communication between speaker and listener and the First Amendment arguably protects the relationship between them, without which speech is impossible.

Outright censorship of extraterritorial political speech would be problematic if it infringes on the right of Americans to consume that political speech. For example, in *Lamont*, the Supreme Court overturned a postal service censorship regime that interdicted and confiscated inbound foreign mail if its content was deemed to be communist political propaganda. The Supreme Court concluded that the interdiction program infringed on the constitutional rights of Americans to receive the extraterritorial speech. It was insignificant that the speaker (or author) was located outside the United States; it was enough for the reader to be located in the United States to trigger the protections of the First Amendment.[29] As the Court noted:

> We rest on the narrow ground that the addressee in order to receive his mail must request in writing that it be delivered. This amounts in our judgment to an unconstitutional abridgment of the addressee's First Amendment rights. The addressee carries an affirmative obligation which we do not think the Government may impose on him. This requirement is almost certain to have a deterrent effect, especially as respects those who have sensitive positions. Their livelihood may be dependent on a security clearance. Public officials like school-teachers who have no tenure, might think they would invite disaster if they read what the Federal Government says contains the seeds of treason. Apart from them, any addressee is likely to feel some inhibition in sending for literature which federal officials have condemned as "communist political propaganda." The regime of this Act is at war with the "uninhibited, robust, and wide-open" debate and discussion that are contemplated by the First Amendment.[30]

Arguably the style of argument from *Lamont* might apply to social media electioneering as well. Although a Russian individual might not have a First Amendment right to engage in political speech aimed at the American marketplace of ideas, an American social media user might have a First Amendment right to receive social media postings on political matters. This view might apply both to political

distribution with regard to U.S. propaganda distributed abroad, (5) limited rights to speak to and associate with aliens located abroad, and (6) limited cross-border free exercise rights." *Id.* It should be noted that this is a list of currently recognized rights; Zick argues, as a normative matter, for a more expansive "cosmopolitan" view of the First Amendment with greater extraterritorial reach.

[29] *See also* Martin v. City of Struthers, 319 U.S. 141, 143 (1943) ("This freedom embraces the right to distribute literature and necessarily protects the right to receive it."); Stanley v. Georgia, 394 U.S. 557, 564 (1969) ("It is now well established that the Constitution protects the right to receive information and ideas.").

[30] *See* Lamont v. Postmaster General, 381 U.S. 301, 306 (1965) (first-amendment right to receive foreign mail free from inspection, concluding that "Just as the licensing or taxing authorities ... sought to control the flow of ideas to the public, so here federal agencies regulate the flow of mail.").

advertisements as well as social media postings. If accepted, this argument would effectively unwind any boundary regulation that prohibits outsiders from engaging in political speech designed to be consumed by American audiences.

Based on *Lamont* and its underlying logic, several scholars have argued that there is a general constitutional right to receive foreign speech in most contexts.[31] However, even those scholars recognize that certain regulatory responses might be consistent with a First Amendment right to receive foreign speech, including social media efforts designed to combat the pernicious effect of fake news.[32] The permissibility of regulation flows from the fact that "the disclosure of political speech by foreign nations, particularly in the electoral context, seems consistent with the truth-seeking and self-governance functions of the First Amendment."[33]

The right to receive foreign speech is not absolute and may be subject to regulation, as long as the regulations survive strict scrutiny. For example, if the right to receive foreign speech were absolute, it would entail absurd consequences. In the immigration context, an absolute right to receive foreign speech would require the government to issue a visa to any individual who wished to speak in the United States. On this theory, denying entry to the person would infringe on the right of Americans to consume the speech of the visitor as would be the case if, for example, the visitor was scheduled to give a speech or lecture at a conference.[34] But clearly the Constitution does not and cannot subordinate immigration law entirely to the First

---

[31] *See* Joseph Thai, *The Right to Receive Foreign Speech*, 71 OKLA. L. REV. 269, 314 (2018) (stating that "open access to foreign information and ideas seems generally consistent with the commonly identified functions of the First Amendment to further truth-seeking, democratic self-governance, and self-realization"); Zick, *supra* note 21, at 945 ("traditional free speech justifications, particularly those concerned with domestic self-governance, were designed to apply to speech by citizens located within the United States who are communicating with other citizens inside the United States").

[32] *See* Thai, *supra* note 31, at 317 (suggesting that "at a minimum, online platforms should work to uncover speech affiliated with foreign states and disclose that affiliation to users" and noting that "[p]latforms are already attempting to do so voluntarily, and most likely could be required to do so").

[33] *Id.* (quoting the Supreme Court's statement in *Citizens United*, 558 U.S. 310, 371, permitting "the electorate to make informed decisions and give proper weight to different speakers and messages").

[34] This argument was rejected in *Kleindienst v. Mandel*, 408 U.S. 753, 768–9 (1972) ("Appellees' First Amendment argument would prove too much. In almost every instance of an alien excludable ... there are probably those who would wish to meet and speak with him. The ideas of most such aliens might not be so influential as those of Mandel, nor his American audience so numerous, nor the planned discussion forums so impressive. But the First Amendment does not protect only the articulate, the well known, and the popular. Were we to endorse the proposition that governmental power to withhold a waiver must yield whenever a bona fide claim is made that American citizens wish to meet and talk with an alien excludable under s 212(a)(28), one of two unsatisfactory results would necessarily ensue. Either every claim would prevail, in which case the plenary discretionary authority Congress granted the Executive becomes a nullity, or courts in each case would be required to weigh the strength of the audience's interest against that of the Government in refusing a waiver to the particular alien applicant, according to some as yet undetermined standard. The dangers and the undesirability of making that determination on the basis of factors such as the size of the audience or the probity of the speaker's ideas are obvious. Indeed, it is for precisely this reason that the waiver decision has, properly, been placed in the hands of the Executive.").

Amendment right to consume speech from foreigners or to associate with them in person.

There are two major reasons why social media regulation would be consistent with the right to receive speech. The first is that social media regulation, unlike the censorship program in *Lamont*, would not be designed to destroy the offending speech. It would be a pure labeling regime. Foreign users would still be able to speak their mind on social media platforms and Americans would still have access to this speech. However, the additional factor is the question of anonymity. As we saw above, the First Amendment protects anonymity to a certain extent, because the right to speak anonymously is often integral to free speech; a requirement to speak without anonymity will often chill speech and dampen political participation. Persons are naturally and understandably fearful of negative reactions to their speech and often fear the consequences of expressing unpopular beliefs, whether those consequences flow from the government or just from a social community. As such, anonymous speech has First Amendment value. Adding anonymity to the mix suggests, perhaps, that American social media users have a right to receive *anonymous* speech over the Internet and that any regulation that dampens anonymous speech would violate the First Amendment.

However, it is doubtful that the proposed social media regulation is, in any meaningful way, a complete barrier to anonymity. The labeling regime simply requires the labeling of foreign speech as such. The regulation does not require that social media content be identified by name and does not require that social media firms censor content that is not identified by name. Rather, it simply directs social media firms to label foreign-sourced material. To argue that this is unconstitutional would require arguing that American social media users have a constitutional right to receive foreign speech whose foreign origin is cloaked behind a veil of secrecy, which is doubtful. The content of the foreign speech is not being restricted – simply labeled.[35] This is a far cry from the censorship at issue in *Lamont*.

Furthermore, anonymity is not an absolute value, as campaign finance disclosures make clear. Donors have a First Amendment right to give money to political campaigns although they do not have a right to do so anonymously; it is perfectly consistent with the First Amendment to require political campaigns to publicly disclose their donors, even if doing so might discourage some individuals from donating money if they fear negative blowback for those donations. The Supreme Court has long recognized that the anti-corruption rationale, articulated in *Buckley*, justifies a campaign finance regulation that necessarily infringes on the right to participate anonymously in the political system through anonymous campaign

---

[35] For a similar argument that such labeling would be constitutional, see Joseph Thai, *The Right to Receive Foreign Speech*, 71 OKLA. L. REV. 269, 318 (2018) (noting that "speaker identity generally can be a valuable indicator to listeners of credibility, quality, knowledge, motivation, and reliability, and the identity of a foreign-state speaker can greatly impact each of these trust factors").

donations. Similarly, the entire apparatus of federal regulations pertaining to lobbying is based on the idea that individuals do not have an unqualified right to anonymously express and receive speech designed to lobby federal officials. If anonymity were required for all cases of political speech, lobbying could not be regulated in its current form.[36]

Of course, social media speech is not the same as campaign donations, and the anti-corruption rationale does not apply with equal force to social media communications as it does to the political donations at issue in *Buckley*. Indeed, *Buckley* was based on the idea that political *spending* should remain unregulated because it did not, and does not, implicate the anti-corruption rationale in the same way as direct campaign *donations*. To the extent that *Buckley* rejected or sidestepped an anti-distortion rationale, this might prove problematic for the constitutionality of social media regulation. Indeed, the best way of justifying the social media regulation is to view it as having an anti-distortion rationale. Foreign speech has a distortionary effect on a political discourse that should be tethered to the American polity; foreign speech risks undermining the very concept of democratic self-governance. To the extent that the Supreme Court has rejected the anti-distortion rationale, one might worry that this is a harbinger of what is to come – a rejection of all campaign regulations applied to foreign speech based on an expansive reading of the First Amendment.

This would be a hasty conclusion. The reason why the Supreme Court has focused exclusively on an anti-corruption rationale is simply because each of its cases has focused on the domestic context. The Court has consistently separated the domestic from the foreign and indicated that the ban on foreign participation is a wholly different affair. If forced to explicitly consider the fate of foreign participation, the Court would likely recognize that there are other values at stake, in addition to the anti-corruption rationale, such as anti-distortion.

Another reason why the prohibition against anonymous donations is not unconstitutional is because it is a content-neutral regulation. The problem with the censorship in *Lamont* was that the government specifically targeted communist propaganda for screening and censorship. In contrast, the proposed social regulation would be content neutral insofar as any foreign-sourced speech would be subject to the same regulation. The political viewpoint in the social media posting would be irrelevant. The only discrimination would be between foreign and domestic speech – a distinction that is based, not on content, but rather on a desire to protect the integrity of elections from foreign interference, rather than a desire to suppress or limit one particular viewpoint.[37] That makes social media labeling far more compelling than the blatant political censorship at issue in *Lamont*.

---

[36] *See* United States v. Harriss, 347 U.S. 612, 625 (1954) (concluding that "Congress . . . is not constitutionally forbidden to require the disclosure of lobbying activities").

[37] Protecting the integrity of the democratic process should be a legitimate governmental enterprise and consistent with the First Amendment. *See* Helen Norton, *(At Least) Thirteen Ways of Looking at*

3. LABELING, DISCLOSURE, AND COMPELLED SPEECH

Since the social media regulation involves the labeling of foreign accounts, it presents unique issues of First Amendment law that are not implicated in other contexts. The government frequently requires disclosures and labels as a regulatory solution to a particular problem and in many cases the individual who is required to include the disclosure or label objects to the compulsory label as a violation of free speech. These are cases of "compelled speech" wherein the government places words in the mouths of a particular speaker – in one sense the opposite of a restriction of speech but no less problematic from the perspective of the First Amendment.

The government has usually prevailed in defending labeling requirements in the context of commercial speech. Consequently, the Supreme Court has blessed required labels on foods, drugs, and associated advertisements. Though the Supreme Court has long since abandoned the antiquated view that commercial speech is unprotected by the First Amendment, it is also not the case that compelled speech in the commercial speech area triggers strict scrutiny. Instead, these cases are usually decided under a standard of intermediate scrutiny – requiring the government to articulate an important interest in crafting the regulations. In the case of required labels in the food and drug context, the government interest is usually preventing consumer deception – essentially an informational interest – so that consumers can make safe and healthy decisions. These regulations do not force the consumers to make a particular choice but rather give the consumers the relevant information to nudge them towards better choices.[38] For this reason, compelled speech in the context of commercial speech receives a lower level of scrutiny than political speech.[39]

However, the government has had a much rougher go at it when it comes to compelled speech claims for political speech, which receive a higher level of scrutiny than cases of commercial speech. For example, in *West Virginia State Board of Education v. Barnette*, the Supreme Court concluded that the state could not force students to salute the flag or recite the pledge of allegiance, both of which were allegedly justified by a government interest in creating national

---

Election Lies, 71 OKLA. L. REV. 117, 121 (2018) (noting that "Even more important, foreign speakers' lies to influence American elections to their own advantage threaten especially grave harm to key constitutional values – particularly if we understand the First Amendment's primary purpose as protecting speech that facilitates the United States' democratic self-governance").

[38] *See* Nigel Barrella, *First Amendment Limits on Compulsory Labeling*, 71 FOOD & DRUG L.J. 519, 541 (2016) (suggesting that the compelled speech cases "can instead be analyzed as concluding that the government may not use compulsory labels to *tell* consumers what to do" but the government "may only *inform* consumers and allow them to make up their own minds").

[39] *See* Zauderer v. Office of Disciplinary Counsel of Supreme Court of Ohio, 471 U.S. 626, 651 (1985) ("The State has attempted only to prescribe what shall be orthodox in commercial advertising, and its prescription has taken the form of a requirement that appellant include in his advertising purely factual and uncontroversial information about the terms under which his services will be available.").

unity.[40] This example of compelled speech was too baldly political for the First Amendment to countenance.[41] It was also not content-neutral because students were required to adopt speech that articulated a particular viewpoint.

Similarly, and predictably, the Supreme Court declared unconstitutional New Hampshire's mandatory "Live Free or Die" motto on car license plates. In that case, although the government had a strong interest in requiring license plates, the government could not articulate a compelling interest for requiring a particular message on those license plates.[42] Like *Barnette*, the *Wooley* case involved an attempt to put a specific political message in the mouths of state residents with automobiles. When described in this way, it is not surprising that the Court could not let the compelled speech stand.[43]

In *Miami Herald v. Tornillo*, the Court struck down a compulsory access law that required newspapers to grant equal space to political candidates to counter the speech of their opponents – essentially an attempt to create a right of equal access for election speech in newspapers.[44] The problem with the regulation was that it ran straight into the editorial discretion of newspaper editors to decide what content to publish in their newspapers; compelling them to print certain words, even if doing so did not involve an endorsement of those views, involved an impermissible hijacking of the editorial independence of the newspaper. This result is particularly note-worthy because the regulation was arguably content neutral and inspired by a government interest in giving the public access to competing viewpoints. In passing the law, the state was trying to protect the integrity of political deliberations

[40] 319 U.S. 624, 633 (1943) ("Here it is the State that employs a flag as a symbol of adherence to government as presently organized. It requires the individual to communicate by word and sign his acceptance of the political ideas it thus bespeaks. Objection to this form of communication when coerced is an old one, well known to the framers of the Bill of Rights.").

[41] 319 U.S. 624, 642 ("If there is any fixed star in our constitutional constellation, it is that no official, high or petty, can prescribe what shall be orthodox in politics, nationalism, religion, or other matters of opinion or force citizens to confess by word or act their faith therein.").

[42] Wooley v. Maynard, 430 U.S. 705, 716 (1977) ("We must also determine whether the State's counter-vailing interest is sufficiently compelling to justify requiring appellees to display the state motto on their license plates. The two interests advanced by the State are that display of the motto (1) facilitates the identification of passenger vehicles, and (2) promotes appreciation of history, individualism, and state pride . . . . where the State's interest is to disseminate an ideology, no matter how acceptable to some, such interest cannot outweigh an individual's First Amendment right to avoid becoming the courier for such message.").

[43] For a discussion of the complexity of the First Amendment as it applies to license plates, see Caroline Mala Corbin, Mixed Speech: When Speech Is Both Private and Governmental, 83 N.Y.U. L. Rev. 605, 609 (2008).

[44] Miami Herald Pub. Co. v. Tornillo, 418 U.S. 241, 258 (1974) ("Even if a newspaper would face no additional costs to comply with a compulsory access law and would not be forced to forgo publication of news or opinion by the inclusion of a reply, the Florida statute fails to clear the barriers of the First Amendment because of its intrusion into the function of editors. A newspaper is more than a passive receptacle or conduit for news, comment, and advertising. The choice of material to go into a newspaper, and the decisions made as to limitations on the size and content of the paper, and treatment of public issues and public officials – whether fair or unfair – constitute the exercise of editorial control and judgment.").

that has been the topic of our discussions. If the government cannot compel a newspaper to give equal space to particular political candidates, in order to give the public access to the information that it needs to promote a political deliberation, then it is unclear (at least at first glance) how the government has the authority to require social media companies to label foreign accounts, especially where the latter is justified by a need to protect the deliberative process.

Finally, in *Turner Broadcasting v. F.C.C.*, the Supreme Court upheld "must carry" rules that require cable operators to carry local and public.[45] In this case, the must carry rules were upheld because, inter alia, the regulations were content neutral. Cable operators were not required to display a particular message but were, instead, simply required to carry some channels from a particular category (local and public channels), irrespective of what content was broadcast on these channels. The primary reason for the government's victory is that content-neutral regulations that have an incidental burden on speech only receive intermediate scrutiny.

In a sense, neither of these two categories of cases are good paradigms for the social media regulation requiring labeling of foreign accounts. On the one hand, the regulation involves more than commercial speech and has far more political impact than requiring a particular label on a carton of milk. On the other hand, though, the compelled speech is far less burdensome than requiring someone to recite the pledge of allegiance, especially where they might disagree with it, or requiring them to display a particular political message on a license plate. The social media labeling regime is in the middle.

In some ways, the closest thing in terms of a labeling regime that would apply to all content, and in that sense is content neutral, would be the 1990s debate over internet filtering systems (such as PICS and POWDER).[46] These systems created protocols that helped internet search pages create filters, which the user could select, that would filter out content that would not be appropriate for younger views.[47] The filter depends on each page having a label that tags the page with a designation that allows the filtering to occur. The primary usage for such a system was parents or teachers at a school. But even users of a mature age might not want to see the content and therefore the filter had a value for populations other than teachers and parents.

---

[45]   Turner Broad. Sys., Inc. v. F.C.C., 512 U.S. 622, 643–4 (1994) ("Insofar as they pertain to the carriage of full-power broadcasters, the must-carry rules, on their face, impose burdens and confer benefits without reference to the content of speech. Although the provisions interfere with cable operators' editorial discretion by compelling them to offer carriage to a certain minimum number of broadcast stations, the extent of the interference does not depend upon the content of the cable operators' programming.").

[46]   PICS stands for Platform for Internet Content Selection. POWDER stands for Protocol for Web Description Resources.

[47]   For a discussion, see R. Polk Wagner, *Filters and the First Amendment*, 83 MINN. L. REV. 755, 793–4 (1999) ("The second, and I suspect more difficult, issue for the PICS-enforcing statute is whether the Court will find it to be 'effective' enough. The government will have to convince the Court that the labeling requirement is going to work at least as effectively as any other equally-restrictive alternative.").

This scheme is much closer to the social media regulation because, in a sense, it involves labeling particular content with a label that might be useful for consumers of the content but could be considered an example of compelled speech – at least if the labeling was required by the government. However, the federal government has not required its use and therefore any potential compelled speech problems associated with it have not been litigated.

The compelled speech doctrine also rears its head in the disclosure context, particularly campaign financing. According to *Buckley v. Valeo*, the government has a compelling interest in preventing corruption and may enact mandatory disclosure regimes, but only in cases that involve "express advocacy."[48] If this standard is applied to social media regulation, then it would appear to not justify the social media regulation of labeling foreign accounts. The regulation would capture within its ambit many communications that do not constitute express advocacy as that phrase was used in *Buckley*. However, it should be noted that the compelled disclosure in campaign finance law is far more intrusive – it requires disclosure of the person's name and amount donated to the campaign – an intrusive regulation to be sure. However, social media labeling does not require disclosure of any identifying information – simply the foreign source of the account. It is therefore not analogous to the typical campaign finance disclosure regime.

Two other doctrines might pose "compelled speech" problems for the social media regulation: anonymity and the right to free association. First, on the question of anonymity, one might argue that social media regulation would prevent users from engaging in anonymous political speech on the Internet because their identity as foreigners would no longer be secret. The Supreme Court has consistently recognized the value of anonymity in protecting political speech, for a variety of reasons. In *McIntyre*, the Supreme Court overturned an Ohio statute prohibiting anonymous campaign literature.[49] The decision was particularly significant because the court distinguished *Valeo* and noted that the Ohio regulation was not limited to deceptive or libelous speech but applied to all speech, in much the same way that social media labeling might limit the possibility for anonymous speech regardless of whether the particular statement in the posting is deceptive or not. The value of anonymity is arguably even more important on the Internet than it is in the corporeal world, since one feature of the Internet is that users are able to communicate anonymously about sensitive topics.[50]

---

[48] *See* Buckley v. Valeo, 424 U.S. 1, 47 (1976).

[49] McIntyre v. Ohio Elections Comm'n, 514 U.S. 334, 341–2 (1995) ("The decision in favor of anonymity may be motivated by fear of economic or official retaliation, by concern about social ostracism, or merely by a desire to preserve as much of one's privacy as possible.").

[50] *See* Catherine Crump, *Data Retention: Privacy, Anonymity, and Accountability Online*, 56 STAN. L. REV. 191, 228 (2003) ("In summary, the values the Court has articulated in support of anonymous speech in real space hold true for the space of the Internet as well. By providing cheap access to anonymous speech, the Internet limits government power by strengthening the voices of the poor and

Second, the right of association, particularly the right of anonymous association, might be impacted by the proposed regulation. Seeing the issue in this way helps bring the rights of the American user to the forefront; it is not the right of the Russian user that is compromised, but rather the right of the American user to associate with anonymous foreigner users.[51] The Supreme Court has certainly recognized that the right to associate anonymously is protected by the First Amendment and is particularly important with regard to unpopular or controversial associations. For example, in *NAACP v. Alabama*, the court declared unconstitutional a registration regulation that required the NAACP to disclose its members to the government.[52] By extension, one might argue that a regulation that requires social media users to be tagged as foreign or domestic makes it harder for people to associate anonymously on Twitter, by following the accounts that they wish to follow, especially if there is a negative connotation associated with being a foreign account.

In conclusion, it is clear that social media regulations would have some impact on anonymity and association.[53] At the same time, though, it is important not to fall victim to the naturalistic fallacy. Some modest changes to the norms of anonymity on social media platforms would promote election integrity while at the same time permitting the free exchange of information and political opinion. Social media users would still be able to correspond with any and all individuals on the Internet. Moreover, the regulations would be content-neutral. Even under strict scrutiny analysis, the regulations should prevail under the First Amendment.

4. FREEDOM OF SPEECH UNDER INTERNATIONAL HUMAN RIGHTS LAW

Up until now, the analysis has focused exclusively on potential constitutional constraints that might prevent the United States from enacting meaningful regulations to combat foreign election interference on social media platforms. However, election interference is not just an American concern but a global phenomenon affecting many democratic societies. Recent news reports have indicated that not

---

unpopular. Because it makes anonymity easy, the Internet lowers the risks associated with contributing to political debate.").

[51] *See* Katherine J. Strandburg, *Freedom of Association in A Networked World: First Amendment Regulation of Relational Surveillance*, 49 B.C. L. Rev. 741, 745 (2008) ("Digital technology has transformed the ways in which civic and political associations are formed and operate.").

[52] Nat'l Ass'n for Advancement of Colored People v. State of Ala. ex rel. Patterson, 357 U.S. 449, 462 (1958) ("It is hardly a novel perception that compelled disclosure of affiliation with groups engaged in advocacy may constitute as effective a restraint on freedom of association as the forms of governmental action in the cases above were thought likely to produce upon the particular constitutional rights there involved.").

[53] *See* Strandburg, *supra* note 51, at 751 (noting that "[t]he anonymity (or, more accurately, pseudonymity) of Internet communication also facilitates the emergence of groups that might never otherwise have formed because potential members might have been deterred from participating until the involvement of a threshold number of others was assured").

just Russia but also China and Iran have conducted substantial information operations over the Internet. Moreover, it may one day come to pass that even small states – states without significant military power – use information operations to compensate for their lack of military strength. If we are indeed entering an era of covert global electioneering, it is crucial to understand not just the domestic sources of law that might limit election regulations but also international sources of law that might similarly constrain domestic regulations.[54] In particular, international human rights law codifies a right to freedom of speech, as well as a right to freedom of association. As the following analysis will show, these rights in some ways track their U.S. counterparts but in important ways depart substantially from American jurisprudence. The result of this analysis is that the international rights are far less dramatic than the First Amendment and therefore the international instruments pose even less of a constraint than the U.S. Constitution.

Article 19 of the ICCPR codifies the right of free speech, while freedom of association is codified in article 22. One notable feature of article 19 is that it explicitly codifies the right to "seek, receive and impart information and ideas of all kinds, regardless of frontiers, either orally, in writing or in print, in the form of art, or through any other media of his choice." Unfortunately, the ICCPR does not have a binding adjudicatory mechanism, so there is little international case law applying those provisions to particular government regulations. At first glance, the use of the term "frontiers" suggests a global application, although this is not surprising since the right being elucidated is an international one. However, the text of article 19 makes clear that restrictions on the right of free speech are permitted if necessary for the protection of the rights of others, while article 22 makes clear that restrictions on association are permitted if necessary in a "democratic society" – a phrase that is echoed in other human rights treaties.

The free speech and association provisions in the European Convention on Human Rights and Fundamental Freedoms (ECHR) have generated a substantial amount of litigation, both in domestic courts and at the European Court in Strasbourg. Consequently, any election regulations contemplated by European states would have to be consistent with the ECHR provisions on free speech and association and would be struck down if they are not in compliance. In many respects, these European provisions dovetail with their counterparts in the ICCPR.

For three reasons that will now be explained in greater detail, the European Convention is less of a constraint than one might otherwise expect. First, the application of rights in the Convention are subject to a "margin of appreciation." Second, freedom of speech is analyzed in the context of necessity – a form of proportionality review that explicitly permits balancing of competing interests. Third, restrictions on free speech are permitted when necessary to protect

---

[54]   See Timothy Zick, *Territoriality and the First Amendment: Free Speech at – and beyond – Our Borders*, 85 NOTRE DAME L. REV. 1543, 1592 (2010) (asking the similar question "whether the First Amendment might be characterized as a universal human right rather than a domestic limitation").

a democratic society – a legal constraint that fits well with the goal of protecting election integrity. Each of these elements will now be addressed.

The "margin of appreciation" is the term used by the European Court to describe the deference that it gives to state parties to solve problems on their own in unique ways.[55] The margin of appreciation is incorporated into the final decision-making process when the Court engages in proportionality review. To an American ear, the term "margin of appreciation" sounds unfamiliar, but in one sense it is not that much different from the concept of a standard of review. American constitutional analysis is divided into three review categories: rationality review, intermediate scrutiny, and strict scrutiny. Margin of appreciation simply reflects a similar idea that the court will give some deference to state parties and will not disturb their regulations unless the Court finds, pursuant to its balancing analysis, that the regulation is substantially more intrusive than it needs to be when judged against the governmental interest. The margin of appreciation is a recognition that what is required in one society might not be required in another and that while the European Convention imposes a minimum floor below which no European state may regulate, the Convention does not require each state to craft and impose the same regulations. The doctrine recognizes and preserves pluralism.

As noted above, restrictions on political (rather than commercial) speech receive strict scrutiny in American courts. In contrast, the ECHR applies the margin of appreciation in all cases, including speech cases, though its application differs depending on the context. As a comparative matter, though, the level of scrutiny applied by a European Court is likely to be less severe than an American court applying strict scrutiny (especially in the free speech context).

Second, the European Court generally decides all human rights cases using the methodology of proportionality review. Proportionality requires the Court to identify the government interest and then decide whether the regulation was necessary to achieve that interest. In making this determination, the Court asks whether the regulation was "necessary" to achieve the government interest, which usually means the "least restrictive" regulation possible.[56] In one sense, this sounds no different from First Amendment "overbreadth" doctrine, which dictates that a regulation cannot be broader than necessary.[57] But the difference is that the application of strict scrutiny by American courts produces a form of First Amendment absolutism, whereby freedom of speech trumps competing interests and rights, making it very difficult for a government regulation to prevail where it infringes on an expressive right. In contrast, European proportionality review takes place against a general presumption that restrictions on speech will be upheld where necessary to achieve

---

[55] *See generally* ANDREW LEGG, THE MARGIN OF APPRECIATION IN INTERNATIONAL HUMAN RIGHTS LAW (Oxford University Press, 2012).

[56] *See generally* YUTAKA ARAI-TAKAHASHI, THE MARGIN OF APPRECIATION DOCTRINE AND THE PRINCIPLE OF PROPORTIONALITY IN THE JURISPRUDENCE OF THE ECHR (Intersentia, 2001).

[57] *See* Henry Paul Monaghan, *Overbreadth*, 1981 SUPREME CT. REV. 1 (1981).

a legitimate governmental objective, even if that regulation is content-driven. So, for example, regulations against hate speech or Holocaust denial are permitted in European societies as a proportional response to a social problem, while U.S. courts would view such regulations as impermissible constraints on the expression of controversial opinions.[58] The result is that many content-based restrictions would be upheld in Europe that would be struck down in the United States.

Finally, and most importantly, the ECHR includes a provision allowing restrictions on the freedom of speech that are necessary in a "democratic" society; the provision then articulates the content of a democracy-enhancing regulation. According to the ECHR, free speech regulations must be prescribed by law, must serve a legitimate purpose, and must be necessary in a democratic society. Article 10(2) lists the following purposes: "in the interests of national security, territorial integrity or public safety, for the prevention of disorder or crime, for the protection of health or morals, for the protection of the reputation or rights of others, for preventing the disclosure of information received in confidence, or for maintaining the authority and impartiality of the judiciary." Some scholars have argued that this provision provides a justification for the regulation of "undemocratic" speech.[59]

At first glance, the list of permissible purposes sounds limited. On closer inspection, though, it becomes clear that the list includes several catch-all provisions that are truly expansive. The most notable provision states that restrictions on free speech are permissible if they are necessary to protect the "rights of others." The rights of others are not further limited, making clear that freedom of expression, far from standing above the rest, is simply one among many rights and remains in conversation with the other rights articulated in the Convention. No similar language of balancing is present in the First Amendment, which is expressed in absolute terms: the government may pass no law abridging the freedom of speech. In contrast, the European Convention makes abundantly clear that freedom of speech must be balanced against other rights in the Convention and that a government is permitted to restrict speech in order to protect another right outlined in the Convention. This

---

[58] For example, in *Pavel Ivanov v. Russia*, Application No. 35222/04, the European Court concluded that Russia could convict an individual of incitement to racial hatred for distributing an anti-Semitic pamphlet. The Court concluded that the applicant "sought through his publications to incite hatred towards the Jewish people. Such a general and vehement attack on one ethnic group is in contradiction with the Convention's underlying values, notably tolerance, social peace and non-discrimination. Consequently, the Court finds that, by reason of Article 17 of the Convention, the applicant may not benefit from the protection afforded by Article 10 of the Convention." *Id.* at para. 1. This case would not have come out the same way in the United States. While incitement to commit violence could be prosecuted in the United States in some contexts, incitement to racial hatred would not.

[59] *See, e.g.*, Caroline Uyttendaele and Joseph Dumortier, *Free Speech on the Information Superhighway: European Perspectives*, 16 J. MARSHALL J. COMPUTER & INFO. L. 905, 923 (1998) ("It might be stated as a general rule that when forms of speech strike at the heart of values deeply cherished in a free and democratic society, doctrinal space for regulation opens up. Indeed, certain expressions may, instead of helping to realize the fulfillment of democracy, undermine or endanger that realization.").

structure removes freedom of speech from its lofty perch as an absolute right and returns it to the realm of terrestrial rights that must accommodate, and be accommodated by, other rights.

One might be concerned that the European version of free speech is almost meaningless, because a government can almost always come up with an argument that its restriction is required to protect the rights of others. Possibly so, but it is important to remember the conceptual power of the concept of necessity. The government intrusion into the protected right (freedom of expression) is only permissible if it is truly necessary, that is, the least restrictive means for protecting the other right. If the restriction is not the least-restrictive alternative, it has slipped from the grasp of necessity and violated the European Convention.

It just remains to decide whether restrictions on election speech could possibly be justified under this scheme. The key to making this argument is to identify another right that is protected by the scheme, so that one can evaluate the balance between the two rights and see if the restriction is truly the least-restrictive means to protecting the other right. The European Convention states in Article 16 that nothing "in Articles 10, 11 and 14 shall be regarded as preventing the High Contracting Parties from imposing restrictions on the political activity of aliens." This makes abundantly clear that freedom of expression cannot be used as an argument in favor of prohibiting foreign electioneering. One hardly needs a complicated legal argument to demonstrate that states are entitled to prohibit aliens from participating in the political process. This would include not just the right to vote, but also the right to contribute financially in an election or the right to engage in other forms of electioneering. In terms of other rights articulated in the Convention, the Protocol to the Convention for the Protection of Human Rights and Fundamental Freedoms states in article 3 that "The High Contracting Parties undertake to hold free elections at reasonable intervals by secret ballot, under conditions which will ensure the free expression of the opinion of the people in the choice of the legislature."[60] Consequently, states may infringe the right to free speech if doing so is necessary to protect the rights of others, in this case the right to participate in a "free election" as protected by article 3 of the Protocol. Furthermore, article 3 explicitly makes a commitment to "conditions" that ensure the "free expression of the opinion of the *people*" – a reference to the connection between self-determination and democratic self-government that stands at the core of this research project. Prohibiting outsiders from participating in an election – or imposing restrictions on their speech – is consistent with the goal of ensuring that the result of the election will express the opinion of the people rather than the opinions of *other* peoples. This structure is far more explicit than anything in the U.S. Constitution regarding the relationship between free speech and democratic ideals.

---

[60] Famously, the U.S. Constitution includes the Guarantee Clause which "guarantees" the people a republic form of government, though the Supreme Court has concluded that the Guarantee Clause is nonjusticiable.

Applying this legal structure to social media regulation, it is clear that social media regulation falls within the ambit of article 3's obligation to conduct an election that expresses the will of the people. Indeed, the proposed regulation outlined in this book is a modest effort to combat foreign election interference by giving social media users information about the foreign source of accounts on the platform so that the deliberative process is not corrupted by outside voices. Furthermore, to the extent that this regulation distinguishes between domestic and foreign sources of information, this distinction is entirely consistent with the Convention's explicit authorization to prohibit aliens from participating in the political process. The proposed social media regulation, and other possible regulations similar to it, are narrowly tailored to solve a particular problem, and in fact stronger and more assertive regulations would probably fall within a state's margin of appreciation. The regulation does not prohibit speech but merely labels it as foreign; the regulation is the least restrictive means for protecting election integrity while preserving free expression to the maximum amount.

All of this adds up to the conclusion that while social media labeling would most likely be constitutional in the United States, its fate in the European context is in even less doubt. While freedom of speech is important in the European constellation of rights, both the Convention text and the jurisprudence that has emerged from it gives states much more freedom to enact democracy-enhancing regulations that might infringe on the right of free speech when compared to the United States. As such, it would be wrong for free speech advocates in either the United States or Europe to claim that social media regulations violate the right to free speech. Indeed, one advantage of the European rights framework is that it helps to clarify that human rights exist on both sides of the equation. The situation is not simply a government regulation on one hand, and an individual right (speech or expression) on the other. Instead, the European framework presents the legal analysis as a true conflict of rights, with a right to free expression on one hand and a right to participatory democracy on the other, balanced against each other.

CONCLUSION

This chapter has laid to rest one anxiety with regulating foreign social media electioneering. Sensible regulations would be consistent with the First Amendment and international human rights law. As the preceding analysis made clear, even the especially hazardous area of political speech is subject to regulation. The case for regulation is easiest under European and international human rights law, but even under the First Amendment, the government is not entirely prohibited from regulating political speech. These two sources of rights use different concepts and different methodologies, but at a deeper level of abstraction both spheres of law circle around a similar standard: government regulations are permissible as long as those regulations are narrowly tailored to achieve a legitimate government interest.

While the European framework is explicit about the fact that the government has a right to engage in actions to protect a "democratic" society, this notion is arguably implicit in the American scheme as well.

Of course, there might be other obstacles or costs associated with social media labeling – apart from the First Amendment issues. This chapter has simply addressed, and hopefully resolved, any First Amendment concerns, but it is important to remember that there are other considerations implicated by social media labeling. For example, there might be additional technical or social costs with the regulations and this chapter has not addressed these concerns. The goal of this chapter was simply to remove any concern that social media labeling would be unconstitutional under the First Amendment. I leave it to others to have a fuller conversation about the exact details of social media regulation. The goal here was simply to open up a space for conversation about social media regulations that might respond to the growing threat of foreign election interference. Other regulations might be possible or even preferable.

Social media labeling could occur in a number of ways. This chapter has focused on a federal requirement mandating the labeling. But another possibility is that the major social media platforms might voluntarily adopt mechanisms to fight foreign electioneering even in the absence of a federal mandate. Voluntary adoption of these or other mechanisms would avoid any First Amendment issue because there would be no state action. In other areas, social media platforms such as Facebook have voluntarily developed mechanisms and programs to respond to the problem of fake news and conspiracy theories promoted on social media. Since social media traffic is largely consolidated in a few major platforms, action by just a few companies could have a significant impact. While lawyers are often disposed towards formal regulations and statutory requirements, informal norms and industry standards can often achieve similar, or even better, results.

7

The Value of Criminal Prosecutions

INTRODUCTION

The best and most plausible antidote to the problem of foreign election interference is sunshine – inform the public immediately about the nature and content of the foreign election interference. This information should ideally reach the public in real time to unwind the negative damage caused by corrosive social media posts. Even public information may not be enough to negate the corrosive effect of widespread misinformation. A certain segment of the population will be primed to believe conspiracy theories and knowing that conspiracy theories are circulating on the Internet – promulgated by a foreign adversary – will not be enough to empower them to resist alluring conspiracies. However, the publicizing of the foreign involvement may be enough to allow *some* people to resist the information, which might be all that we can hope for. In life, sometimes we need to choose between the best among a landscape of imperfect solutions and this may be one of those moments.

Criminal prosecutions also play an important role in disclosing information to the public, as one part of a larger strategy of depriving foreign election interference of its effectiveness. This chapter focuses on the role that criminal prosecutions played during the Mueller investigation into Russian interference and how similar criminal investigations might be harnessed as a general response to election interference. Section 1 discusses, in a general way, how criminal investigations can help to keep the public informed about critical social problems – and the limitations of using the criminal justice system as a disclosure and transparency regime. Section 2 then analyzes the missteps made by the Obama Administration in failing to use criminal investigations – or any other meaningful tool – to provide meaningful disclosure to the public about the scope of Russian information operations conducted over social media platforms. The rest of the chapter then pivots to solutions and best practices that might harness the power of criminal investigations to disclose critical information to the public. In particular, Section 3 focuses on recent changes to the Justice Department policies regarding disclosure of foreign influence operations. As will be discussed below, many of these changes are laudable, though the changes did not go far enough to address the problem; the new policy contains so many caveats and exceptions that the policy may not actually achieve its stated goal: to increase disclosure of foreign operations. Finally, Section 4 looks at structural factors in the intelligence community to understand that community's hesitation about relying on the criminal justice system, and how this reluctance might be overcome in the future. This section notes that no single federal agency currently has primary authority for identifying, and defending against, foreign election interference. The chapter therefore ends with a question: Should Congress create a new independent agency or commission tasked with combating foreign election interference? Until that happens, however, the Justice Department needs to use criminal investigations to keep the public informed.

1. CRIMINAL PROSECUTIONS AS TRANSPARENCY

The great criminal law scholar Herbert Packer once wrote that criminal law was dominated by two paradigms: crime control and due process.[1] The first model, crime control, is the idea that society, and its government, has created a system of criminal justice in order to control crime – to put it crudely, to get people who commit crimes off the streets and into prison. The second model, due process, is the idea that the criminal justice system exists as a constraint on executive action – a judicial stop on unchecked power, ensuring that decisions about prosecution and incarceration are made fairly, based on evidence, and the rule of law. Crime control and due process stand in constant tension, both important in their own right, but also in eternal conversation with each other. In thinking about these models, one might be tempted to believe that criminal prosecutions are just about punishment and fairness, but in fact criminal prosecutions have important and far-reaching implications that can fundamentally reorder the relationship between individuals and the society that they live in. The Packer models are certainly capacious enough to accommodate these connections, though contemporary discourse often obscures them.

For example, criminal law theorists are fond of pointing out the expressive function of criminal punishment. Punishment can serve many functions: it can deter future lawbreaking, it can ensure that offenders receive their just deserts (retributivism), or both. It can also express society's view of the offender's conduct. That "expression" can be understood in many ways – it could be an expression of disapproval of the conduct, an expression of solidarity with the victim or victims, or an expression of disapproval of the offenders themselves, though this latter possibility is controversial because the criminal justice system is supposed to adjudicate

---

[1] See Herbert Packer, *Two Models of the Criminal Process*, 113 U. PA. L. REV. 1, 6 (1964) (developing "two competing systems of values," discussing the tension between two accounts that "attempt to give operational content to these conflicting schemes of values," and noting that "[j]ust as the models are not to be taken as describing real-world situations, so the values that underlie them are not to be regarded as expressing the values held by any one person").

allegations of criminal behavior or criminal conduct, rather than passing judgment on the character of individual defendants. In any event, expressivist theories of punishment have highlighted the communicative function of the criminal law: its capacity to express something or communicate a message from society to a diverse group of audiences: to the offender, to the victim, to future offenders, or to future victims.[2] Although the details of these accounts are often different, a common framework for them is that the criminal justice system can communicate a message from society to particular individuals.

While much of the expressivist program is no doubt correct, it has had one unfortunate byproduct: it has a tendency to crowd out additional accounts of the communicative functions of the criminal law. In the following paragraphs, I will lay out an account of the criminal law that allows and encourages the government to disclose and publicize to the public important information about what is happening in local communities and what the government is doing to address these problems. While it would seem as if communication to the public about these problems can and should happen through other avenues, the very public nature of the criminal justice system (the open court requirement) makes the criminal justice system an ideal venue for public disclosure of important information.

Despite their public nature, governments at all levels (federal, state, local) operate as massive bureaucracies. Information about some of their operations is classified or confidential (think, for example, of information about personnel decisions, or confidential deliberations of government officials that are exempted from the reach of open records statutes), but most of their operations are officially public in nature. From the perspective of the regular public, however, much of the supposedly "public" information is never released or, if it is released, is rarely digested by the public. There are multiple reasons for this phenomenon, but at least some of the reasons include the fact that bureaucratic information is hard to understand in lay terms. Also, the vast volume of raw public information makes it hard to focus on the truly consequential information. Significant information is often lost in a sea of data dumps. Newspaper editors and journalists often play a key role in acting as an intermediary to the public, sifting through the massive pile of information to find the significant information and then explaining its significance to the public. Unfortunately, changes in the economic marketplace (lack of advertising dollars, etc.), have decimated the local journalism industry, meaning that there are fewer newspaper, radio, and television reporters to perform this function. And although some websites have increased their hiring as these websites increase their market

---

[2] For a discussion of expressivism as a justification for punishment, see Dan M. Kahan, *What Do Alternative Sanctions Mean?*, 63 U. CHI. L. REV. 591, 597 (1996). For a discussion of expressivism in law generally, see Elizabeth S. Anderson and Richard H. Pildes, *Expressive Theories of Law: A General Restatement*, 148 U. PA. L. REV. 1503, 1504 (2000) (arguing that "expressive concerns figure into normative theories of individual conduct: what makes an action morally right depends on whether it expresses the appropriate valuations of (that is, attitudes toward) persons"). *Compare with* Matthew D. Adler, *Expressive Theories of Law: A Skeptical Overview*, 148 U. PA. L. REV. 1363 (2000).

share, with a few exceptions these websites do not perform a similar function as local newspaper reporters do. The result is that there are fewer individuals combing through public information and explaining its relevance to the public.

The criminal justice system plays an important role within this overall dynamic. Criminal prosecutions receive widespread attention, and moreover they take place in a context that is dramatic – the fate of an individual defendant being prosecuted by the government and punished by a court. The public not only has access to information about courtroom activities but, more importantly, the adversarial system makes stories about court cases much more digestible for the public. Narratives – stories – are important for understanding information, and the criminal justice system includes a built-in narrative with personal stakes for its characters: victims who seek vindication and justice, and defendants whose liberty is at stake depending on the outcome of the case. So, it is very easy for the public to understand information that comes out through the context of a criminal trial.

Of course, none of this is to suggest that the public has immediate and total access to everything that occurs in the criminal justice system. A few high-profile cases receive the greatest attention and low-level street crimes, especially drug transactions, receive little attention. Even though a defendant might be prosecuted for jumping a turnstile or selling a small amount of narcotics, no one will hear or read about the case because it contains none of the shock value of a high-profile murder case. Nonetheless, these street-level crimes, in the aggregate, raise important structural issues regarding broken windows policing and the daily life of residents in particular communities. This dynamic is particularly acute in many urban areas, where the criminal justice system is so massive, and the caseload so heavy, that the public rarely pays attention to thousands of low-level but important criminal cases. Urban life, even in the criminal justice system, yields a form of anonymity that can frustrate the goals of public disclosure.

Still, the criminal justice system in general is an important source of information for the public. Because of the cultural and legal expectation that courts will operate in a public and transparent fashion, the courts function as a natural entry point for the public to learn about the type of criminal behavior that is occurring in a community and the government's response to it. Indeed, to take just one example, the criminal justice system has provided the public in New York City with important information about the use of stop-and-frisk *Terry* stops by police officers. This information gave local activists the empirical tools they needed to advocate for a change in policy, to file lawsuits against the City of New York alleging constitutional violations and negotiate a successful resolution with city officials.[3] Part of the reason why information about stop-and-frisk activity was so easily accessible to the public was because the information was part of the criminal justice system.

---

[3] *See* Floyd v. City of New York, 959 F. Supp. 2d 668, 672 (S.D.N.Y. 2013).

Another example is the social problem of domestic violence. Information about complaints of domestic violence, including situations where the police respond to calls of distress for police or medical services, have transformed how experts and the public alike understand the contours of domestic violence. Some of these cases resulted in arrests, prosecution, and conviction, but even the cases where the police were called but no arrests were made were significant in themselves. In response to analysis, some police departments instituted new policies that required police officers to make arrests in these circumstances even if the police faced an "unco-operative" victim, that is, a victim who objected to the arrest of their partner and announced their intention not to cooperate with prosecutors. Experts and the public were able to advocate for changes in policy because they had access to important data through the criminal justice system. In addition to the empirical studies, the public learned about the significance of the problem – and the government's response to it – by reading press reports about domestic violence arrests. As scholars such as Jeannie Suk have noted, the application of the criminal law transformed what was once considered "private" behavior into a matter of public concern by inserting the machinery of the criminal justice system into private homes.[4] In this case, again, the public learned about the nature of a social problem only because the criminal justice system played an important role in publicizing the issues at hand.

Of course, I am not suggesting that issues not addressed by the criminal justice system are never publicized or never become matters of public concern. Of course not. There are plenty of examples of social or economic problems, and government responses to them, that are known to the public even without the involvement of the criminal justice system. This includes everything from tax policy to the regulation of food products to thousands of other government actions in between. The claim that I am defending is simply that as a comparative matter, the criminal justice system often makes public access to information easier and more compelling than it would be otherwise.

Applying this rubric to the problem of election interference, the thesis that I want to advance is that criminal investigation and criminal prosecution both have an important role to play in publicizing information about foreign election interfer-ence. This is not to say that criminal prosecution should be the only method of public disclosure. Indeed, prior chapters suggested that social media posts originat-ing from foreign sources should be labelled as foreign – a disclosure regime that would be far more sweeping than anything that could be accomplished in the

---

4   It should be noted that Professor Suk is somewhat critical of this development. *See* Jeannie Suk, *Criminal Law Comes Home*, 116 YALE L.J. 2, 66 (2006) ("A distinctive feature of the criminal law expansion described in this Article is the invocation of the public interest to justify the control of home space and intimate relationships within it. This expansion, often on the basis of an alleged misdemea-nor, takes place in a world in which 'violence' is defined down to include incidents not causing physical injury. Through it, the state excludes people from their homes, reallocates property interests, reorders intimate relationships, and imposes de facto divorce – without seeking the consent of the parties involved and through the coercive power of the criminal law.").

criminal justice system. Nonetheless, the publicity surrounding criminal justice investigations and prosecutions is an additional tool that could be used to get information about foreign election interference into the right hands – the public.

Even if individuals are never put on trial, convicted, or punished, the indictment itself has an important signaling function to the public. An indictment can provide information about the nature of the foreign involvement and the methods that the foreign actor used to infiltrate American political discourse. For example, if particular social media platforms were used to accomplish the interference, the details of these social media efforts will be outlined in the indictment. Although the public is not likely to read a lengthy and complex indictment, journalists will perform an important intermediary function to act as a conduit to the public.

One might object that a criminal indictment is not required to provide the press or the public with information about foreign election interference, especially if a trial is not going to take place. A government report or some other form of disclosure could accomplish the same task. This much is true, but it is only partially true. As a comparative matter, criminal prosecutions and indictments provide an *additional* level of public disclosure, one that is uniquely suited to getting crucial information into the public domain and to the attention of the public. Far more than any other organ of government, the judicial process attracts public attention. In the absence of a criminal prosecution, the public receives less information than they would otherwise about the underlying social problem and the government's response to it.

The indictments issued by the office of Special Counsel Robert Mueller support this conclusion. In the absence of the indictments issued by that office, the public would not have received as much information about, for example, the troll farm activity conducted by the IRA. Although this information was ultimately disclosed in the Special Counsel's final report, the indictment provided more timely information and also attracted widespread attention. Indeed, it appears that prior to the appointment of the special counsel and his pursuit of the IRA indictment, much of the government's specific information about the IRA either would have remained undisclosed or, if it was disclosed, would not have attracted the same level of attention from the public.

As noted in prior chapters, the greatest single response to foreign election interference is to unmask its foreign source, that is, to prevent a foreign state from interfering *covertly* in the American political system. By publicizing the nature of the foreign interference, the government will rob the interference of its greatest effectiveness because the covert nature of the influence operations will be removed. As noted above, it is not enough for the government to release the information in an abstract way; the public must absorb the information so that it has the relevant information to evaluate the disclosure and transparency. One way to help achieve this disclosure is through criminal prosecutions. Ideally, criminal prosecutions, whether trials or just indictments, should occur in a timely way so that the public has access to the information contained in the indictments when it is most relevant.

Trials conducted later in time will not have the desired effect of disclosing critical information to the public, though late prosecutions are better than no prosecutions at all, and may serve other laudatory aims, including deterrence, retribution, and incapacitation. To maximize the disclosure impact of these prosecutions, however, prosecutors need to understand the crucial role that prosecutions play in public disclosure in cases of election interference.

2. MISSED OPPORTUNITIES

Unfortunately, the Justice Department during the Obama Administration missed an opportunity to use the machinery of the criminal justice system to publicize, and ultimately counteract, the scope of Russian election interference. Instead, the FBI, Justice Department, and other federal agencies stuck to the counterintelligence script of collecting information about Russian active measures and then discussed using covert methods for counteracting those active measures. This included confidential warnings issued to President Putin and other covert measures that were never disclosed. Many criticized the Obama Administration for doing little to combat Putin's campaign of election interference. Whether this criticism is legitimate or not, it is undeniable that the measures taken by the Obama Administration were not publicly disclosed, at least initially, and that the Obama Administration did not place a premium on public disclosure in its efforts to push back against Putin's interference. These actions reveal that Obama and his intelligence agencies viewed this situation almost entirely through the established lens of counterintelligence activity. This is the old model and it did not work.

The better avenue is to publicize the active measures and disclose them to the public in the hopes that greater publicity will blunt the sharp edge of the foreign information operations. In order to counteract the impact of information operations, the public must receive information about these operations. Moreover, the information must be specific and detailed. Ideally, that information would be available on the Internet and physically tied to the *product* of those information operations.

At the time when the FBI, the Justice Department, and other counterintelligence departments began investigating Russian interference in the 2016 election, these departments kept the conclusions of their investigations confidential. Quite famously, FBI Director James Comey did not disclose, during the campaign, that the FBI was investigating members of the Trump campaign to determine whether any individual was coordinating or otherwise connected to the Russian influence operation. Members of the intelligence community apparently briefed President Obama and senior White House officials about Russian interference on an ongoing basis. Based on this information, President Obama took certain steps, many of which remain classified, such as warning President Putin that if Russia tampered with the tallying of votes, the United States would consider this an armed attack (or an act of war) and that the United States would respond with military force in that instance.

The United States reportedly made preparations for future cyber-attacks against Russia's power grid, in order to send a message to Russia about election interference.[5] All of this was done privatively, however. Obama said little publicly about Russian interference, even as top intelligence and counterintelligence officials were fully aware that the Russians were using social media platforms as part of their active measures campaign. There appears to have been no meaningful effort to help the electorate separate political statements that originated abroad from bona fide expressions of American political deliberation.[6]

Of course, there were several reasons why the Obama administration failed to give more publicity to the active measures campaign. First, the Obama administration apparently believed that publicizing and discussing Russian interference would be perceived as a political intervention – one that would support candidate Hillary Clinton and that would harm candidate Donald Trump. Setting aside for the moment the question of whether presidential statements would have been perceived as such, the more important question is whether more public disclosures were warranted given the corrosive consequences of the Russian active measures. Providing information to the public about the active measures might have negated some of the impact of those active measures. Instead, the Obama Administration kept to the traditional counterintelligence script, which is to say little to nothing about intelligence operations conducted by foreign powers.

Second, the FBI was not just investigating a foreign intelligence operation, it was also investigating whether U.S. individuals were complicit in that effort. This makes the publicity question more complicated, since the Justice Department has a policy not to discuss ongoing criminal investigations. The reasons for this reticence are numerous, well known, and certainly legitimate. Publicly disclosing information about an ongoing criminal investigation might compromise the investigation, taint a jury pool during a future trial, and might unfairly damage the reputation of the investigatory target. The latter issue is particularly important in cases where the target is never charged and has no opportunity to vindicate his or her character at a public trial. In this case, the FBI did not want to speak publicly about an investigation that was initiated to determine whether specific individuals were involved with Russian election interference.

However, it is important to remember that this was no ordinary criminal investigation. It was, instead, a dual-track investigation: a counterintelligence investigation

---

[5] *See* David E. Sanger and Nicole Perlroth, *U.S. Escalates Online Attacks on Russia's Power Grid*, N.Y. Times (June 15, 2019) (noting that "officials described the previously unreported deployment of American computer code inside Russia's grid and other targets as a classified companion to more publicly discussed action directed at Moscow's disinformation and hacking units around the 2018 midterm elections").

[6] The U.S. Senate released a report in 2019 that substantially criticized the federal government's response to Russian election interference, including the federal government during the Obama Administration.

and a criminal investigation at the same time.[7] The goals of the two investigations were not always compatible. The goal of the counterintelligence investigation was to reveal the extent of foreign intelligence operations and protect the United States by counteracting the effects of that operation. The goal of the criminal investigation was to determine criminal culpability and lay the groundwork for a future prosecution in the event that the Justice Department had gathered enough evidence to warrant presenting charges to a court. In the end, the goals of the second investigation managed to eclipse the goal of the first investigation. Although the Justice Department will not admit this, the policies, procedures, and institutional culture of the department gave priority to the criminal investigation, and insufficient attention has been paid to situations where the two paradigms conflict. As this chapter will explain, a more sophisticated and nuanced procedure would recognize that not only should the goal of neutralizing the electoral interference not take a back seat to the criminal investigation, the opposite is advisable: criminal investigations should be placed in service of neutralizing election interference because they can play a valuable role in publicizing the specifics of election interference.

Of course, it is not surprising that the conflict between these two paradigms was poorly handled, because traditionally the conflict is not manifested. Historically, the approach of maintaining confidentiality was good for counterintelligence investigations and also appropriate for criminal investigations. That is because most counterintelligence investigations were designed to *restore* secrecy and confidentiality of U.S. classified information, so both tracks counseled in favor of radical silence. But not anymore. In a world of information operations, counterintelligence requires a more nuanced approach. It requires balancing, in a sophisticated way, the dual goals of publicity required to defeat information operations and confidentiality appropriate in criminal investigations.

3. REVISIONS TO THE JUSTICE MANUAL

The federal government's approach to foreign election interference in 2016 was wanting, mostly because the United States has never faced foreign interference of this magnitude or this immediacy. The federal government was caught flat-footed, never having experienced a foreign influence operation with this degree of sophistication, resources, and audacity. Knowing that a new era of foreign influence operations has dawned, some departments of the federal bureaucracy have realized

---

[7] There is some confusion on this point still to this day and the situation is far from clear. *See* Aditya Bamzai, *Counterintelligence Investigations and the Special Counsel's Mandate: Part I*, Lawfare (May 26, 2017) ("The Rosenstein Order, however, appears to delegate a counterintelligence investigation to the Special Counsel under the criminal-prosecution-focused Part 600 regulations, thereby creating some confusion on the appropriate scope and type of investigation. By seemingly directing Mueller to conduct a counterintelligence investigation while at the same time limiting his authority to the criminal investigations authorized by the Part 600 regulations, the Rosenstein Order points in different directions on the scope of the Special Counsel's mandate.").

that the old playbook is outdated and needs to be rewritten. Although foreign interference arguably impacts many federal departments, this section will focus on the Justice Department and changes to its policy structure, including the adoption of a new policy dealing with foreign influence operations. The Justice Department (DOJ) is arguably on the frontlines of foreign election interference because it is the federal government's leading counterintelligence agency. The changes to DOJ policy are impressive and a step in the right direction, although not nearly enough. Audacious foreign influence operations require a restructuring of a complacent Justice Department and a revision of its twentieth-century regulations, and that process has only just begun.

In 2017, the Justice Department realized that its approach to investigating foreign election interference was flawed and required a different approach from its traditional counterintelligence mission.[8] Specifically, the Justice Department outlined a new policy that would allow disclosure of "foreign information operations" in some circumstances.[9] The policy was the outgrowth of a Justice Department Task Force report on the issue.[10] The new policy was codified in the "Justice Manual," the document that contains all DOJ policies for federal prosecutors and the agents that work with them.[11] As will be explained below, the change in policy was a welcome development but did not go far enough. The carefully worded clauses in the new provision allow for public disclosure but it is unclear if the provision will be enough to overcome the institutional pressures to keep counterintelligence operations secret.

The new policy was codified in the Manual as section "9–90.730 – Disclosure of Foreign Influence Operations." The policy defines foreign information operations as including "covert actions by foreign governments intended to sow divisions in our society, undermine confidence in our democratic institutions, and otherwise affect political sentiment and public discourse to achieve strategic geopolitical objectives."[12] The policy goes on to note that "[s]uch operations are often empowered by modern technology that facilitates malicious cyber activity and covert or anonymous communications with U.S. audiences on a mass scale from abroad."[13]

---

[8] For a discussion of the changes, see Rod Rosenstein, Speech at Aspen Security Forum (July 19, 2018) (discussing the "multifaceted challenges of cyber-enabled crime," and the Justice Department's new "strategies to detect, deter and disrupt threats" including informing "victims and the public about dangers").

[9] For a description of the new policy, see Eliot Kim, *Summary: Justice Department Policy on "Disclosure of Foreign Influence Operations,"* LAWFARE (Oct. 16, 2018).

[10] *See* U.S. Department of Justice, Report of the Attorney General's Cyber Digital Task Force 7 (2018) (noting that "[c]riminal charges also provide the public with information about the illegal activities of foreign actors we seek to hold accountable"). However, the report also states that the department's framework for responding to foreign information operations contemplates disclosure to the public and the private sector "where appropriate." *Id.* at 8.

[11] The Justice Manual was formerly known as the AUSA Manual.

[12] Justice Manual § 9–90.730.

[13] *Id.*

The policy then states that the general goal of the policy is to "investigate, disrupt, and prosecute the perpetrators of illegal foreign influence activities where feasible" and to "alert the victims and unwitting targets of foreign influence activities."[14] However, this goal is substantially qualified because alerting victims and targets will only be conducted "when appropriate and consistent with the Department's policies and practices, and with our national security interests."[15] The policy also notes that disclosure may not be possible or prudent because of "investigative or operational considerations, or other constraints."[16] This suggests, unfortunately, that in many cases the Justice Department will not alert victims and targets of influence operations. The devil is in the details, in particular how other Justice Department "policies and practices" will interact with this provision and potentially disrupt its effectiveness. There are many other policies and practices that counsel in favor of silence, confidentiality, and secrecy during the course of an investigation, and the new policy will only have "bite" if it, in fact, takes precedence over competing policies and practices of the Justice Department. This is especially true when one considers that government officials working in the intelligence and counterintelligence arena are rarely disciplined for withholding information from the public, but can face draconian consequences if they erroneously release information or even if they deliberately release information that someone else believes should have been kept secret. This dynamic creates a powerful pull towards secrecy.

Despite the wishy-washiness of the umbrella language, the policy articulates a general statement in favor of disclosure as a method for combating foreign information operations:

> It may not be possible or prudent to disclose foreign influence operations in certain contexts because of investigative or operational considerations, or other constraints. In some circumstances, however, public exposure and attribution of foreign influence operations can be an important means of countering the threat and rendering those operations less effective.[17]

The policy then provides a list of contexts where disclosure might be permissible. These include:

1. To support criminal investigation and prosecution of federal crimes.
2. To alert victims.
3. To alert "unwitting recipients of foreign government-sponsored covert support, as necessary to assist in countering the threat."
4. To alert technology companies whose platforms were used for influence operations (such as Facebook or Twitter).
5. To alert Congress.

[14] *Id.*
[15] *Id.*
[16] *Id.*
[17] *Id.*

6. To alert "the public or other affected individuals, where the federal or national interests in doing so outweigh any countervailing considerations."

The last example is particularly vague because it relies on a balancing exercise that weighs national interests against unspecified "countervailing" interests. It is unclear what countervailing interest could outweigh an all-things-considered judgment that the national interest requires disclosure. The Justice Manual gives one example where this balancing exercise permits disclosure and another example that counsels against disclosure. In the first example, disclosure would be appropriate when the foreign operation: "threatens to undermine confidence in the government or public institutions; risks inciting violence or other illegal actions; or may cause substantial harm, alarm, or confusion if left unaddressed." Examples where the balancing exercise counsels against disclosure are situations where the disclosure would "amplify or otherwise exacerbate the foreign government's messaging" or could "re-victimize the victim."[18] While the latter two examples are unobjectionable as matter of intent, the problem is that a counterintelligence department raised on secrecy can always assert that disclosure would "exacerbate" the messages of the foreign information operation, with little empirical evidence to support this conclusion. Without empirical evidence, it is hard to definitively say whether disclosure will or will not exacerbate the foreign message; this is a counterfactual question. But more importantly, the example misconstrues the rationale for disclosure. Disclosure will never dampen the foreign message. What makes disclosure important is that it can counteract the impact of the foreign operations by making sure that the public understands which messages in the political landscape have a foreign source. This does not silence the foreign message; it merely blunts its effectiveness.

The policy also includes a number of caveats that are justifiable on their own, but which cause concern that the policy will rarely lead to an effective disclosure. The Justice Department policy indicates that the following principles will be kept in mind prior to making the disclosure decision:

1. The disclosure decision will not be affected by "partisan political considerations" and disclosure should not be made for the "purpose" of conferring "advantage or disadvantage on any political or social group or any individual or organization."
2. The Justice Department can and should protect "intelligence sources and methods, investigations, and other U.S. government operations."
3. Disclosure will only be made when the federal government can attribute the information operation to a foreign state "with high confidence." Conversely, if the information operation is conducted by an entity other than a foreign state, or if no attribution to a foreign state can be successfully made, the Justice Department will not engage in disclosure *under this policy* (though this leaves open the possibility for disclosure under another policy).

[18] *Id.*

4. The approach of an election is a relevant consideration. Just as the Justice
   Department must consider the impact on the election of the timing of
   a criminal charge or prosecution, so too the Justice Department must consider
   the possibility that an "overt investigative step" regarding a foreign influence
   operation might have an impact on an election that is closely approaching. In
   other words, the Justice Department is supposed to avoid political consequences and one way to ensure this is to refuse to engage in overt actions,
   whether investigatory or prosecutorial, late in the election cycle.

These principles, each one sensible in the abstract, raise a number of concerns in
their application. For the first one, it is important to note that the policy uses the
word "purpose" in the context of avoiding the conferral of a political advantage. In
the context of foreign election interference, revealing the existence of an information operation will necessarily – by definition – have political consequences for one
side or the other. As the policy says, the government's disclosure of the outside
interference should not be made with the purpose of conferring a political advantage, depending on what one means by "purpose" in this context. Certainly, it should
be permissible for the government to reveal the existence of an information operation in order to protect democratic institutions and neutralize the impact of the
foreign operation. Neutralization will inevitably have political consequences
because the foreign operation likely was conducted with a desire to help one side
of the election and hurt the other. This raises the possibility, or even the probability,
that the Justice Department will refuse to disclose the existence of the foreign
operation out of concern that the department will be criticized for itself interfering
in the political process. The result is the creation of an institutional bias towards nondisclosure, when the institutional bias should be the opposite.

For the second one, the protection of "intelligence sources and methods, investigations, and other U.S. government operations," this exception might apply in
almost every case. Depending on how the exception is understood and applied, it
might swallow the rule. In almost every case, intelligence sources and methods will
be implicated by the disclosure. Moreover, it is virtually impossible for outside
agencies or government branches to successfully mount an objection to an intelligence community assertion that it must protect intelligence sources and methods.
The outside actors almost never have the relevant information to successfully
challenge this assertion. The reality is that the exception becomes an unreviewable
trump card to block the release of information. Although one hopes that the Justice
Department will not rely on this exception too often, the reality is that it is almost
impossible to challenge its use in concrete cases.

The third principle is problematic depending on how the Justice Department
interprets the requirement of attribution with "high confidence." Although the
requirement sounds perfectly reasonable in the abstract, the requirement opens
up several opportunities for insidious nondisclosure. For example, imagine

a situation where the Justice Department concludes that a foreign influence operation is under way and believes that the operation has been conducted by one of two countries. Although the government is sure that the influence operation originates from one of these two countries, the government is not sure which one. In other words, the government might have a high degree of confidence that one of the two countries is responsible, but a lower degree of confidence with regard to each country. This situation is entirely predictable, given the difficulties of attribution discussed in prior chapters. The Department could use this situation as a rationale for nondisclosure because it does not have a high degree of confidence in its attribution of the operation to country *x*. This result, while arguably consistent with the policy, is absurd, because the American people would benefit from knowing about the influence operation, even if attribution can only be made to a pair of countries. Disclosure would help neutralize the impact of the influence operation and would protect democratic institutions.

The fourth principle, not taking an important overt step just prior to an election, sounds unobjectionable but on deeper inspection makes little sense. Imagine that a foreign state has launched an influence operation in order to help one candidate. If the federal government only unmasks the operation in the weeks before the election, or only makes a confident attribution assessment in the weeks before the election, it would seem that the federal government should act quickly in the remaining time left before the election. It seems odd to say that the government should refrain from acting simply because an election is approaching. Indeed, the approach of the election simply adds urgency to the situation and may require even bolder action to counteract the impact of the foreign operations.

The Justice Department policy on disclosing foreign influence operations refers to the DOJ policy on prosecution of election offenses, which includes a rule of "prosecution, not intervention."[19] The earlier policy has a completely different rationale because it states that the Justice Department is not tasked with ensuring electoral integrity or preventing abuses but merely prosecuting them after the fact. Specifically, the policy states that:

> Because the federal prosecutor's function in the area of election fraud is not primarily preventative, any criminal investigation by the Department must be conducted in a way that minimizes the likelihood that the investigation itself may become a factor in the election. The mere fact that a criminal investigation is being conducted may impact upon the adjudication of election litigation and contests in state courts. Moreover, the seizure by federal authorities of documentation generated by the election process may deprive state election and judicial authorities of critical materials needed to resolve election disputes, conduct recounts, and certify the ultimate winners. Accordingly, it is the general policy of the Department not to conduct overt investigations, including interviews with

---

[19] *See, e.g.*, U.S. Dept. of Justice, Federal Prosecution of Election Offenses 9 (8th edn., 2017).

individual voters, until after the outcome of the election allegedly affected by the fraud is certified.[20]

Although this paragraph also includes a footnote stating that the policy does not apply to "covert investigative techniques," this merely suggests that the department can continue to collect information during this time period as long as the public remains unaware of the activity. This footnote clearly does not change the rule with regard to public disclosures, since disclosures by definition are known to the public. This policy is deeply disturbing and the fact that it is referenced in the new policy suggests a tension in DOJ policy and reveals that its institutional culture will require a major reorientation to solve the problem of foreign influence operations.

The prior policy on the federal prosecution of election offenses was mostly a response to campaign finance violations and similar offenses of election fraud – each of which could be prosecuted after an election. It those cases it was a safe bet that the violations would have only a minor effect on the election, but a major investigative move by the Justice Department could, in theory, have a massive impact on the election. For this reason, one can understand why the Justice Department believed that doing nothing was sometimes the safest course of action, at least on the eve of an election, because the cure could be worse than the disease. But this situation is a far cry from responding to a foreign influence operation that might frustrate the collective right of self-determination by fundamentally altering the nature of the country's democratic deliberations. In the case of foreign election interference, responses need to happen before the election because otherwise the foreign operation has not been neutralized – it has been allowed to succeed. And the fact that the operation has only been uncovered in the weeks before the election is not a good reason to give the foreign adversary a pass and keep their operations from the public. In other words, the sanitizing effect of public disclosure is equally valid in the weeks before the election, perhaps even more so. The Justice Department's reference to the prior policy saying the exact opposite is a worrisome omen and does not inspire confidence that the Department will act aggressively to combat foreign election interference on the eve of a major federal election.

In the end, the new federal policy on disclosure of foreign influence operations was a good first step, but the particular way that it was drafted leaves so many holes that a federal bureaucrat who fails to disclose a foreign operation can certainly justify that decision. Given the institutional culture against disclosure of foreign operations, what is needed is something far bolder: a clear statement that explicitly establishes a presumption in favor of disclosure in the context of foreign influence operations designed to attack democratic institutions. The best way to defeat these operations is to disclose them, and criminal indictments against foreign agents is one of the best ways of doing that, even if the defendants cannot be apprehended and brought to trial. Criminal indictments have an important role to play in disclosing

[20] *Id.*

the foreign involvement and they should be pursued vigorously. To make one point about federal prosecutions, the cases against the IRA troll farm were pursued by Special Counsel Robert Mueller and his team. One has to ask whether the Justice Department would have pursued this case if the Special Counsel had not been appointed by Deputy Attorney General Rod Rosenstein. It is significant that the Justice Department was not already investigating and indicting these individuals in the months leading up to the federal election of 2016, because the federal government was certainly aware of the Russian social media activity. Changes are required. The new DOJ policy is a step in the right direction but not nearly enough.

4. STRUCTURAL REFORMS TO THE INTELLIGENCE COMMUNITY

Is it possible to transform an agency built on secrecy and turn it into an engine of transparency? Can a department previously dedicated to counterintelligence understand that counterintelligence requires working directly with the public to disclose information? What we need is a completely new model for counterintelligence that upends decades, perhaps even centuries, of received wisdom of how to conduct counterintelligence. The new model would be counterintelligence for the age of misinformation.

The current model for counterintelligence is based on an obsolete assumption about the nature of the threats posed by intelligence operations. FBI counterintelligence operations are usually conducted without any public involvement because the nature of the threat was the theft or disclosure of sensitive information. Usually this theft of information involves either SIGINT, through some digital surveillance or computer intrusion, or HUMINT through the recruitment of an American source, possibly an employee or contractor working for an intelligence agency. So, for example, the Russians recruited FBI counterintelligence agent Robert Hansson to disclose classified information and documents to Russian intelligence operatives. The American public received little information about the investigation into this breach while the investigation was ongoing. In general, even during the prosecution phase, the FBI is incredibly hesitant to release information in open court. For this reason, the FBI is sometimes hesitant to engage in prosecutions at all, and often prefers a negotiated plea bargain so that it can avoid the public disclosures inherent in a criminal trial. The reasons for this reticence are tied to the ultimate harm of these intelligence operations: the theft and disclosure of classified information. In this context, disclosure to the American public (and by extension the world community) of these intelligence operations would only advance the interests of the foreign intelligence agency and would work *against* the interests of the counterintelligence agents who are trying hard to protect secrecy. For this reason, the model of counterintelligence has been to maintain, preserve, and protect secrecy. The problem is that this model, which is deeply entrenched in counterintelligence law, policy, informal norms, and institutional culture, is utterly inappropriate for countering information operations. This can be seen most clearly in the Russian active measures campaign against the 2016 elections.

The question is whether the counterintelligence community can be reformed to encourage departments and individuals to make better decisions to protect the United States from the corrosive consequences of information operations. This is no easy task. Major structural reforms would be required. When confronted with a foreign intelligence operation, the agency should first assess whether the intelligence operation is designed to steal confidential information (extract information) or whether the intelligence operation is designed to promote certain views (implanting information or views) through an information operation. If the operation involves the latter, either completely or partially, a different set of procedures should be triggered. Those procedures should require an immediate assessment of the goal of the foreign information operation and the possible countermeasures that might be taken to neutralize the impact of the information operation. Front and center in these discussions should be the public disclosure of the foreign source of the information operation, so that the public knows what information in the public marketplace of ideas has come from a foreign source. Methods of public disclosure include, but are not limited to, official statements released through government websites, paid public service announcements on traditional media, and, as discussed above, criminal indictments and prosecutions of individuals involved in the information operations, even if those individuals are located outside the country and are unlikely to be extradited to face trial. In the past, criminal indictments were disfavored in cases where it seemed unlikely that the government could secure the defendant's presence for trial. But in today's world of information operations, these criminal indictments have a new rationale: disclosing to the public a foreign power's involvement in American political deliberations.[21]

For the FBI, this task will be hard, but certainly possible. The FBI is already a creature of the Justice Department and its institutional culture already understands the value of criminal prosecutions and the goals of transparency and public disclosure. However, the FBI counterintelligence operations have largely been dominated by the institutional culture of the CIA and other intelligence agencies, rather than the institutional culture of the rest of the Justice Department. A strategic reorientation of the culture would entail imposing the cultural norms of the criminal justice side – publicity and transparency – over to the counterintelligence side.

For other agencies that engage in counterintelligence work, including the NSA, the structural reforms might be a bridge too far. These agencies are so thoroughly embedded in intelligence work that secrecy is part of their DNA. It would be so hard

---

21   See Jill I. Goldenziel and Manal Cheema, *The New Fighting Words? How U.S. Law Hampers The Fight Against Information Warfare*, 22 U. PA. J. CONST. L. 81, 138 (2019) (suggesting that "disclosure guidelines should be incorporated into any statute involving surveillance to fight information warfare").

to change that culture that one might argue that change is impossible. Indeed, another solution would be to create a separate division, agency, or entity, that is designed to receive the intelligence from these agencies and then work to disinfect the foreign interference. The new agency would implement transparency by getting the information about the foreign involvement in front of citizens and voters. The virtue of this proposal is that intelligence agents designed to protect secrets would not be tasked with disclosing sensitive information – the exact opposite of their skillset. Instead, a group of individuals who are proven communicators, with the appropriate skills, would work to counteract the information operation by making sure that the voting public knows about it.

To take just one example, it was reported in 2019 that a "Vets for Trump" Facebook page was being operated by agents of Macedonia, not by American servicemembers, as its title suggests. An intelligence agency that unmasks this deception as part of a foreign active measures campaign could hand off this piece of information to an agency that would work to ensure that everyone on that Facebook page learns that the forum is actually a sophisticated operation conducted by a foreign government. The details of how this information would be disclosed would be conducted by the new agency, whose members would have the relevant expertise on how to present this new information to social media users. Of course, any government agency would be saddled by bureaucratic inefficiencies, but an inefficient effort would be better than no effort at all. If at least some social media users are scared away by the government warnings, the agency will have succeeded in partially neutralizing the impact of the foreign influence operation.

Arguably, the FBI and the Justice Department are poorly suited to combating foreign election interference. The same can be said of every other department of the federal government. As of now, there is no federal agency that has both the competence and the authority to combat foreign election interference.[22] There are multiple agencies whose mission is partly related to foreign information operations, but the phenomenon does not fall squarely within any of these agencies or departments.[23] The result is a set of overlapping bureaucracies with little coordination and no institutional "ownership" over analyzing the problem and implementing a solution to it.

A simple canvassing of a few different federal agencies demonstrates how the problem of foreign election interference falls through the cracks. For example, one might think that the Federal Election Commission should, in theory, protect the overall integrity of federal elections, but its mission is mostly to protect elections against domestic threats such as campaign finance violations. Altering the mission of

---

[22] *See* Herbert Lin, *On the Organization of the U.S. Government for Responding to Adversarial Information Warfare and Influence Operations*, 15 I/S: J.L. & POL'Y FOR INFO. SOC'Y 1, 36 (2019) (suggesting that "no existing entity could do the job").

[23] *Id.* at 37 (2019) (noting that "some responsibilities are unclear and that information flow will be impeded in possible operational scenarios").

the FEC to counteract foreign election interference would be controversial and contrary to its current expertise, which is focused on domestic violations. In contrast, intelligence agencies have the opposite problem: these agencies have the expertise to identify and analyze foreign intelligence operations, but these agencies have nothing to do with domestic elections and no competence to regulate or protect them. Coordination between intelligence agencies and election agencies is hard to accomplish because it runs against the enforced separation between domestic agencies and intelligence agencies focused on foreign threats – a separation that was instituted and maintained in order to preserve civil liberties and make it impossible for intelligence agencies to collect intelligence on domestic individuals. The result is that the relevant competence is split not just between two different agencies but between two different *types* of agencies with not just a history but an obligation to remain separate from each other.[24] It is unclear how to bridge this separation without breaking the wall that civil libertarians worked so hard to construct. In any event, *some* federal agency, whether a new or existing one, needs to be tasked with responding to foreign election interference.

Other agencies in the federal government are similarly ill-equipped to handle the problem. As Herb Lin has noted, the Federal Trade Commission has authority over deceptive business transactions, including financial fraud, but election fraud falls outside its purview because it does not involve a pecuniary loss. The Election Assistance Commission was created to help election authorities with election infrastructure issues, although this does not include information operations (though it does include more traditional cyber-security defense).[25] The Defense Department focuses on foreign attacks, but these are usually kinetic or direct cyber-attacks, rather than information operations. The National Security Administration (NSA) has the capacity to detect and analyze foreign information operations over computer networks (including social media) but has no legal capacity for responding to these threats because it focuses on direct cyber-defense of computer systems. Many departments or agencies have responsibility for some isolated aspect of election interference, but no one department has wholesale responsibility over the situation.

One solution is to create an interagency working group to allow coordination in responding to foreign information operations. Working groups have been used in other situations to break down artificial barriers, promote cooperation, and share information within the federal bureaucracy. In some situations, the working groups have worked, while in other situations the working group has had insufficient institutional or bureaucratic resources to solve problems. It is doubtful in this case that an interagency working group would have the bureaucratic clout and legal authority to accomplish what needs to be done. Just as Congress passed substantial

---

[24] For a discussion of this issue, see *id.* at 31 (concluding that "in most cases, the fit between ... authorities/mission/expertise and the cyber-enabled ... [information operation] conducted by adversaries in the United States is not good").

[25] *Id.* at 36.

reforms that created the Department of Homeland Security after the 9/11 attacks, so too Congress needs to pass reforms to create a new federal structure for responding to and neutralizing foreign influence operations.

A new federal department in charge of election security could be given the express authority to protect elections from foreign interference. This could include cyber-defense initiatives to protect election infrastructure, but it should also include an explicit directive to take domestic actions necessary to neutralize foreign interference on social media platforms. Since the department would take substantial action in the domestic arena, it is important that the department be located outside the NSA, which is justifiably uncomfortable with domestic action.

One problem with this department is that it could be corrupted to serve partisan political interests. The identification and neutralization of foreign interference must be neutral, apolitical, and nonpartisan. If, say, a president was to order this new agency to combat some sources of foreign interference but not others, the department would not be successful in its mission. More disturbingly, the department could become an *instrument* of foreign election interference, with domestic complicity, if it combats some election interference but not others with a particular political goal in mind. In other words, the department could be advertently or inadvertently captured by the very forces that it should be regulating and combating.

Consequently, the best structure for this new initiative would be an independent administrative agency, like the FTC or FEC, with administrators who are appointed by both parties and serve lengthy terms, and who do not serve at the direct pleasure of the President. Although political pressure is still possible, an independent agency is probably the best chance of achieving nonpartisan equity. The FEC operates under a rule that no more than three members can be appointed by the same political party, and voting rules ensure that every official action of the FEC has at least some bipartisan support. The reason for these rules in the context of the FEC is obvious: election regulation and protection must have broad bipartisan support otherwise the actions will be viewed as having a partisan motivation. The same rationale applies with even greater force to a new commission with a mandate to stop foreign election interference.

There are some costs with this independent commission approach. A pure executive department would have greater access to the President and arguably more clout within the Executive Department. However, the value of political independence and objectivity far outweigh the costs associated with distance from the presidency. Furthermore, the existence of voting commissioners runs the risk that the commission will become bogged down by gridlock and inaction.[26] The default move for such a commission might be to do nothing. To solve this problem, another option is

---

[26] *See* Pichaya P. Winichakul, *The Missing Structural Debate: Reforming Disclosure of Online Political Communications*, 93 N.Y.U. L. Rev. 1387, 1389 (2018) (arguing that "the FEC's failure to detect and enforce against Russian political online communications is due to inaction and capture, two issues that stem from structural, not substantive, issues at the FEC").

to have an independent agency with a single administrator that requires Senate confirmation (rather than commissioners).[27] Selecting among these two options requires weighing political independence versus executive clout. The independent agency with a single administrator would be less independent but likely more forceful in its actions (for good or for bad).

Until the federal bureaucracy can be reformed to create a new agency in charge of combating foreign election interference, we need to work with the existing tools. In the existing structure, the Justice Department and the FBI are the best options, and for this reason this chapter has focused on the benefits of criminal investigations. Criminal investigations provide much needed transparency to the public, thereby blunting the sharp edge of covert foreign operations on the Internet. Public disclosure via criminal investigations is not everything, but right now it is the best option until more structural reforms are implemented.

CONCLUSION

This raises a larger question: Is the public disclosure of information about foreign information operations enough to stop these operations? Of course not. The response needs to be multifaceted. Legal tools at the international and domestic level are required. States need to defend their elections with every coercive mechanism consistent with the international rule of law. Sanctions and other countermeasures need to be imposed against states that violate the collective right of self-determination. The public disclosure of information, including the use of criminal prosecutions, is just one tool among many to combat foreign election interference. But it is an important one.

This chapter has focused on disclosure because it requires a reframing of some of the basic assumptions regarding the criminal justice system: What is it for? What can it accomplish? As described in this chapter, the criminal justice system is about more than just criminal accountability and punishment: it also has an important role to play in public information disclosure about threats to democratic institutions. The criminal justice system, at least in this area, needs to be subtly reformed to maximize this potential.

---

[27]   *Id.* at 1418 ("Congress, through legislative solutions other than the Honest Ads Act, as well as other entities such as private companies and states, could take important steps to address the structural issues that have plagued the FEC in its enforcement of online disclosure rules.").

8

Soliciting Foreign Interference

INTRODUCTION

Prior chapters have focused almost exclusively on the collective dimension – the role and responsibility of nation-states for conducting influence operations that interfere in another state's election. The collective focus is entirely justifiable for international lawyers, since international law is mostly concerned with the question of state responsibility. But the domestic political conversation has focused on individuals: which individuals "colluded" with Russia, which individuals might face legal exposure for their involvement with Russia's influence operations in the United States, which individuals were investigated by the FBI and why. Although the fate of individuals might appear to be beyond the scope of the international legal analysis, there are several reasons to focus on the conduct of individuals. To the extent that individuals actively encourage or promote foreign participation in American elections, how should the law treat these individuals?

To answer this question, the present chapter focuses on one particular legal category of participation, the *solicitation* of foreign involvement. The goal of the chapter is to subtly reorient much of the political discourse on election interference, including the debate over impeaching Donald Trump. Much of the debate has focused on technical details of federal criminal law – an important debate but one that obscures and masks the deeper political significance of an individual's potential complicity in foreign election interference. As the following analysis will make clear, solicitation of foreign interference represents a betrayal of public trust because it threatens to undermine the people's right of self-determination – a foundational norm of our constitutional order.

Section 1 of the chapter focuses on candidate Trump's solicitation of Russian email hacking during his speech in Florida in July of 2016 – a speech that set the tone for much of what was to come during the Trump presidency. Likewise, Section 2 focuses on an even more daring solicitation: President Trump's solicitation of interference from Ukraine during a call with its President, Volodymyr Zelensky. This phone call produced an internal rift within the Trump Administration and finally broke the logjam on impeachment in the Democratic Party, resulting in a fast-track impeachment process in the House of Representatives. Section 3 looks at the legal status of the domestic norm against soliciting foreign interference. Ultimately, I argue that for the removal of all doubt, Congress should pass a new statute criminalizing the solicitation of foreign involvement in elections. Then, Section 4 responds to the argument that such a statute could not be applied against the President because doing so would conflict with the President's constitutional authority to conduct foreign relations. The President's authority in this area is strong but it is not absolute; and it is certainly not absolute in the context of protecting the machinery of democracy, which falls squarely within the zone of permissible congressional regulation. Nonetheless, there are extensive political and legal barriers that prevent the Justice Department from prosecuting a sitting President, even one who committed solicitation of foreign interference. Finally, Section 5 examines the ultimate remedy of impeachment as a tool for sanctioning a President who solicits foreign involvement in an election.

1. SOLICITATION OF EMAIL HACKING

In July of 2016, Donald Trump, then a candidate for the presidency of the United States, held a news conference in Florida. During the news conference, Trump made the following public statement: "Russia, if you're listening, I hope you're able to find the 30,000 e-mails that are missing. I think you will probably be rewarded mightily by our press. Let's see if that happens. That will be next." In this statement, Trump asked a foreign sovereign state to intervene in the 2016 election – a shocking turn of events that was without precedent. Nonetheless, nothing happened to Trump. He was elected and he never faced criminal consequences for this solicitation. Why? This section explains the legal consequences of Trump's solicitation of Russian interference and why there was no criminal accountability for it.

Hillary Clinton's presidential campaign was hobbled by reports that the FBI was investigating her use of a private email server while she worked for the State Department and conducted government business. In the media, Clinton's Republican opponents argued that she (and her staff) had mishandled classified emails. Republican operatives successfully kept two stories alive during her campaign: first, that she had mishandled the Benghazi situation in Libya, leading to the violent death of the American ambassador there, and later misled Congress and the public about it; and, second, that her use of the private email server was designed to cover the tracks of corrupt behavior. During public campaign events, these talking points were summarized and echoed with chants of "lock her up!" None of these charges were substantiated in formal investigations, but nonetheless the talking points successfully energized the Republican base and may have contributed to Trump's election.

The FBI conducted an investigation of Clinton's use of the private server (to determine if classified documents were mishandled in violation of federal law). On July 5, 2016, FBI Director James Comey publicly announced in a news conference that the FBI had closed the investigation and decided not to file any charges, though he also stated that Clinton's handling of the emails, though not criminal, was nonetheless "reckless." This statement kept the story alive in the political discourse.

It was against this background that Trump made his famous July 2016 speech in Florida. Trump's reference to "missing" emails referred to emails that were not recovered by the FBI during its investigation. In making this speech, Trump was asking for Russia not only to intervene in the 2016 election but also to engage in computer hacking – a violation of federal criminal law. Despite the bald-faced nature of the request for intervention, Trump faced no criminal prosecution for his comments.

The incident was briefly discussed in Special Counsel Mueller's report. Although it is not clear which legal avenues were pursued by Mueller's team, it is likely that federal prosecutors investigated the speech as a potential campaign finance violation. This legal theory was based on the idea that the Russian assistance in this situation constituted a "thing of value" because any effort that resulted in the disclosure of the Clinton emails would assist Trump's campaign because the new emails would prolong the email server story to the detriment of the Clinton campaign. By Trump requesting a "thing of value" from the Russians, Trump arguably engaged in a conspiracy to commit a campaign finance violation.

This legal theory raises several thorny legal problems. The first is whether the Russian assistance could be considered a "thing of value" under current election law. Some of the president's supporters have suggested that the concept of something of "value" is not so malleable, but there is certainly no case law directly on point that stands for the proposition that this type of assistance is clearly *not* a thing of value. The second is whether Trump's statements were enough to form a conspiracy with the Russians. A conspiracy requires an agreement between two or more individuals to commit an unlawful act, but a conspiracy need not be formed by an explicit agreement in writing; an informal agreement is possible and can be formed by the slightest of communications. By making the speech itself, Trump could have formed an agreement with the Russians. Third, some have questioned whether the Russians were even listening to the speech and whether Trump's behavior had any impact on Russian intelligence efforts. However, the Mueller report is clear that GRU intelligence agents started probing Clinton email accounts "within approximately five hours" of the speech and that no prior attempts to hack that domain address were detected prior to the speech. Consequently, it appears that the Russians were indeed listening and that they took up Trump's invitation. Even though causation is not a legal requirement, it appears that there was a clear causal connection between Trump's speech and Russian interference efforts against the Clinton campaign.

Strangely, though, the public discourse surrounding this event may have missed the most salient legal category for understanding the significance of Trump's behavior. That category is criminal solicitation. A solicitation is a request by one individual for another individual to commit a crime. Unlike a conspiracy which requires an agreement between two or more individuals, a solicitation has no such requirement of an agreement. For solicitation, it is enough that the requesting individual made the request; it is irrelevant whether the person who received the request agreed to perform the crime. Although both solicitation and conspiracy are inchoate crimes, because neither require that the target crime be brought to fruition, a criminal solicitation is in many ways less developed than a conspiracy, which is further on the road to the completion of the target offense.

Solicitation is codified in the federal code under 18 U.S.C. 373:

> Whoever, with intent that another person engage in conduct constituting a felony that has as an element the use, attempted use, or threatened use of physical force against property or against the person of another in violation of the laws of the United States, and under circumstances strongly corroborative of that intent, solicits, commands, induces, or otherwise endeavors to persuade such other person to engage in such conduct, shall be imprisoned not more than one-half the maximum term of imprisonment or . . . fined not more than one-half of the maximum fine prescribed for the punishment of the crime solicited, or both; or if the crime solicited is punishable by life imprisonment or death, shall be imprisoned for not more than twenty years.

One thing to note about the federal solicitation statute is that it is explicitly limited to crimes of violence (i.e. a crime that involves the use or threat of physical force). So, asking someone to commit a robbery or a murder would violate federal law, regardless of whether the robbery or murder is ever brought about. Solicitation of nonviolent offenses is not covered by federal law, at least not the general solicitation statute, though they may be criminalized by topic-specific federal statutes that explicitly refer to solicitations. Perhaps it is for this reason that the Special Counsel never seriously analyzed, in his report, whether candidate Trump engaged in a criminal solicitation.

Unfortunately, this analysis is incomplete. Trump's speech was given in Florida and Florida's criminal law provision on solicitation is far broader than its federal counterpart. Florida Penal Law 777.04 states that: "A person who solicits another to commit an offense prohibited by law and in the course of such solicitation commands, encourages, hires, or requests another person to engage in specific conduct which would constitute such offense or an attempt to commit such offense commits the offense of criminal solicitation, ranked for purposes of sentencing as provided in subsection (4)." The limiting clause of violent offenses is noticeably absent in the state statute and with good reason. General criminal law is mostly reserved to the states and there are fewer constitutional constraints on what conduct may be penalized by state legislatures. In contrast, federal penal statutes must be justified by some affirmative grant of legislative authority to Congress articulated in the Constitution. For this reason, state penal statutes are usually general in nature, while federal statutes are often drafted in much narrower terms to comply with the Constitution's restrictions on federal power. Against this background, it makes perfect sense that a state solicitation provision would be far broader than a federal solicitation statute.

There appears to be no evidence that Mueller's team seriously analyzed whether Trump's speech violated Florida law. Although federal prosecutors would not have jurisdiction to prosecute an offense committed under state penal law, federal prosecutors could refer a case to state prosecutors if federal prosecutors developed information that a potential state crime was committed. Indeed, the Justice Department routinely refers cases to state prosecutors when federal prosecutors receive credible information that a state crime may have occurred. In the event that such a referral occurred, the Special Counsel report should have disclosed the referral and explained the basis for the referral, that is, why the Office of the Special Counsel believed that a crime might have occurred. If no referral took place, I believe this was a legal oversight. As it stands, it is unfortunate that the Special Counsel appears to have ignored the application of garden-variety state penal law to Trump's extraordinary request for Russian assistance during his July 2016 speech. It is possible that a full investigation by state authorities, or a full analysis of Florida state penal law, would reveal a legal obstacle to applying the general solicitation statute to this incident. But at first glance it would appear that the state statute was violated.

2. THE UKRAINE AFFAIR

As noted above, Trump's solicitation of foreign assistance was not punished, and he remained undeterred. His next solicitation was far more brazen but less public. During a phone call with the newly elected Ukrainian president, Volodymyr Zelensky, Trump asked for assistance from the Ukrainian government, specifically, an investigation into Joe Biden and his son Hunter. Trump also asked for help locating a computer server that according to conspiracy theories was located in Ukraine. Although it is unclear why Trump was asking for the computer server, it seemed to be related to an investigation conducted by the Justice Department into the origins of the federal government's investigation of Russian interference in the 2016 election.

Numerous federal officials, including Secretary of State Mike Pompeo, were listening in to the conversation between Trump and Zelensky, and White House aides kept detailed notes of the conversation. In the summer of 2019, an employee of the CIA filed a whistleblower complaint that alleged that the conversation was part of an improper scheme by Trump to solicit foreign interference in the 2020 election.

The whistleblower complaint was received by the CIA inspector general, who decided that the substance of the complaint contained allegations that were substantial, urgent, and should be turned over to Congress. The Director of National Intelligence declined to disclose the complaint to Congress, forcing the inspector general to inform Congress of the complaint's existence. In response to the resulting controversy, the White House ultimately disclosed a transcript of the phone call between Trump and Zelensky. Though the transcript is neither complete nor verbatim, it does nonetheless provide a clear portrait of an intentional solicitation of foreign assistance. For example, the relevant part of the transcript includes Trump's request for assistance regarding the server:

> **The President:** I would like you to do us a favor though because our country has been through a lot and Ukraine knows a lot about it. I would like you to find out what happened with this whole situation with Ukraine, they say Crowdstrike . . . I guess you have one of your wealthy people . . . The server, they say Ukraine has it. There are a lot of things that went on, the whole situation. I think you're surrounding yourself with some of the same people. I would like to have the Attorney General call you or your people and I would like you to get to the bottom of it. As you saw yesterday, that whole nonsense ended with a very poor performance by a man named Robert Mueller, an incompetent performance, but they say a lot of it started with Ukraine. Whatever you can do, it's very important that you do it if that's possible.

At another point in the conversation, Trump asks for the Ukrainian President to investigate Biden and his son:

> **The President:** Good because I heard you had a prosecutor who was very good and he was shut down and that's really unfair. A lot of people are talking about that, the way they shut your very good prosecutor down and you had some very bad people involved. Mr. Giuliani is a highly respected man. He was the mayor of New York City, a great mayor, and I would like him to call you. I will ask him to call you along with the Attorney General. Rudy very much knows what's happening and he is a very capable guy. If you could speak to him that would be great. The former ambassador from the United States, the woman, was bad news and the people she was dealing with in the Ukraine were bad news so I just want to let you know that. The other thing, there's a lot of talk about Biden's son, that Biden stopped the prosecution and a lot of people want to find out about that so whatever you can do with the Attorney General would be great. Biden went around bragging that he stopped the prosecution so if you can look into it . . . It sounds horrible to me.

In response to these requests, Zelensky told Trump that:

> the next prosecutor general will be 100% my person, my candidate, who will be approved, by the parliament and will start as a new prosecutor in September. He or

she will look into the situation, specifically to the company that you mentioned in this issue. The issue of the investigation of the case is actually the issue of making sure to restore the honesty so we will take care of that and will work on the investigation of the case.

When news of Trump's solicitation leaked, Trump's defenders argued that the phone call was not improper because there was no suggestion of quid pro quo during the conversation. In other words, under this view, Trump's behavior was only problematic if he offered something specific – or threatened something specific – in return for the favor that he was requesting (the investigation of the Bidens). There is ample evidence of a quid pro quo during the conversation, because Trump discussed foreign aid to the Ukraine and implied that it was conditional on the fulfillment of the favor. Indeed, news reports indicate that Trump and Giuliani worked to freeze previously planned aid to Ukraine in the weeks leading up to the phone call, strongly suggesting that the aid was being used as leverage against Ukraine. During the call, Trump specifically brought up foreign aid to Ukraine:

The President: Well it is very nice of you to say that. I will say that we do a lot for Ukraine. We spend a lot of effort and a lot of time. Much more than the European countries are doing and they should be helping you more than they are. Germany does almost nothing for you. All they do is talk and I think it's something that you should really ask them about. When I was speaking to Angela Merkel she talks Ukraine, but she doesn't do anything. A lot of the European countries are the same way so I think it's something you want to look at but the United States has been very very good to Ukraine. I wouldn't say that it's reciprocal necessarily because things are happening that are not good but the United States has been very very good to Ukraine.

In response, Zelensky noted that he needed the United States to continue its military aid and made specific reference to anti-tank missiles that the Ukrainians needed to fight Russian-backed rebels in Eastern Ukraine: "I would also like to thank you for your great support in the area of defense. We are ready to continue to cooperate for the next steps specifically we are almost ready to buy more Javelins from the United States for defense purposes."

White House Chief of Staff Mick Mulvaney confirmed during a press conference that Trump held up the foreign aid to Ukraine because he wanted to pressure Zelensky into turning over the DNC email server. (Right-wing websites have pushed a conspiracy theory that the foreign intervention in the 2016 election was conducted by Ukraine, which then blamed Russia for the intervention and that there is a computer server that proves it.) Specifically, Mulvaney stated that:

[Did] he also mention to me, in the past, that the corruption related to the DNC server? Absolutely, no question about that. But that's it. And that's why we held up the money. . . . The look back to what happened in 2016 certainly was part of the thing that he was worried about in corruption with that nation. And that is absolutely appropriate.[1]

Mulvaney also stated that the quid-pro-quo arrangement was not inappropriate because "We do that all the time with foreign policy . . . I have news for everybody: Get over it. There's going to be political influence in foreign policy."[2] This last comment explicitly conceded the connection between the deployment of foreign aid and the desire to use that aid in a way that would benefit Trump's political fortune. Later, in a subsequent statement, Mulvaney attempted to walk back his comments; he claimed that there was no quid-pro-quo arrangement, but by that point the damage was already done. Mulvaney had admitted that the foreign aid to Ukraine was linked to Zelensky helping Trump win reelection.

Although the conversation clearly exhibited an implicit quid-pro-quo arrangement that promised continued United States aid to Ukraine only in the event that Ukraine conducted an investigation into the Bidens, the whole issue of the quid-pro-quo arrangement is irrelevant to the deeper pathology represented by Trump's phone call, and it is this deeper reason that probably triggered the whistleblower's profound discomfort with Trump's behavior. The reason the call was problematic was because Trump was once again soliciting foreign intervention in a federal election. Since Trump escaped meaningful consequences for his July 2016 solicitation in Florida, Trump repeated the gambit a second time, this time during the diplomatic phone call. But the basic building blocks of the request were the same: asking a foreign power to intervene in the election in a way that would be beneficial to candidate Trump or President Trump. The real story is the solicitation of foreign involvement, not the quid pro quo.

Legal commentators had a hard time articulating a particular criminal provision that was violated by Trump's conduct during the call. One possibility is a campaign finance violation, although this again raises the question of what constitutes a "thing of value" and whether an investigation of the Bidens would be a thing of value to the Trump campaign. Certainly, a foreign investigation of Biden would be beneficial to Trump's campaign and therefore arguably a thing of "value." A second possibility is that Trump was attempting to bribe Zelensky into engaging in a particular action by dangling foreign aid in exchange for assistance to his campaign. Certainly, conversations of this sort when conducted by an American businessperson and a foreign politician might implicate the Foreign Corrupt Practices Act, which penalizes bribery of foreign officials by Americans overseas. The problem with this legal approach was that Trump was not offering to provide money to Zelensky personally but rather was trying to provide something beneficial to the government of Ukraine (the foreign aid). This inverts the standard paradigm for extraterritorial bribery,

[1] See Aaron Blake, *Trump's acting chief of staff admits it: There was a Ukraine quid pro quo*, WASH. POST (Oct. 17, 2019).
[2] *Id.*

which usually involves the conferral of a private benefit to a foreign official in order to receive a benefit from the foreign state (which the official arranges). In contrast, in this situation, Trump was dangling a public benefit to Ukraine in order to receive a private benefit for his campaign. While this is clearly inappropriate, it does not fit the paradigm of typical cases of foreign bribery. Similarly, the application of extortion statutes suffers from similar problems. The federal extortion statute says that: "Whoever, being an officer, or employee of the United States or any department or agency thereof, or representing himself to be or assuming to act as such, under color or pretense of office or employment commits or attempts an act of extortion, shall be fined under this title or imprisoned not more than three years, or both; but if the amount so extorted or demanded does not exceed $1,000, he shall be fined under this title or imprisoned not more than one year, or both."[3] Did Trump violate this statute? Possibly, although extortion requires a threat, which is more than just a quid pro quo (as in a bribery case) and rises to the level of a forceful threat. Although there is more than one definition of extortion in the federal code, 18 U.S.C. § 1951 is a representative example and defines extortion as "the obtaining of property from another, with his consent, induced by wrongful use of actual or threatened force, violence, or fear, or under color of official right." Trump clearly did not threaten Zelensky with physical force or violence although some might argue that Trump attempted to procure the consent of Zelensky under color of "official right." Also, there was a coercive quality to Trump's dealings with Zelensky, in the sense that he threatened to withhold the foreign aid, which might support a finding of extortion.

A more promising legal avenue is to argue that Trump committed "honest services" fraud. Honest services fraud is a catch-all provision in the federal code to prosecute cases of public corruption. Under the federal code, "Whoever, having devised or intending to devise any scheme or artifice to defraud, or for obtaining money or property by means of false or fraudulent pretenses, representations, or promises, transmits or causes to be transmitted by means of wire, radio, or television communication in interstate or foreign commerce, any writings, signs, signals, pictures, or sounds for the purpose of executing such scheme or artifice, shall be fined under this title or imprisoned not more than 20 years, or both."[4] A subsequent provision clarifies that "the term 'scheme or artifice to defraud' includes a scheme or artifice to deprive another of the intangible right of honest services."[5] Federal prosecutors have used this provision to prosecute public officials for graft and other forms of corruption. However, recent Supreme Court cases have limited the reach of this once capacious federal statute, and those cases now require a quid-pro-quo arrangement in order to sustain a conviction. In *McDonnell v. United States*, the Supreme Court concluded that:

---

[3]   18 U.S.C. § 872.
[4]   18 U.S.C. § 1343.
[5]   18 U.S.C. § 1346.

an "official act" is a decision or action on a "question, matter, cause, suit, proceeding or controversy." The "question, matter, cause, suit, proceeding or controversy" must involve a formal exercise of governmental power that is similar in nature to a lawsuit before a court, a determination before an agency, or a hearing before a committee. It must also be something specific and focused that is "pending" or "may by law be brought" before a public official. To qualify as an "official act," the public official must make a decision or take an action on that "question, matter, cause, suit, proceeding or controversy," or agree to do so. That decision or action may include using his official position to exert pressure on another official to perform an "official act," or to advise another official, knowing or intending that such advice will form the basis for an "official act" by another official. Setting up a meeting, talking to another official, or organizing an event (or agreeing to do so) – without more – does not fit that definition of "official act."[6]

The Supreme Court's famous narrowing of the "honest services" provision was designed to distinguish criminal corruption from "normal political interaction between public officials and their constituents."[7] However, it does not seem likely that Trump's behavior could be described as a normal political interaction between himself and a constituent. On the other hand, some have suggested that presidents often need to threaten, cajole, bribe, or extort foreign leaders during the exercise of foreign diplomacy.

But the key distinction in that regard is that the President might be required to threaten, cajole, bribe or extort foreign leaders for the benefit of the country that the President represents. During Trump's phone call with Zelensky, he appears to have attempted to engineer a situation for his *personal* political benefit as opposed to a benefit for the country. The latter course of conduct (securing a benefit for the country) might be a legitimate goal of statecraft but securing a personal benefit for one's political campaign is an altogether different matter. This fact has led some lawyers, including former prosecutor Barbara McQuade, to argue that "Trump's alleged solicitation of a personal benefit – dirt on Biden – in exchange for performing an official act – the release of military aid – deprives the public of his honest services as president."[8] Trump cannot defend his behavior by arguing that his conduct during the phone call represented "normal" diplomatic behavior. However, it is still an open question whether a federal court would allow a prosecution under the honest services provision of federal law for Trump's twisted form of diplomacy, given that most other prosecutions under the provision involved quid-pro-quo bribes from constituents in exchange for official acts that would benefit the constituent.

---

[6]   McDonnell v. United States, 136 S. Ct. 2355, 2371–2 (2016).

[7]   Id.

[8]   *See* Barbara McQuade, *Trump's Call to Ukraine May Constitute "Honest Services Fraud"* – A Core Crime of Public Corruption, JUST SECURITY (Sept. 25, 2019).

Trump's phone call with Zelensky almost certainly constituted a solicitation of a foreign government for assistance in a federal election. Although Trump, and his supporters, may try to interpret the conversation differently, the passages quoted above make clear that, by seeking an investigation of his chief political opponent in the upcoming election, Trump was seeking assistance for his political campaign rather than seeking a public benefit for the nation. This brief canvassing of federal statutes makes clear that none of the available statutes directly addresses this unprecedented situation, though each of the statutes could be interpreted in a way that covers Trump's conduct. Although foreign participation in domestic elections is regulated and policed through a number of federal statutes and regulations, Trump's phone call is not a *paradigmatic* violation of any of them. This throws into sharp relief the existence of a major lacuna in federal law. Broader norms of political democracy, and international law, prohibit foreign interference in domestic elections, yet an individual's solicitation of that interference is not necessarily a crime under federal law, though depending on the factual circumstances more specific statutes might apply.

3. THE DOMESTIC NORM AGAINST FOREIGN PARTICIPATION

Whether Trump committed a crime or not during his Florida speech or his phone call with Zelensky, these two incidents reveal a painful truth about the contemporary legal landscape: there may be gaping holes in the U.S. legal regime regarding the solicitation of foreign assistance in a federal election. Mueller's team apparently investigated the incident under campaign financial laws, and the federal conspiracy statute, and decided not to make a more aggressive legal conclusion regarding Trump's liability for the speech. In doing so, they apparently ignored Florida state penal law. But making reference to Florida state penal law should not have been necessary in the first place, because in an ideal world, Congress would have drafted and enacted a specific federal statute criminalizing solicitation of foreign interference in a federal election. If such a statute had existed prior to Trump's phone call with Zelensky, the legal analysis of the phone call would be much simpler.

A new federal statute criminalizing the solicitation of election interference would finally liberate this topic from the long shadow of campaign finance regulations, which unnecessarily complicate enforcement of this conduct. For example, campaign finance regulations prohibit requesting something of "value" because these regulations are, after all, *finance* regulations. However, a new federal solicitation statute could be liberated from the "value" requirement and could penalize soliciting foreign assistance regardless of whether that assistance has any "value" or not. Furthermore, the solicitation statute could jettison the entire rubric of "assistance" and instead criminalize the solicitation of foreign interference – thus making clear that the harm that is being prohibited is not really assistance at all but rather the solicitation of *interference*. This would then liberate prosecutors from needing to establish that the foreigner was acting in a way that would assist the candidate who was soliciting the interference. In other words, the asking for interference, regardless of who that interference would benefit, would be itself illegal under the statute.

Finally, a new solicitation statute should be explicit that the prohibited offense is an *inchoate* crime. In the context of the criminal law, "inchoate" is a technical term meaning that the offense is preparatory and need not result in the target offense. In the context of soliciting foreign interference, the statute would apply even in the absence of any causal connection between the solicitation and the foreign interference; indeed, no foreign interference would need to happen *at all* for the statute to apply. The mere asking for foreign interference is the crime itself, regardless of what happens next. As a criminal law concept, solicitation is usually justified by the need to allow early intervention by authorities into a burgeoning criminal behavior because the target offense is sufficiently dangerous. Foreign election interference fits this criterion perfectly for the reasons already identified in this and previous chapters because the interference has the capacity to frustrate the people's right to self-determination. Early intervention is not just permissible but essential.

Why did Congress not pass such a statute before? Arguably because Congress never imagined that a presidential candidate would use a press conference to publicly ask a foreign power to intervene in a federal election – a shocking result that calls into question the very nature of national elections as an expression of the American people's political will. Nor did Congress anticipate that a President would use an official phone call to ask a foreign government to investigate a political rival. But, Congress' excuse of ignorance or failure of imagination cannot be used again. Congress can anticipate this problem because it just happened, and will happen again, unless Congress passes a statute criminalizing the solicitation of foreign assistance in an election. The Watergate scandal triggered a wave of governmental reforms that were designed by Congress to scale back executive power and to reassert Congress' prerogative to regulate intelligence agencies. One wonders if the ultimate legacy of Trump's presidency will be a second wave of congressional reforms. Many of Trump's actions involved constitutional or political norms that many assumed would never be violated because the political costs of violating them were too high. Trump has demonstrated the weakness of that logic because he used a new equation to build a path to victory in 2016. Congress may respond by passing new legislation designed to prohibit what was previously considered unthinkable. Criminalizing the solicitation of foreign election assistance should be first on that agenda.

Free speech absolutists might argue that such a prohibition would violate the First Amendment. Solicitation is just words, after all, and the Constitution protects the people's right to say whatever they want. This argument was already discussed, and rejected, in the chapter on freedom of speech in election regulations, but a few words are worth repeating here. The first is that the argument is hopelessly overbroad because all solicitation statutes penalize mere speech and state solicitation statutes are clearly constitutional. A spoken word can be a criminal act and if the

Constitution forbids their criminalization, then the entire edifice of criminal law would crumble, since criminals often use language to complete criminal transactions.[9] More importantly, protecting American elections from the distortionary effect of foreign participation is a compelling government interest that not only justifies – but indeed demands – federal regulation. Foreign participation in federal elections violates the core principle of self-determination outlined in this book, that is, the notion that elections in a democracy are designed to allow a political community to select its own destiny. This democratic process of self-determination entails, by necessity, boundary regulations to protect the participatory rights of insiders and prohibit outsiders from influencing the process. It would be an odd result if outsiders were prohibited from participating in elections, but insiders were still allowed to solicit that outside assistance. Logically the two should go together. Solicitation of foreign assistance, just as much as the underlying foreign assistance, should be not just prohibited but also criminal in nature.

Indeed, the argument for criminalizing solicitation is greater than the argument for criminalizing the actual interference by the foreign actor. While both actions (the solicitation and the underlying interference) undermine the exercise of political self-determination, the solicitation happens from someone *within* the political community. That individual is a member of the political community, and the solicitation of outside assistance in the political process involves a profound violation of the relationship between the individual and the political *demos* to which he or she belongs. Although it might be an exaggeration to describe this as an act of disloyalty to the state, it is nonetheless an act that has profoundly corrosive consequences for the political community. It ruptures the relationship between the individual and the political community, and that rupture provides an additional reason to criminalize the solicitation.

The costs of failing to criminalize the solicitation of foreign assistance are just too high. Trump's behavior has flouted a deeply engrained political norm, but if that norm is not codified in federal law, it will create a de facto precedent that these solicitations are permissible. If this behavior were to be regularized, the result could be catastrophic to the political order, with candidates on both sides of a campaign rushing to solicit foreign assistance from world powers with whatever resources (threats, promises, bribes) that each candidate has at his or her disposal. This would create an arms race among candidates – a worldwide "Amazing Race" to solicit foreign assistance wherever it could be located. When combined with the growing arsenal of cyber-tools to engage in social media information operations, these solicitations could radically increase the frequency and depth of foreign interventions in the political process.

---

[9] *See, e.g.*, Chaplinsky v. State of New Hampshire, 315 U.S. 568, 571–2 (1942) (noting that "[t]here are certain well-defined and narrowly limited classes of speech, the prevention and punishment of which have never been thought to raise any Constitutional problem").

4. DOES THE PRESIDENT HAVE AUTHORITY TO INVITE FOREIGN INTERVENTION?

Some legal scholars have suggested that the President's conduct of foreign relations is neither subject to regulation nor subject to second-guessing, precisely because the President has Article II authority to direct the country's diplomatic posture. Under this argument, there is no basis for either the Justice Department, or Congress, to question Trump's behavior during the call when Trump solicited Zelensky's assistance. For example, Professor Jack Goldsmith has written that "The president's power to act in confidence is at its absolute height when he has a classified conversation with a foreign leader" and that "[p]utting it brutally, Article II gives the president the authority to do, and say, and pledge, awful things in the secret conduct of U.S. foreign policy. That is a very dangerous discretion, to be sure, but has long been thought worth it on balance."[10] Similarly, Secretary of State Mike Pompeo defended Trump's conversation with Zelensky, arguing that presidents make deals with foreign leaders all the time and that this conversation was no different.

Both of these arguments rely on an unsustainable and ill-advised view of the president's foreign affairs power. They are based on the unstated and undefended assumption that just because the president is relying on an Article II authority – such as the president's authority to conduct foreign relations – then that power is absolute and not subject to any other constitutional constraint by another branch's exercise of its powers. Article II makes the president commander-in-chief of the armed forces and also authorizes him to "make treaties," but nothing in the text of Article II gives the president *exclusive* control over foreign affairs.

Despite the lack of a clear textual grant of exclusive authority over foreign affairs, Supreme Court decisions over several decades have blessed the President's primary role in that domain. To take just one example, in *Zivotofsky v. Kerry*,[11] the Supreme Court concluded that the power to recognize foreign governments and/or foreign states belonged with the Executive Branch. In *Zivotofsky*, Congress had passed a statute directing the Executive Branch to list "Israel" as the place of birth in the passport of any American born in Jerusalem. By this seemingly obscure ministerial act, Congress was taking a stand on the contested question of Israel's sovereignty over Jerusalem – a question that the U.S. State Department had repeatedly refused to take an official stance on, believing that such a stance might endanger delicate diplomatic efforts to resolve the dispute between the Israelis and the Palestinians. The Supreme

---

[10] *See* Jack Goldsmith, TWITTER, September 19, 2019, 6:20pm (https://twitter.com/jacklgoldsmith/status/1174721033485594626). Goldsmith continued: "So what is to be done? Imagine that Trump engaged in an act of national treachery: he casually blew a source for no good reason (or a venal one), or he betrayed the nation in a Manchurian Candidate sort of way . . . . I don't think there is a legal avenue to correct such a betrayal of national trust by the Chief Executive and Commander in Chief. That is one of the accommodations the Constitution makes for the benefits of a vigorous presidency who can conduct foreign policy in secret."

[11] 576 U.S. 1059 (2015).

Court concluded that the statute was unconstitutional because it infringed on the President's authority to control recognition decisions specifically and conduct of foreign affairs more generally.

In making this determination, the Supreme Court engaged in a methodology that repeatedly recognized the Executive Branch's primacy in the conduct of foreign relations. First, the Court noted that several clauses of the Constitution grant foreign affairs powers to the presidency. This includes not just the right to "make" treaties but also the right to "nominate" and "appoint" ambassadors to foreign nations, upon advice and consent of the Senate. From these examples, the Supreme Court concluded that "the President himself has the power to open diplomatic channels simply by engaging in direct diplomacy with foreign heads of state and their ministers."[12] In deciding whether the executive branch's recognition power is "exclusive," that is whether it prevails over inconsistent recognition decisions made by Congress, the Supreme Court looked to historical precedent and noted that although there were a few precedents to the contrary, the bulk of historical precedents supported the conclusion that recognition was an executive – not congressional – power.[13] The Court also relied on the "functional" consideration that the United States must speak with "one voice" in recognition decisions – a consideration that assumes that the Executive Branch is inherently unified while Congress is inherently divisible. This argument is often used to justify Executive primacy over all of foreign affairs, not just the recognition power.[14] However, this point ignores the fact that although Congress has a different decision procedure, the output of its decisions are just as unified as the output of the Executive Branch.

On this basis, scholars have argued that any congressional attempt to regulate or limit the executive's conduct of foreign affairs must be unconstitutional. As noted above, this argument relies on a form of Article II absolutism, that is, the assumption that because diplomatic relations are assigned to the President, it cannot be restrained or regulated in any way by Congress. For example, Goldsmith has suggested that it would be unconstitutional for a statute to "give an NSA employee monitoring intercepts (or whatever) the authority to disclose to Congress the classified communications of POTUS with a foreign leader."[15] Similarly, advocates for a strong executive branch sometimes argue that "regular" criminal law provisions

---

[12]   Zivotofsky v. Kerry, 135 S. Ct. 2076, 2086 (2015).

[13]   The use of history as a recognized methodology for determining separation-of-powers questions goes back to Justice Jackson's concurring statement in *Youngstown* that a "a systematic, unbroken, executive practice, long pursued to the knowledge of the Congress and never before questioned, engaged in by Presidents who have also sworn to uphold the Constitution, making as it were such exercise of power part of the structure of our government, may be treated as a gloss on 'executive Power' vested in the President by s 1 of Art. II." Youngstown Sheet & Tube Co. v. Sawyer, 343 U.S. 579, 610–11 (1952).

[14]   *See* ERIC A. POSNER AND ADRIAN VERMEULE, THE EXECUTIVE UNBOUND: AFTER THE MADISONIAN REPUBLIC 27 (Oxford University Press, 2010) (noting that the "executive can act with much greater unity, force, and dispatch than can Congress, which is chronically hampered by the need for debate and consensus among large numbers").

[15]   *See* Goldsmith, *supra* note 10.

cannot, and should not, be applied against the President, because doing so would infringe on the President's Article II powers.

In making these arguments, Article II advocates often cite the "clear statement rule," which requires that a congressional statute should only be applied against the President if there is a clear statement in the statute explicitly stating that it applies to the President. For example, in *Franklin v. Massachusetts*, the Supreme Court noted that "[o]ut of respect for the separation of powers and the unique constitutional position of the President, we find that textual silence is not enough to subject the President to the provisions of the APA" and then announced that it would require "an express statement by Congress before assuming it intended the President's performance of his statutory duties to be reviewed for abuse of discretion."[16] The clear statement rule has been invoked in other cases as well.[17] It is an example of constitutional avoidance in the context of separation of powers; federal courts should only confront a direct confrontation between congressional power and Article II authority if the conflict (the application of the statute to the President) is abundantly clear. The clear statement rule was also invoked by Bill Barr in his memorandum arguing that the President could not be guilty of obstruction of justice for firing James Comey (because that act fell within his executive authority).[18] The Justice Department's Office of Legal Counsel has also articulated the existence of the clear statement rule.[19] In his Report, Special Counsel Robert Mueller concluded that, contrary to Barr's argument, the federal obstruction of justice statute could apply to official presidential actions.[20] Mueller's argument in this section was subject to extensive public debate by constitutional scholars.[21]

[16]   505 U.S. 788, 800–1 (1992).

[17]   *See, e.g.*, Pub. Citizen v. U.S. Dep't of Justice, 491 U.S. 440 (1989).

[18]   *See* Bill Barr, Memorandum to Deputy Attorney General Red Rosenstein and Assistant Attorney General Steve Engel on Mueller's "Obstruction" Theory, June 8, 2018 (arguing that "'the Clear Statement Rule' Long Adhered To By the [Justice] Department, Preclude[s] Its Application to Facially-Lawful Exercises of the President's Constitutional Discretion").

[19]   *See* Office of Legal Counsel, Memorandum Opinion for the Counsel to the President, Application of 28 U.S.C. § 458 to Presidential Appointments of Federal Judges, at 351 (1995) (referring to a "well-settled principle that statutes that do not expressly apply to the President must be construed as not applying to the President if such application would involve a possible conflict with the President's constitutional prerogatives").

[20]   *See* Robert S. Mueller III, Department of Justice Special Counsel, *Report On The Investigation Into Russian Interference In The 2016 Presidential Election* 170 (2019) ("Congress can permissibly criminalize certain obstructive conduct by the President, such as suborning perjury, intimidating witnesses, or fabricating evidence, because those prohibitions raise no separation-of-powers questions. The Constitution does not authorize the President to engage in such conduct, and those actions would transgress the President's duty to 'take Care that the Laws be faithfully executed.' In view of those clearly permissible applications of the obstruction statutes to the President, [the] holding that the President is entirely excluded from a statute absent a clear statement would not apply in this context.") (internal citations omitted).

[21]   *See, e.g.*, Jack Goldsmith, *The Mueller Report's Weak Statutory Interpretation Analysis*, LAWFARE (May 11, 2019) (noting that the "clear statement rule is not beyond criticism, and, indeed, it has many critics" and "perhaps why so many commentators who have analyzed the application of the obstruction statutes to the president have elided or downplayed the rule" but ultimately concluding

The same lawyers who objected to Mueller's application of the obstruction of justice statute might similarly object that the President cannot be subject to a congressional statute criminalizing the solicitation of foreign interference in an election. Their argument would have the same structure as their earlier arguments about the obstruction of justice statute. They might say that the President has constitutional authority to conduct foreign relations and that a proposed solicitation statute cannot be applied against him absent a clear statement. They might even go so far as to suggest that even in the presence of a clear statement, the statute might be unconstitutional because it infringes on the President's Article II power.

These arguments are problematic and should be rejected for the following reason. None of the precedents applying the clear statement rule involved the application of criminal statutes. It is one thing to require a clear statement rule in a separation of powers context. But the neutral application of a valid criminal statute is not a separation of powers issue. By their very nature, criminal statutes are designed to apply to everyone, regardless of official status or role. In the shadow of the criminal law, the President is just one among many individuals. The application of the criminal law to the chief executive does not implicate a conflict between congressional authority and Article II power. Rather, the application of the criminal law simply involves the neutral application of criminal regulation to all individuals in the polity. To deny this fact is simply to assert an imperial vision of the presidency as sitting above the criminal law and capable of exercising Article II authorities without any interference at all. Our structural Constitution does not grant such monarchial authority to the chief executive.

If the proposed solicitation statute were tested in a federal court, the evaluation of its constitutionality would consider historical precedents. As noted above, a long chain of unbroken congressional acquiescence is sometimes treated, under the *Youngstown* framework, as a "gloss" on executive power. Although there is a history of congressional deference to the executive on matters of diplomatic relations, there is no history of congressional deference on matters regarding boundary regulations for elections. Congress enacts campaign finance regulations; Congress defines, by statute, criteria for citizenship; Congress enacts regulations regarding elections and voting. The machinery of democracy is very much within the purview of congressional regulation and not something that Congress has deferred to executive action.

5. IMPEACHMENT AS A RESPONSE FOR SOLICITING FOREIGN INTERFERENCE

With or without a statute criminalizing the solicitation of foreign interference, holding a President responsible for this violation would be extremely difficult. The official

that "if one is following the law, one cannot do this"). Similarly, see Josh Blackman, *The Special Counsel's Constitutional Analysis: Clearing up the Clear Statement Rule*, LAWFARE (May 17, 2019) (noting that the 1995 OLC opinion "did precisely what I would expect an executive branch lawyer to do: read Supreme Court precedent to provide a charitable accounting of presidential power").

position of the Office of Legal Counsel is that a sitting President cannot be indicted while in office. Although this legal conclusion is just a mere departmental "opinion," it is nonetheless considered binding policy on the Justice Department. What this means is that the Justice Department, and its prosecutors, is not permitted to file an indictment against a sitting President – unless the Office of Legal Counsel opinion is withdrawn or revised. A state attorney general or a local prosecutor would not be bound by internal Justice Department policies, but the proposed solicitation statute would be a federal law. Consequently, the only prosecutors with jurisdiction to bring a case against a President would be forbidden, by policy, from pursuing such a case. However, even if no indictment is possible as a matter of policy, the Justice Department, through a Special Counsel, could still *investigate* the President. However, Trump's phone call with Zelensky came after the Special Counsel investigation by Robert Mueller was already closed. Consequently, there is currently no executive branch-led criminal investigation of Trump's solicitation of foreign interference. In fact, after the phone call was reported to the Justice Department, lawyers there quickly determined that no investigation into the incident was warranted.

Congress has many tools to induce a noncompliant executive branch to follow federal law. One possibility is to play constitutional hardball – to use congressional powers to stop a President from inviting foreign assistance. For example, Congress could threaten to shut down the government, by wielding the power of the purse, until the Executive Branch changes its behavior.[22] However, this strategy carries some risks; Congress might be blamed by the electorate for shutting down the government if the Executive branch fails to comply and a stand-off persists for many weeks. Constituents might be especially angry if the government shutdown prevents the delivery of much-needed public services.

The ultimate constitutional tool for Congress to induce compliance is to impeach the President for soliciting foreign interference in a federal election. This is a drastic step, although as demonstrated above, many of the other tools for establishing criminal responsibility will be difficult or impossible to deploy against a sitting President. Indeed, the legal view that a sitting President is immune from federal prosecution is based on the idea that impeachment and removal from office is the sole and *exclusive* remedy for presidential lawbreaking. Regardless of whether this view is legally correct or not, it is currently the view of the Justice Department, making impeachment the only viable option for holding the President accountable.[23]

---

[22] *See generally*, Kate Stith, *Congress' Power of the Purse*, 97 YALE L.J. 1343, 1347 (1988).

[23] *See* U.S. Dep't of Justice, Memorandum Opinion for the Attorney General, A Sitting President's Amenability to Indictment and Criminal Prosecution, 24 Op. O.L.C. 222 (2000) (noting that "the Framers themselves specifically determined that the public interest in immediately removing a sitting President whose continuation in office poses a threat to the Nation's welfare outweighs the public interest in avoiding the Executive burdens incident thereto" and concluding that "[t]he constitutionally prescribed process of impeachment and removal, moreover, lies in the hands of duly elected and politically accountable officials").

In the following paragraphs, I lay out how such an impeachment effort could be successfully articulated. Because of the language of the Impeachment Clause and its reference to "Treason, Bribery or other high Crimes and Misdemeanors," the public discourse surrounding impeachment often revolves around the question of whether the President has engaged in an identifiable crime under the federal criminal code. So, for example, there is an engrained tendency to ask whether the President's conduct during his phone call with Zelensky constituted a crime. As noted above, the conversation then focuses on detailed arcana, that is, whether a Ukrainian investigation of Biden would constitute a "thing of value" for purposes of campaign finance law. Although this assistance may very well constitute a thing of value, focusing on this point dramatically understates the profound nature of the political violation in this case. In order for impeachment to make sense as a response to a violation of the core principles of political autonomy and self-determination – the very concepts at the center of this book – then the impeachment inquiry needs to shed its reliance on the technical requirements of the criminal law.

Scholars have long argued that presidents may be impeached for conduct that would not constitute a crime under the criminal code.[24] The impeachment process is designed to allow removal of a president who betrays the nation in some fundamental way, either through corruption, disloyalty, or some other form of self-dealing behavior. In the case of Trump, impeachment is only justified if his behavior involved a political wrong of the highest order.[25] Focusing on potential campaign finance violations fails to communicate the political stakes at issue. The only way to make the political argument is by appealing to the core principles articulated in this book: the right of the people to select their own political destiny through the democratic process and the free functioning of elections.

Viewed in this way, Trump's behavior compromised the essential machinery of democracy by inviting foreign participation in the political system. This behavior fundamentally compromised the capacity of the American people to exercise their right to self-determination. In order to explain why impeachment is a necessary act, Congress needs to focus on the role that boundary regulations play in the democratic system in general and voting in particular. By definition, the people's right to self-determination requires the implementation of rules that prohibit external actors from participating in American elections. If foreign interests are allowed to distort

---

[24] *See* CHARLES L. BLACK, IMPEACHMENT: A HANDBOOK (Yale University Press, 1974); R. BERGER, IMPEACHMENT: THE CONSTITUTIONAL PROBLEMS (Harvard University Press, 1973); CHARLES EVANS HUGHES, THE SUPREME COURT OF THE UNITED STATES 19 (Columbia University Press, 1928); Julie R. O'Sullivan, *The Interaction Between Impeachment and the Independent Counsel Statute*, 86 Geo. L.J. 2193, 2216 (1998) ("The weight of modern authority also clearly favors the view that impeachments were designed to address political – and not necessarily criminal – wrongs.").

[25] Hon. Elizabeth Holtzman, *Abuses of Presidential Power: Impeachment As A Remedy*, 62 U. MIAMI L. REV. 213, 226 (2008) ("The Impeachment Clause is what allows us to preserve our democracy in the face of attempts to subvert the Constitution."); Josh Chafetz, *Impeachment and Assassination*, 95 MINN. L. REV. 347, 422 (2010) (discussing impeachment as the remedy for a President's "destruction of republican liberty").

the political process, the result of an election will express the will of the foreign actors rather than the will of the American people. When seen in this light, the victim of Trump's phone call, and his solicitation of assistance from Zelensky, was not Biden but rather then American people, whose right to self-determination was violated by the solicitation of foreign interference.

The centrality of the people's right of self-determination in a democratic order explains why impeachment is an appropriate remedy for a President's solicitation of foreign interference. No other method is currently available to hold a President accountable for this solicitation. Furthermore, the underlying violation has the potential to undermine the machinery of democratic self-government, thus making the violation a matter of urgent concern for the Congress to address. Congress needs to act in order to vindicate the people's right to self-determination and to protect the democratic process from falling victim to foreign interests. In the absence of congressional action, the President would continue to solicit foreign interference in the political process, potentially resulting in massive distortion of future elections.

This articulation of the political necessity for impeachment throws into sharp relief the inadequacy of technical discussions of criminal offenses under the federal code. No amount of campaign finance violations will articulate the true harm caused by solicitations of foreign assistance, which in this case involved a perversion of foreign policy by substituting personal interests at the expense of national goals. This is a supporting argument that yields the same result – an argument in favor of impeachment. The conduct of foreign policy, especially communications with foreign leaders, is supposed to carry out national objectives. When a President engages in those conversations in order to prioritize personal (rather than national) ends, then the President violates his constitutional oath of office by engaging in a form of corrupt self-dealing.

Some have suggested that America's national interests are whatever the President says that they are, so that it is incoherent to suggest that the President has acted contrary to the national interest (at least where foreign policy is concerned).[26] Under a version of this view, if the President believed that the United States should request Ukrainian investigations of Biden, this basically became a national interest as soon as the President uttered the words, because foreign policy – even *erratic* foreign policy – is a presidential prerogative. Although Presidents are owed a certain amount of deference in the context of national foreign policy, this argument cannot be applied to the subversion of boundary regulations that define our democratic process and protect the people's right to self-determination. The President has some authority,

---

[26] See Jack Goldsmith, *On What Grounds Can the FBI Investigate the President as a Counterintelligence Threat?* LAWFARE (Jan. 13, 2019) (noting that "[i]t is not unusual for a president to make controversial policy decisions that could, in some quarters, be viewed as causing harm to the national security interests of the United States," including "Trump's . . . attacks on allies and international institutions, his lies and erratic behavior, and the like" but concluding that "these actions – and indeed the very determination of the U.S. interest in the conduct of U.S. foreign policy – are presidential prerogatives").

concurrent with Congress' role in foreign affairs, to determine the national interests of the United States. But those interests may never unwind democratic institutions that are designed to bring expression to the people's right of self-determination.[27] If these systematic protections were subject to presidential prerogative, the President could unilaterally transform a functioning democracy into a sub-democratic regime. Whatever it was, Trump's solicitation of Ukrainian interference was not a valid expression of presidential prerogative.

In December 2019, the House of Representatives approved two articles of impeachment against President Trump. The first article was titled "Abuse of Power," though the underlying text of that article alleged that Trump "solicited the interference of a foreign government, Ukraine, in the 2020 United States Presidential election" and that Trump "engaged in this scheme or course of conduct for corrupt purposes in pursuit of personal political benefit." This solicitation, according to the first article of impeachment, "undermined the integrity of the United States democratic process" and therefore required Trump's removal from office. Setting aside for the moment whether Senators were right or wrong to vote in favor of Trump's removal from office, it is important to note that the first article of impeachment accurately captured the distinctive harm of Trump's behavior, that is the solicitation of foreign interference in the electoral process in a way that compromised the American people's right of self-determination and the democratic mechanisms designed to actualize that collective right. It is significant that even some Senators who voted against Trump's removal, such as Sen. Lamar Alexander, did so after concluding that Trump solicited foreign interference and that doing so was, in Alexander's words, "inappropriate" and undermined "the principle of equal justice under the law."[28] Although the impeachment did not result in Trump's removal from office (and Alexander endorsed Trump's reelection), the process nonetheless signaled an assessment that a domestic actor's solicitation of foreign interference is corrosive to the machinery of democracy.

Several Trump supporters in the Senate argued against removal, arguing that the issue of Trump's behavior should be put before voters and decided at the ballot box in the 2020 presidential election. The problem with this view is not that it allegedly understates the level of harm caused by Trump's "inappropriate" behavior, but rather that it ignores the particular *type* of harm caused by the solicitation of foreign interference. That solicitation has, as its goal, the contamination of the political process, so it is a bit fanciful to then rely on that democratic process as

---

[27] *Compare with id.* (arguing that Trump's "persistent refusal to acknowledge … Russia's 'ongoing, pervasive efforts to undermine our democracy'; and more … are all part of his ultimate discretion to conduct foreign policy and U.S. intelligence operations … [and] therefore, cannot pose a threat to [our] national security as a justification for a counterintelligence investigation" and concluding that although this "may sound like an extreme conclusion … it might follow from Article II").

[28] Senator Alexander Lamar (R-Tenn.), Statement on Impeachment Witness Vote, January 30, 2020.

a remedy for this class of political misbehavior. Indeed, the whole assumption behind campaign finance and other electoral regulations is that they must be enforced by actors who are external to, or at the very least distanced from, the democratic process. If no such external enforcement is impossible, then the solicitor of foreign interference is in a position to corrupt the very system that is supposed to act as a check against that misbehavior. This pernicious possibility suggests that the process of impeachment and removal is a uniquely appropriate tool for resolving cases of soliciting foreign election interference, rather than relying on the next election.

CONCLUSION

This chapter has explored the legal issues that arise when an individual solicits a foreign power to intervene in an American election. The rest of the book laid out a conception of election interference that was defined mostly from the raw materials of international law. Specifically, the core thesis of the book is that election inter-ference violates a people's right to self-determination – a collective right protected under international law. In contrast, this concluding chapter focused more on domestic law and the fate of solicitation of foreign interference as a violation of domestic law. First, the chapter looked at existing statutory frameworks that might prohibit such conduct. Second, the chapter considered the enactment of a new federal statute that would resolve whatever uncertainty exists over solicitation by explicitly criminalizing solicitation of foreign interference. By focusing on domestic statutory frameworks, the chapter pivoted away from international law. In doing so, though, the chapter retained the conceptual machinery of the prior chapters, insofar as the people's right to self-determination was the background principle that justifies the criminalization of solicitation.

Furthermore, the right of self-determination is a creature not just of interna-tional law but of domestic law as well. In international law, the right to self-determination is a collective right. In domestic law, the American people's right to self-determination could be described as a collective right, although that term has no particular purchase in domestic law. A more appropriate label would describe the right to self-determination as a foundational constitutional norm that underlies the American political system. Typically, American political and constitutional theorists have described this foundational norm as "popular sover-eignty," though it is the same basic idea under two labels.[29] The right to self-

---

[29]   See, e.g., Akhil Reed Amar, The Central Meaning of Republican Government: Popular Sovereignty, Majority Rule, and the Denominator Problem, 65 U. COLO. L. REV. 749 (1994) ("The central pillar of Republican Government, I claim, is popular sovereignty."); Christian G. Fritz, Alternative Visions of American Constitutionalism: Popular Sovereignty and the Early American Constitutional Debate, 24 HASTINGS CONST. L.Q. 287, 290 (1997); Brett W. King, Wild Political Dreaming: Historical Context, Popular Sovereignty, and Supermajority Rules, 2 U. PA. J. CONST. L. 609, 612 (2000).

determination is just as much a part of American legal culture as it is a part of international law. The difference is simply that its codification in international law is at the level of legal doctrine, such as the International Covenant on Civil and Political Rights, whereas in domestic legal culture the right is a foundational norm at a deeper level of abstraction.

Conclusion

1. THE ROLE OF SELF-DETERMINATION IN THE ARGUMENT

Although the topic of this book is election interference, the star of the analysis was self-determination. The concept of self-determination pulls the argumentative weight of the book's thesis. In some sense, the book is one attempt to return self-determination to its rightful place in the edifice of international law. This raises an obvious point. Why does self-determination need restoration in the first place? Why has self-determination fallen from its perch?

I will not delve too deeply into the historical question here. However, it is important to note that some historians of international law have argued that while self-determination was once invested with great emancipatory potential, the legal codification of self-determination was sufficiently watered down. Abstractly construed, self-determination might be viewed as a justification or excuse for wars of liberation or, even more broadly, a right to rebellion. But tellingly, the 1970 Declaration of the Principles of International Law Concerning Friendly Relations and Co-operation Among States included the following provision: "Nothing in this Declaration shall be construed as prejudicing in any manner the provisions of the Charter or the rights and duties of Member States under the Charter or the rights of peoples under the Charter, taking into account the elaboration of these rights in this Declaration." Similarly, the United Nations Declaration on the Rights of Indigenous Peoples includes the following language in article 46: "Nothing in this Declaration may be interpreted as implying for any State, people, group or person any right to engage in any activity or to perform any act contrary to the Charter of the United Nations or construed as authorizing or encouraging any action which would dismember or impair, totally or in part, the territorial integrity or political unity of sovereign and independent States."

As Joseph Massad has argued, these provisions "therefore limited the general understanding of self-determination in international law further as one that grants the right to independence by transforming this right when applied to indigenous population as one that grants them only the right to 'self-government' and political participation within existing states."[1] In essence, self-determination has been watered down from a preeminent right to one that must be balanced against other rights and responsibilities recognized by international law.

The most significant example of a counterbalancing legal concept is sovereignty. Self-determination and sovereignty stand in eternal tension with each other as legal concepts that potentially destabilize and undermine each other. In order for self-determination to have real teeth, it needs to prevail over sovereignty, in the sense that a people without their own state should have the right to break up – via force if necessary – the territory of their parent state. On the other hand, for sovereignty to be fully respected under international law, the territorial integrity of existing states must be acknowledged and legally protected, even if alternative arrangements might be more just or more likely to advance the goals of nationalism. If international law prioritizes self-determination over sovereignty, then the result is global instability. On the other hand, if international law prioritizes sovereignty over self-determination, the result is an entrenchment of global arrangements that are the historical product of empire and colonialism. Neither alternative is particularly attractive.

Until now, international law has tried to chart an intermediate course. It has recognized the value of self-determination but also tried to assert some limits on the concept. Self-determination can push a people on the path to statehood, but that path is not automatic and does not apply in many cases. The link between self-determination and secession is not automatic. In making this observation, I am not trying to push a particular view of self-determination and its relationship to sovereignty. Rather, I am simply observing that the relationship between these two core concepts of international law is fraught and contested. And it is one reason why international law has such a tortured relationship to self-determination and why that legal concept has withered.

Self-determination's sidetracking is an unfortunate development, because there are legal problems that could be solved with the ideas that self-determination brings to the table. This book has been dedicated to the proposition that election interference is precisely such a problem. Election interference has defied easy interpretation and analysis in the international legal doctrine, and one reason is because few lawyers look to self-determination as a primary framework.

As noted in prior chapters, self-determination is an explicitly political concept. It is designed to legally support a *political* project – the effort by a people to establish, demand, or negotiate a political arrangement that allows them control over their own destiny, at least as to matters that are necessary for their survival as a people. This includes, among other things, matters of religion, culture, language, and other social practices.

At the same time, this book has demonstrated that election interference is an inherently political problem. The distinctive harm of election interference has less

---

[1]   *See* Joseph Massad, *Against Self-Determination*, 9 HUMANITY (2018).

to do with sovereignty and territorial incursions, and much more to do with interference in an inherently political process – the democratic machinery of government. That machinery is designed to actualize the most sacred element of representative democracy: select among a slate of candidates and by extension select among competing visions for the future. Election interference potentially compromises the selection of the choice since the choice is designed to express the will of the political community that is holding the election.

The book has hopefully drawn out, in explicit detail, the tight connection between the distinctive harm of election interference and the legal category used to analyze it. The interference in the political process is the center of the story, which is why self-determination provides a far better analytical framework than sovereignty. Although it is not strictly necessary in every case, it is helpful for legal analysis to use concepts and terms that match the facts on the ground. When the legal and commonsense terms match up, the law has an intuitive appeal because the justifications for legal regulation are transparent for all to see. To take just one example, criminal law terms such as murder or robbery add legal precision to terms whose moral significance are inherently obvious, but the criminal law borrows these terms from the domain of morality where they already have normative significance. Conversely, when legal concepts do not mirror the facts on the ground, lawyers must engage in a translation exercise to explain to the public why a set of technical and obscure legal concepts should be used to regulate a phenomenon that has a real-world existence. In the case of election interference, using the concept of self-determination highlights the political nature of the harm in a way that matches the reality on the ground. That should count as a virtue of the legal theory presented in this book.

2. THE CASE STUDY APPROACH

This book outlined a legal answer to the general problem of election interference. However, the book mostly focused on Russian interference during the 2016 election, rather than looking at a wide number of cases of election interference, past and present. In other words, the entire book used a case study approach to understanding election interference. As a methodology, case studies are vulnerable to many objections. These objections include the idea that any one example of a phenomenon might be a product of one-off factors that will not be repeated in future instances. Therefore, any solutions will only be responsive to the case study example, rather than the general phenomenon. There is a similar objection that experts and legislators sometimes regulate in response to the latest crisis, but that dynamic is destined to produce obsolete solutions. There is no guarantee that the prior crisis will be repeated. Legislators and experts should regulate for the *next* crisis, not the prior one.

For election interference, one might worry that a legal theory built from a case study of Russian interference will produce a legal analysis, and policy solutions, that

2. *The Case Study Approach*

only apply to Russian interference. Election interference in the 2020 election might be much different. Other countries might engage in election interference in future years using different tools. Social media platforms might become passé; troll farms might be obsolete in five years. And states that engage in tomorrow's election interference might be motivated by other strategic reasons. They might not seek to elect certain candidates or sow division in the political landscape; they might seek outcomes that we cannot imagine today. Consequently, the legal analysis might be completely different. In other words, I might have constructed a legal argument regarding Russia's interference in the 2016 election, but not a generalizable legal analysis of election interference as a phenomenon. Furthermore, I might have proposed policy solutions that would have mitigated the 2016 interference but that are poorly designed for solving future interference in 2020, 2024, and 2028, whatever that interference will look like.

This is a perennial worry in legal scholarship but the concentration on Russian interference in 2016 was a justifiable choice – and likely the only real option for pursuing the legal analysis. Although it is always difficult to predict the future, it seems right to say that Russia's interference in the 2016 election represented a sea change in foreign interference. The use of social media tools had not existed a generation before. More importantly, that methodology is likely to be used in future elections for the foreseeable future. Although Facebook, Instagram, and Twitter might evolve, social media is here to stay, and electioneering on the Internet – in whatever form that might take – is likely a permanent redefinition of how democratic deliberation takes place. States engaged in election interference in future elections are likely to steal Russia's playbook. Consequently, the legal analysis inspired by Russia's election interference is likely to apply to future cases as well.

Prior chapters identified the following characteristics of Russia's strategy for election interference: creation of social media accounts specifically designed to look like U.S. individuals; large number of tweets and retweets engaging in divisive political rhetoric; supporting candidates perceived as likely to pursue policies that dovetail with Russian strategic interests; and supporting candidates, issues, and messages likely to be damaging to the *opponent* of the preferred candidate, even if those messages come from the opposite end of the political spectrum and are not directly consistent with Russian strategic interests. The Russians also used online advertisements, created new advocacy groups based on social media membership, and even sponsored rallies and protests. The details might change in the future, but the overall strategy is likely to be repeated by other foreign nations in future elections. The strategy is designed to leverage the anonymity of the Internet and the ability of social media users, whether from a troll farm or an automated bot, to create accounts that suggest an American origin. There is every reason to believe that this form of election interference will be used for the foreseeable future.

Similarly, there is every reason to believe that the policy prescriptions outlined in prior chapters will help mitigate future interventions. For example, the prohibition on soliciting election interference will deter U.S. citizens from reaching out to foreign powers to interfere on behalf of a political campaign. Similarly, the Justice Department can use criminal prosecutions to inform the public about future cases of election interference. Finally, the intelligence community needs to build systemic capacity for information disclosure to combat future cases of election interference. Each of these prescriptions is forward-looking, even though informed by evidence of past abuses.

If anything, it is the current state of the law that is the product of regulating prior threats. The Foreign Agent Registration Act (FARA) was designed to counter the threat posed by Nazi propaganda efforts.[2] Campaign finance regulations, and specifically the prohibition on foreign contributions, were enacted in response to concerns that foreign donations were corrupting the political process.[3] As described in prior chapters, neither of these regulatory regimes is particularly on point for regulating social media electioneering by foreign powers. The legal landscape needs to be altered to account for the election interference of today and tomorrow.

Similarly, the international legal rules regarding cyber-attacks and political interference were not designed with the goal of regulating foreign election interference. In fact, just the opposite. The rules regarding cyber-attacks are still in development and somewhat contested, though the rules are being discussed in relation to cyber-attacks against military targets, civilian infrastructure such as electrical grids, or financial institutions. Election interference was not foremost on the minds of the drafters of the Tallinn Manual.[4] Also, the rules regarding political interference are ancient but most recently articulated in the ICJ *Nicaragua* judgment, which discussed the required element of coercion. But the *Nicaragua* judgment involved a very direct form of political interference, the funding of political opponents fighting a guerilla war against their government. Again, this was far afield from election interference on social media platforms. Today's law is arguably anachronistic and out of step with contemporary dangers. Using the case study approach, and focusing on Russian interference, helps to train our gaze squarely on the new flavor of political interference on the Internet.

3. THE FUTURE OF FOREIGN ELECTION INTERFERENCE

This discussion leads naturally to the future of election interference. It should be clear, by now, that election interference was not limited to the 2016 election. Russia

---

[2] *See* BRADLEY W. HART, HITLER'S AMERICAN FRIENDS: THE THIRD REICH'S SUPPORTERS IN THE UNITED STATES 16 (Thomas Dunne Books, 2018).

[3] For a discussion, see Ben Freeman, *America's laws have always left our politics vulnerable to foreign influence*, WASH. POST (Oct. 18, 2019).

[4] However, interference in election operations (casting of ballots, vote counting, etc.) was certainly mentioned in it. *See, e.g.*, Michael M. Schmitt and Liis Vihul (eds.), TALLINN MANUAL 2.0 ON THE INTERNATIONAL LAW APPLICABLE TO CYBER OPERATIONS (2017).

has intervened during both the 2018 and 2020 election cycles and other states have engaged in election-related information operations as well.

For example, on October 21, 2019, Facebook announced that it had detected on its platform a coordinated effort of election interference from Russia. Facebook refers to this behavior as "coordinated inauthentic behavior," a term invented by Facebook that is rather opaque because Facebook removes some types of deceptive content on its platform but leaves other forms of deception intact. One thing that Facebook apparently considers contrary to its user standard is deception about identity. Facebook responded by taking down the pages that it identified as being a part of the effort. The tech firm said that the operations "created networks of accounts to mislead others about who they were and what they were doing." In addition to deactivating the groups and pages (93 Facebook accounts, 17 Facebook pages, and four Instagram accounts), Facebook also announced that it notified "law enforcement, policymakers and industry partners," although it is not clear what this means, especially because Facebook said that it was not removing "the content they posted."

Unfortunately, the Russian activity on Facebook is not alone. Iran has recently joined the fray and Facebook has responded by deleting several groups that it identified as being coordinated inauthentic behavior originating in Iran. The election interference material flowing from Iran is particularly noteworthy, as it seems that Iran was not deterred when some of its material was removed from Facebook in 2018. During that election, Facebook received a tip from cyber-security firm FireEye, which flagged for Facebook the activity of "Liberty Front Press," a group of linked social media accounts that purported to be from an independent Iranian news organization but, in reality, was an organ of Iranian state media.[5] Facebook ultimately removed 652 pages, groups, and accounts.[6] According to FireEye's analysis, the group leveraged "inauthentic news sites" that spread "anti-Saudi, anti-Israeli, and pro-Palestinian themes, as well as support for specific U.S. policies favorable to Iran, such as the U.S.–Iran nuclear deal."[7]

According to a recent academic report, the use of political information operations is endemic, and more than seventy countries engage in the practice.[8] If left unchecked, the majority of information on the Internet may be coordinated and manipulated, and the amount of "genuine" material may be swamped by the amount of content generated by information operations. The use of autonomous

---

[5] *See* Nathaniel Gleicher, *What We've Found So Far*, FACEBOOK (Aug. 21, 2018).

[6] *See Taking Down More Coordinated Inauthentic Behavior*, FACEBOOK (Aug. 21, 2018).

[7] *See* FireEye Intelligence, Threat Research, Suspected Iranian Influence Operation Leverages Network of Inauthentic News Sites & Social Media Targeting Audiences in U.S., UK, Latin America, Middle East (August 21, 2018).

[8] *See* SAMANTHA BRADSHAW AND PHILIP N. HOWARD, THE GLOBAL DISINFORMATION ORDER: 2019 GLOBAL INVENTORY OF ORGANISED SOCIAL MEDIA MANIPULATION (2019) ("We found evidence of organised social media manipulation campaigns in 70 countries, up from 48 countries in 2018 and 28 countries in 2017. Some of this growth comes from new entrants who are experimenting with the tools and techniques of computational propaganda during elections or as a new tool of information control.").

algorithms allows state agencies to generate content on an unprecedented level. Although several states have access to this technology, China appears to have leveraged the technology more aggressively than other states.[9]

These developments paint a scary picture. Far from an isolated political and cultural moment, foreign election interference appears to be a new feature of statecraft. Its ubiquity might lead some to a state of resignation – to accept it as an established element of international relations and not something that international law can regulate or extinguish. This would be a mistake. There are many international behaviors that are inevitable: war is one example. But the ubiquity of the phenomenon is not a good reason to forgo regulation. International law should recognize the distinctive harm of election interference, just as it recognizes the distinctive harm of armed conflict and seeks to reduce the number and the intensity of military conflicts. So too with election interference. International law (and domestic law) should seek to reduce the number of interferences and mitigate their impact. Hopefully this book can serve as an opening salvo in that effort.

---

[9] *Id.* ("Beyond domestically bound platforms, the growing sophistication and use of global social networking technologies demonstrates how China is also turning to these technologies as a tool of geopolitical power and influence.").

Index

active measures, 30, 111, 112, 113, 176, 177, 186, 187
advocacy
  express, 162
advocacy organizations, 6, 11, 111
Al-Assad, Bashar, 14
anonymity, 138, 139, 147, 157, 162, 163, 173, 217
anti-distortion rationale, 128, 129, 158
appreciation, margin of, 165
armed attack, requirement, 43, 44, 47, 48, 50, 51, 52, 53, 54, 55, 62, 65, 176
armed attack, requirement of, 7, 55, 61
armed conflict, 7, 36, 41, 46, 49, 50, 51, 52, 56, 58, 60, 61, 62, 65, 79, 220
  international, 49, 92
  non-international, 49, 50, 52, 92
Assange, Julian, 15, 16
association, right to, 163
attribution, problem of, 30, 32, 47, 114, 137, 138, 180, 181, 182, 183

Barela, Steve, 81
Basque, 94
Biden, Joe, 197, 198, 209
Black Lives Matter, 19
Blumenthal, Richard, 59
Bolton, John, 59
bot accounts, 19, 20
boundary regulations, 8, 9, 116, 118, 119, 120, 128, 136, 144, 203, 207, 209, 210
Brazile, Donna, 13
Brownlie, Ian, 32
Buckley v. Valeo decision, 125
Butina, 25, 132, 134
Butina, Maria, 24, 25, 26

Canada, 122
carrying arms openly, 58
Carter, Ash, 60

Catalonia, 94
censorship, 125, 154, 155, 157, 158
Central Intelligence Agency, 58, 112, 114, 186, 195
Cheney, Dick, 59
China, 4, 44, 111, 164, 220
Citizens United decision, 124, 125, 127, 128, 129, 132, 145, 149, 150, 151, 152, 156
citizenship
  criteria for, 120
Clausewitz, Carl von, 36
clear statement rule, 206, 207
Clinton, Hillary, 1, 2, 11, 12, 13, 14, 15, 16, 17, 18, 29, 33, 34, 35, 36, 82, 100, 101, 177, 192, 193
cluster munitions, 46
CNN, 13, 59, 125
coercion, 4, 5, 7, 53, 68, 72, 76, 78, 79, 80, 81, 82, 83, 84, 85, 88, 174, 190, 218
cognitive dissonance, 27
collateral damage, 42, 45, 46, 56, 57
colonialism, 108, 215
combatant's privilege, 42, 46, 56, 58
Comey, James, 176, 206
Concord Catering, 30, 31
constrained maximization, 5
Contras, 76
control
  effective, 4, 31, 32, 33, 81, 115
  overall, 32, 81
Corfu Channel Case, 70, 71, 76
corruption, 14, 101, 102, 118, 127, 128, 129, 130, 141, 142, 150, 157, 158, 162, 197, 199, 200, 209
counterintelligence, 9, 176, 179
countermeasures, 4, 48, 53, 62, 63, 64, 65, 134, 186, 190
covert action, 5, 8, 24, 36, 47, 58, 64, 77, 113, 131, 132, 134, 164, 175, 176, 179, 180, 190
Craig, Gregory, 132
Customary international law, 6, 47

Index

speech
  anonymous, 162
  commercial, 159
  compelled, 160, 161, 162
  hate, 166
Stevens, John Paul, 125
Stolen Valor Act, 154
Stone, Roger, 15, 21, 23
strict scrutiny, 156
Syria, 14, 34

Tallinn Manual, 47, 48, 50, 52, 53, 54, 61, 62, 73, 79, 80, 83, 84, 85, 86, 87, 218
Tea Party, 19
Torshin, Aleksandr, 24
Trail Smelter arbitration, 86
transparency, 8, 17, 23, 37, 46, 58, 119, 120, 130, 131, 132, 133, 135, 136, 138, 139, 140, 141, 142, 145, 147, 170, 175, 185, 186, 187, 190
troll farm, 1, 2, 19, 20, 21, 26, 28, 29, 64, 74, 78, 82, 101, 112, 118, 119, 134, 137, 138, 140, 143, 175, 185, 217
Trump, Donald, 1, 2, 9, 10, 11, 12, 13, 14, 15, 16, 18, 20, 21, 22, 23, 25, 29, 34, 35, 36, 59, 60, 75, 82, 126, 132, 176, 177, 187, 191, 192, 193, 195, 197, 198, 199, 200, 201, 202, 203, 204, 208, 209, 210, 211
Tsagourias, Nicholas, 103
Twitter, 1, 11, 13, 15, 18, 19, 20, 21, 22, 26, 27, 61, 82, 112, 136, 137, 139, 140, 143, 152, 163, 180, 204, 217

Ukraine, 9, 26, 33, 34, 63, 132, 191, 195, 196, 197, 198, 200
UN Charter
  Article 2(4), 43, 53, 55, 56
  self-defense, 43, 44, 45, 52, 53, 55, 63, 65
Uniform Code of Military Justice, 148
Universal Declaration of Human Rights, 91
usurpation, 7
usurpation of governmental function, 68, 69, 85, 86, 87, 89

Vattel, Emmerich de, 70, 85
Virtual Private Network, 12
voting
  prohibition on foreign, 8, 102, 119, 120, 145

Walzer, Michael, 42, 46
warfare
  kinetic, 40, 49, 53, 54, 55, 57, 58, 60, 65, 188
Westphalian legal order, 7, 67, 70, 72, 88
Wikileaks, 15, 17, 23, 26, 82, 101, 119

X-Agent, 12
X-Tunnel, 12

Zelensky, Volodymyr, 191, 195, 196, 197, 198, 199, 200, 201, 204, 208, 209, 210